THE COLUMBIA GRANGER'S® GUIDE
TO POETRY ANTHOLOGIES

OTHER COLUMBIA UNIVERSITY PRESS REFERENCE BOOKS

The Columbia Granger's Index to Poetry, Ninth Edition.
Edith P. Hazen and Deborah J. Fryer, eds.

The Concise Columbia Book of Poetry.
William Harmon, ed.

The Concise Columbia Dictionary of Quotations.
Robert Andrews, ed.

The Concise Columbia Encyclopedia, Second Edition.

Recent American Opera: A Production Guide.
Rebecca Hodell Kornick

THE COLUMBIA
GRANGER'S®
GUIDE TO POETRY
ANTHOLOGIES

WILLIAM KATZ
LINDA STERNBERG KATZ

COLUMBIA UNIVERSITY PRESS
NEW YORK

Columbia University Press
New York   Oxford
Copyright © 1991 Columbia University Press
All rights reserved

Library of Congress Cataloging-in-Publication Data

Katz, William A., 1924–
The Columbia Granger's guide to poetry anthologies.

"Based on the ninth edition of The Columbia Granger's index to poetry"—Pref.
Includes bibliographical references (p.) and index.
1. Poetry—Collections—Bibliography. 2. English poetry—Bibliography. 3. English
poetry—Translations   from   foreign   languages—Bibliography.   I.   Katz,   Linda
Sternberg.   II. Hazen, Edith P. Columbia Granger's index to poetry.   III. Title.
Z7156.A1K38 1990   [I'N1111] 016.80881   90-2469
ISBN 0-231-07244-9

Casebound editions of Columbia University Press books are Smyth-sewn and printed
on permanent and durable acid-free paper

⊗

Book design by Jennifer Dossin

Printed in the United States of America
c 10 9 8 7 6 5 4 3 2 1

For whom the poets sing — Will, Chris, Randy, and us all

CONTENTS

PREFACE

THE COLUMBIA GRANGER'S® GUIDE TO POETRY ANTHOLOGIES is
based on the ninth edition of THE COLUMBIA GRANGER'S® INDEX TO
POETRY. Librarians and researchers use that index for a variety of pur-
poses, among them to find a poem whose title, first line, author, or
subject they know. There, they have access to over a hundred thousand
poems in nearly four hundred anthologies, so it is quite likely that
searchers will succeed in their quest.

One feature of THE COLUMBIA GRANGER'S® that has been very pop-
ular with librarians is the choice by its editors and consultants of the
anthologies they consider particularly commendable. Such notation led
naturally to the present guide. Why not go beyond the starring of a few
anthologies and provide a full description and evaluation of all the an-
thologies indexed by THE COLUMBIA GRANGER'S®? Which are the
noteworthy anthologies of recent American poetry? What are the distinct
virtues of the several anthologies of women's poetry? of poetry for chil-
dren? of Chinese poetry in translation? No book offers this service at
present. This one fills that need and will be as useful in its own way as
THE COLUMBIA GRANGER'S® has proved to be throughout this century.

What makes an exceptional anthology? We used the same criteria that
librarians use when they review reference books: comprehensiveness;
ease of use; authority of editor and publisher; presence of such trappings
as introduction, notes, indexes, and biographical information; and, al-
ways underlying everything, the excellence of the poems chosen.

A fairly accurate indication of the purpose, scope, and proposed au-
dience of an anthology can be found in its introduction. One can readily
recognize the serious approach to the selection of poems from an intro-
duction that makes interesting points about them and quotes from them
to support the observations. We have found numerous introductions that
are exceptionally interesting in themselves and also make one want to
read the poems they are introducing. We comment on them and quote
from them whenever we feel they help us summarize an opinion.

We point out the method of organization adopted by the editor or
editors. Is it chronological? topical? alphabetical by author? Much can be
conveyed about an anthology by these simple descriptions. Does the

book have illustrations? Is there prose with the poetry? Is the purpose of the anthology mainly for students and teachers, or is it designed for all kinds of poetry readers? We have covered all such essential features of the anthologies in the ninth edition of THE COLUMBIA GRANGER'S® INDEX TO POETRY.

How original is an anthology? It may be the first anthology of a particular type of American poetry; another may be the first collection to identify a new group of young poets, a "movement"; another may be the first anthology of a nation's poetry in translation. Evaluating such collections is more difficult than evaluating anthologies the bulk of whose poetry is known.

This brings up the question of balance. In an anthology that, for example, claims to include the best of English poetry, one looks for a preponderance of works endorsed by historical opinion, as well as for some adventurous discoveries made by the compilers. The goal is to strike an effective balance between classical, generally praised work and fresh, new additions to the canon.

Clear examples of the artful maneuvering between old and new choices can be found in most of the Norton introductory series, as well as in the numerous Faber and Faber and Oxford University Press offerings. Furthermore, there are scores of collections from small presses that succeed in supplying noncanonical poetry, primarily because they accept the challenge of extending the public's artistic horizons. In all cases, our judgments reflect the criteria used by librarians and critics to evaluate books of non-fiction.

We hope that in THE COLUMBIA GRANGER'S® GUIDE TO POETRY ANTHOLOGIES we have defined the standards that will help potential readers and buyers make informed choices.

THE COLUMBIA GRANGER'S®
GUIDE TO POETRY ANTHOLOGIES

AFRICAN POETRY

The Penguin Book of South African Verse. *Jack Cope and Uys Krige, ed.*
(1968) Penguin Books. 332p., o.p.

The compilers note that "poetry is something of an obsession in South
Africa." They go on to trace the development of the form from the
earliest known peoples through the current generations. One learns, for
example, that Afrikaans literature begins only in the twentieth century,
strongly influenced by nineteenth-century English and Dutch poets. The
compilers edit *Vandag*, a magazine in which many of these poems first
appeared, including numerous ones by women poets. The strife in South
Africa over the years has resulted in a severe curb on certain poets.
Many, for this reason and others, went into exile. Of more than a dozen
in this category, among the most famous are Roy Campbell and William
Plomer. For those who stayed, "there has been little inclination towards
experiment for its own sake. Men and women of all races write verse in
English — and the language as a medium has collected undertones of
protest." Those poems not in English are translated by the compilers,
and these are primarily in the Afrikaans section, where some fifteen
poets are found. The other two sections, with about double that number
of voices, are devoted to English and African works.

Poems from Black Africa. *Langston Hughes, ed.* (1963) **Indiana
University Press. 160p., o.p.**

Edited by a distinguished American poet, this is a successful effort to
explain black Africa to the English-speaking world. The majority of the
English-, French-, and Portuguese-speaking poets are not, even today,
that well known. Hughes was not creating celebrities; he was delivering
their concerned messages. The collection, from the anonymous "oral
traditionals" to the modern age, is, as he says, "a rediscovery of self, a
turning within for values to live by, rather than a striking outward in
revenge for past wrongs." Also, Africa is made up of many peoples and
many histories, all of which move along different paths. The translations,
where necessary, are excellent. Most of the poems can be enjoyed as

1

much as songs and vivid portraits of people and places as they can be seen as examples of "a poet's endeavor to recover for his race a normal self pride."

When My Brothers Come Home; Poems from Central and Southern Africa. *Frank Mkalawile Chipasula, ed.* **(1985) Wesleyan University Press. 280p.**

A Malawian poet and editor gathers together the work of fifty-one poets. Each is represented by four or five typical poems. The countries include Angola, Botswana, Malawi, Mozambique, Namibia, South Africa, Zambia, and Zimbabwe. The greatest number of poets, fourteen, are from South Africa; the fewest from Botswana (one) and Namibia and Zambia (two each). All the poems were written in English with the exception of poems from Angola and Mozambique, former colonies of Portugal. These appear in translation. Explaining the content of his particular choices, the editor says, "This is not a mere extension of Western literary traditions; instead, it reflects in its major themes and attitudes the contentious relationship between Europe and Africa. The major recurrent themes are Negritude; protest against colonial domination and apartheid; anger and bitterness over oppression . . . [and] love, hope, the beauty of the land, and the pathos of the human condition." Each poet is introduced with a brief biographical and bibliographical sketch.

AFRO-AMERICAN POETRY

American Negro Poetry. *Arna Bontemps, ed.* (**Rev. ed., 1974**) **Hill and Wang. 252p., pap.**

A highly selective, yet totally representative collection of modern American black poetry and poets. The editor-poet collaborated with Langston Hughes in a similar work, *The Poetry of the Negro,* that goes back to the eighteenth century for inspiration. Drawing from the Harlem Renaissance of the Twenties for more than half of the anthology, Bontemps then turned to some lesser-known voices of the 1940's and 1950's. Among the poets are Paul Lawrence Dunbar, Hughes, and Arna Bontemps himself. Later come Gwendolyn Brooks, then LeRoi Jones, and Julia Fields. Most of the poetry reflects the racial struggles of the black people and the longing and need for freedom, respect, and economic advancement. Two unexpected prose writers are Richard Wright and Frank Yerby, both respectable poets, although Yerby appears considerably less sure of himself than most of the other poets in the anthology.

The Black Poets. *Dudley Randall, ed.* (**1971**) **Bantam Books. 355p., pap.**

In the introduction to *The Poetry of Black America,* Gwendolyn Brooks calls fellow poet Dudley Randall "poet-publisher-anthologist-fatherfigure, and platform provider." The description is apt. Concentrating on poets "turning away from white models and returning to their roots," Randall salutes black poetry under several broad headings. He begins with folk poetry, including folk seculars and spirituals, a fitting reminder of how much we owe to these early composers and poets. Where would American culture be today without, for example, "John Henry" or "Deep River"? Signed verses, which Randall labels "literary poetry," make up most of the collection. Such "forerunners" as Paul Lawrence Dunbar soon give way to the "Harlem Renaissance" and finally in the 1960's to such poets as Nikki Giovanni, Ishmael Reed, and James Randall. Unlike larger anthologies, this one is limited to the better-known poets. The result is highly selective, yet highly satisfying. In its way, it represents the heart of the heart of the country.

Black Sister; Poetry by Black American Women, 1746–1980. *Erlene Stetson, ed.* **(1981) Indiana University Press. 312p. $22.50; pap.**

Most anthologies of black American poetry include the work of women, but often, because of constraints of space, represent them with only one poem each. Here, the various talents of black American women are more fully displayed. Beginning with eighteenth- and nineteenth-century poets, we have four poems by Phillis Wheatley, seven each by Frances E. W. Harper and Henrietta Cordelia Ray. The twentieth-century poets include Angelina Weld Grimké, Alice Dunbar-Nelson, Helene Johnson, Margaret Walker, Mari Evans, and the great Gwendolyn Brooks; younger poets are Sonia Sanchez, Lucille Clifton, and Ntozake Shange. This is a collection of the highest quality. All the poets who appear here are well worth the time of the general reader.

The Book of American Negro Poetry. *James Weldon Johnson, ed.* **(Rev. ed., 1931) Harcourt Brace Jovanovich. 300p., pap.**

First published in 1922, this was immediately considered an important collection. The revised edition introduced readers to a new group of poets, including Countee Cullen, Sterling Brown, and, of course, Langston Hughes. The preface was changed, but Johnson's view of black poetry was essentially unaltered in 1931. He had faith in the intellectual capacity of his poets, in the messages they had to deliver. He included all points of view, even those one suspects he may not have entirely agreed with. The result is one of the more satisfactory collections, even though by now it is much dated. Limiting himself to poets in the United States, Johnson included a few who were less than expert at their craft. But even here the message was often so powerful that it overcame the roughness of style. Johnson was a true poet, selecting other vibrant poets to add to the clamor for black artistic recognition and understanding. He achieved his goal.

Caroling Dusk; an Anthology of Verse by Negro Poets. *Countee Cullen, ed.* **(1927) Harper & Brothers. 237p., o.p.**

An early effort to pay tribute to black poets, this collection was strongest in its focus on many younger poets who have since become basic to American poetry and culture. But it also included some fairly poor

choices, particularly one Albert Rice. But this came from the daring
spirit of the compiler who wanted to represent not only well-known writ-
ers, but also relative beginners. Cullen published several volumes of his
own work in the 1920's and 1930's that apparently suffered from many
of the same artistic faults as his choices in this collection. This is more of
historical/literary interest than a good place to turn for representative
black poets. It is a more useful reference work for libraries, but not of
real value to general readers today.

**Celebrations; a New Anthology of Black American Poetry. *Arnold
Adoff, ed.* (1977) Follett. 285p., o.p.**

This anthology, prepared by a teacher in the New York public
schools, is aimed primarily at students. It can, however, also be appre-
ciated by anyone who is interested in current black poetry. Some eight-
five writers, male and female, are represented by two hundred forty
poems. All were written in this century, and many are by highly regarded
black writers. These include Robert Hayden, Sterling A. Brown, Dudley
Randall, Gwendolyn Brooks, Ishmael Reed, Amiri Baraka, and Audre
Lorde. The poems are arranged thematically into such sections as
"Young Soul," "True Love," and "Myself When I Am Real." The taste of
the compiler is reliable and challenging.

**Collected Black Women's Poetry. Vols. I-IV. *Joan R. Sherman, ed.*
(1988) Oxford University Press.**

This work in four volumes, from The Schomburg Library of Nine-
teenth Century Black Women Writers, reprints some historically inter-
esting writing, often in the format in which it first appeared, right down
to the title-page. The collection begins in the nineteenth century, with
particular focus on the years 1890 to 1910. Literary historians call this
the "Black Woman's Era." Only a handful of poets are represented in the
four volumes, and nine of them were published in the last decade of the
nineteenth and first decade of the twentieth century. Christian idealism
and morality dominate many of the poems, although there is an occa-
sional reference to contemporary racial problems. Most of the poets have
obvious technical ability, but unfortunately, aside from the short intro-
ductions, there are few notes to help one interpret the obscure material
covered by the majority of the writers. The result is an anthology of
historical value, and of great interest to professionals, but of limited
interest to most other readers.

The Forerunners; Black Poets in America. *Woodie King, Jr., ed.* (1975) **Howard University Press. 126p.**

The "forerunners" are the poets who "carried the baton of poetic tradition from the Renaissance in the forties and fifties and created the foundation for the writers of the sixties and seventies." Arrangement of the sixteen poets is alphabetical — a poor choice as it does not place the poets in time. But there is a nice touch: after brief biographical notes for the poets, each one has written a paragraph or two about his or her views on the black poet. Sometimes (particularly in the case of Gwendolyn Brooks or Arna Bontemps), this gives the reader a better understanding of the whole movement and also of the individual voice. The strength of this anthology, one of many welcome collections of black verse, lies in the excellence of the selection. These are the best authors, and there is just enough of their poetry to be the best of the best. This is a grand place to start on a trip through Afro-American literature.

I Am the Darker Brother; an Anthology of Modern Poems by Negro Americans. *Arnold Adoff, ed.* (1968) **Macmillan. 128p.**

The subtitle is slightly misleading by this time, since the poems are no longer particularly modern, but they are, as the editor states, "easily available to both Negroes and whites." Beginning with Langston Hughes's familiar "Me and the Mule," the sixty short poems are arranged under six broad, rather ambiguous, subject headings. The indexes to first lines and to authors are more helpful. There are short biographical sketches for each of the thirty writers included. Hughes is most copiously represented with seven poems, followed closely by Robert Hayden and Conrad Kent Rivers. Other excellent poets whose work will be found here include Gwendolyn Brooks, Margaret Walker, and Raynold Patterson. Many of the others were born at the close of the nineteenth or beginning of the twentieth century. The selection is of a high order and fulfills the purpose of introducing younger people (grades seven and up) to black poets. Effective line drawings add to the pleasure of the volume.

Jump Bad; a New Chicago Anthology. *Gwendolyn Brooks, ed.* (1971) **Broadside Press. 190p., pap.**

The famous black poet Gwendolyn Brooks offers a collection of a dozen Chicago black voices, all of whom share youth (at the time of publication most of them were in their twenties). They were "involved in an exciting labor, a challenging labor; admitting that it is not likely all blacks will immediately convert to Swahili, they are blackening English. Some of the results are effective and stirring . . . True black writers speak as blacks, about blacks, to blacks." There are several prose pieces in this volume, and the reader is advised to read Don Lee's "Black Critic" and "Black Writing" for excellent background material on the attitudes and hopes of most of the poets in the collection. Each of the poets is represented by four or five pieces. By now, much of the poetry seems dated but is still of social interest and remains a basic reference for anyone studying the thought of the late 1960's and early 1970's.

The Poetry of Black America; Anthology of the 20th Century. *Arnold Adoff, ed.* **(1973) Harper & Row. 552p.**

Among the collections of black poetry this is outstanding. As Gwendolyn Brooks explains in the introduction, "The collection opens with elder heralds and songmakers . . . but what surprises, of a less anthologized nature, are available." For if W. E. B. DuBois and Paul Lawrence Dunbar are represented well, so are the poets of what Brooks calls "intensified anger, fed by amazed observation and voracious reading." A decade or so later some of these unknown writers were found in almost all collections, others dropped out of sight, and still others enjoy a small, but loyal audience. This sharp presentation of black poetry gives the reader an amazingly varied view of life, of history, and, of course, of fine artistry. There are about one hundred and fifty poets represented, usually with at least a half dozen poems. The short biographical notes show an amazing number born in the 1920's and 1930's, with few coming from the years before. Noticeably, there is a fine share of outstanding women poets. This basic anthology should be revised to include the poets of the 1970's and 1980's. It is recommended for all libraries.

The Poetry of the Negro, 1746–1970. *Langston Hughes and Arna Bontemps, eds.* **(Rev. ed., 1970) Doubleday. 645p., o.p.**

Here, black poetry is considered in its manifestations not only in the United States, but in such related areas as the Caribbean. Its most questionable section consists of poems by whites writing about blacks. It is not that the whites are critical; on the contrary, most are sympathetic. But should they be included in a book devoted to black poets? At any rate, one hundred sixty poets offer here a cross section of their work. While the translations of some of the poems are excellent, the selection of some of the individual poets is doubtful. The percentage of excellent poetry is probably no more and no less than in any ambitious anthology of this type, i.e., one that tries to cover so many years with representative poets and poetry from each era.

3000 Years of Black Poetry. *Alan Lomax and Raoul Abdul, eds.* **(1970) Dodd, Mead. 263p., pap.**

One of the fathers of folk song and poetry collecting, Lomax exerted a strong influence here. The collection opens with primitive songs from black Africa, followed by "Black Ravens of the Arab World." It is only on page sixty-five that individual European names are tied to poems, and then only for about ten pages. After Spanish, Russian, and French black poetry, the reader is introduced to the Creole of Latin America and the Caribbean. Modern African and American poetry make up the last third of the book, and only sixty pages are given to such well-known black poets as Paul Lawrence Dunbar, Langston Hughes, and Gwendolyn Brooks. The anthology captures the spirit and the culture of a people from almost the beginning of history to the present, although the search for continuity is sometimes stretched. To call Ahkenaton a black is to open an argument about the role of Egypt in history that has yet to be settled. Where this collection does triumph is in the selection and the wide scope of its poets and their writings. A major work.

AMERICAN POETRY
Comprehensive Collections

America Forever New; a Book of Poems. *Sara Brewton and John E. Brewton, comps.* **(1968) Thomas Y. Crowell. 270p.**

This attempt to capture American themes divides the poetry into sub-sections concerned with the land itself, with the immigrants who came here and the different concepts of liberty they brought with them, with the diversity of the continent, including portraits of American cities, and with the overriding sense of progress in America. Some wonderful poets have been included in the various sections: Carl Sandburg, Emily Dickinson, Robert Frost, Richard Wilbur. But there are also many trivial poems included, and they tend to diminish the treatment of the subject. One can still enjoy, however, the outpourings of the real artists that this land produced.

America in Poetry. *Charles Sullivan, ed.* **(1988) Harry N. Abrams. 207p.**

Handsome, glowing illustrations are the hallmark of this unusual book of poetry about America. The poems, limited as they are by the narrow subject matter, are of varying quality, but the illustrations are of the highest caliber: paintings by Edouard Manet and Winslow Homer, Currier and Ives lithographs, watercolors by John Marin, and pastels by James McNeill Whistler. All the drawings and paintings concern aspects of American life over the ages, and the poems intensify those visual representations. The poems are often by very good poets: Emily Dickinson, Edgar Allan Poe, John Hollander, Carl Sandburg. But many other less-renowned and less-talented poets are also featured, diminishing somewhat the aesthetic appeal of a book that movingly and beautifully attempts to give a sense of what America has been like over the past two centuries.

Anthology of American Poetry. *George Gesner, ed.* **(1983) Avenel Books. 735p., o.p.**

The table of contents begins with "Poets of America" and chronologically lists the major, traditional figures from Anne Bradstreet and Philip Freneau to Theodore Roethke and John Updike, but there is no indication of what poems are to be found under their names. Next comes a list of a half dozen broad subjects with poems listed, but no indication of authors. Before each poet's entry there is a brief biographical sketch, and the choice of poems centers around typical American themes. So, this is more than your average anthology of American poets. It is a collection totally dedicated to American ideas, landscapes, history, personalities. From the first entry, "The flesh and the spirit" to the last, "A visit from St. Nicholas," it is totally, completely, and without question the American dream in poems. As such, it is a marvelous work for schools and many individuals, but those with a more adventuresome nature will wish to turn to other, less parochial works.

The Best Loved Poems of the American People. *Hazel Felleman, ed.* **(1936) Doubleday. 670p., pap.**

Conservative almost to a fault, this anthology includes the basic choices of not only the editor but of laypersons who contributed ideas about what to include. The compiler spent fifteen years on *The New York Times Book Review* answering "queries" put to the section by readers. Many of the poems in this anthology are based upon those same queries, i.e., requests by readers for the reprinting of favorite poems. The choices, too often, are precisely the kind of poems that one finds in the newspapers and that tends to age quickly. Many of the old standards are included, but probably the best use of this book now is in the library where it is a good guide to once much-loved but now forgotten poems.

The Gift Outright, America to Her Poets. *Helen Plotz, ed.* **(1977) Greenwillow Books. 204p., o.p.**

Helen Plotz, a noted anthologist, hit upon a fertile theme: the response of poets to America and things American. She divides her subject into the topical categories of: "Columbus," "Indians," "Settlers," "Regions" and "History," as well as "The Idea of America." She then chooses poems from the earliest writings on this continent to the most modern, to demonstrate these themes. The poets featured include Philip Freneau, Henry Wadsworth Longfellow, and Ralph Waldo Emerson from older times, to Adrienne Rich, Muriel Rukeyser, and Lawrence Ferlinghetti from modern times. The poems, organized as they are around these potent national classifications, are most compelling, and the great variety of authors included in this rather slim volume is a testament to the editor's assiduous search to illustrate these subjects. These poems are not only fascinating for revealing the impact the concept of America had on writers over the centuries, but also, since they are poems of the highest quality, for providing a great deal of aesthetic enjoyment and intellectual stimulation.

The Little Treasury of American Poetry. *Oscar Williams, ed.* **(1948) Scribner's. 860p., o.p.**

This was the first member of a family of pocket-sized volumes that later included *A Little Treasury of British Poetry* and *A Little Treasury of Modern Poetry*. Its arrangement is chronological, beginning with "American Indian Poetry" and "The Chief Poets from Colonial Times to the Present" and ending with "Poetry of the Forties." Anne Bradstreet has four entries, beginning with her "The flesh and the spirit." Close to one hundred pages are given to Walt Whitman, while Emily Dickinson, Richard Eberhart, and W. H. Auden have between twelve and twenty-five pages. The choice of the balance of the poets ranges from good to excellent, and the reader has a splendid overall view of American poetry up to the mid-1940's. There are some fascinating, now much-dated, photographs of the poets and an index of authors and titles. In the introduction, Williams observes that the growth of American poetry "may lead us to expect even more exciting work in the future." He was correct, as a glance at the anthologies of American poetry after his time will demonstrate.

The New Oxford Book of American Verse. *Richard Ellmann, ed.* **(1976) Oxford University Press. 1,076p.**

Its great size and its editor's good taste make this volume unsurpassable as a survey of American poetry from its earliest days to the present time. A massive anthology, it provides long sections on all the major American poets, as well as shorter sections on minor ones. There are well over fifty poets here, stretching from the early years of the Republic to contemporary times. Among the writers given particular emphasis are Ralph Waldo Emerson, Walt Whitman, Emily Dickinson, and Robert Frost. The poems by these writers and by the others who are featured are superb. All of T. S. Eliot's "The Wasteland" is printed, as are extended selections from Ezra Pound's "Cantos." More modern writers included are Richard Wilbur, Adrienne Rich, Denise Levertov, and A. R. Ammons. There is an appropriate balance between the past and recent generations.

The Oxford Book of American Verse. *F. O. Matthiessen, ed.* **(1950) Oxford University Press. 1,130p.**

A renowned collection, this displays ideal selective judgment. The distinguished editor-critic begins with America's first poet, Anne Bradstreet (1612-72) and moves through the centuries to close with Robert Lowell. The sixty influential voices represent the canon, although here and there are important poems rarely found in collections. The rule "fewer poets, with more space for each" creates a compelling profile of American poetry. Space allotted to each poet varies, but the usual number is twenty to twenty-five poems for each. There is an evocative, critical introduction that provides an excellent overview of poets and poetry. The standard of printing is up to the usual Oxford high quality, and there are supporting indexes. The dominant theme is one of intelligence and sensibility in poetic discourse. An ideal choice for high school, public, and academic libraries, as well as for the average reader.

Poems of American History. *Burton Egbert Stevenson, ed.* **(Rev. ed., 1922) Houghton Mifflin. 704p.**

There are some good poems about American history here, as well as numerous mediocre ballads and refrains that sing America's glory. It is a fine collection for library reference shelves, particularly for locating a difficult-to-find, lesser-known title, but it is a poor choice for today's individual reader because most of the poems are so badly dated. Lesser-known events and personalities are stressed over and over again, and much of the poetry is poor. Conversely, one can say the collection truly reflects American attitudes at the turn of the century, when the first edition was published.

The Treasury of American Poetry. *Nancy Sullivan, ed.* **(1978) Doubleday. 838p.**

Born before Shakespeare died, Anne Bradstreet was among America's early settlers and was considered its first major poet. Here readers are introduced to the special tone that made her truly American and not simply reflecting English style. It is the quest for the American voice that inspires this large and, for the most part, traditional collection. There are some one hundred poets represented. About three hundred pages are devoted to poets before the twentieth century, while the remainder (beginning with Edward Arlington Robinson and Robert Frost) are distinctly modern. William Carlos Williams is given fourteen pages, while Ezra Pound has eleven and T. S. Eliot nineteen. With the end of the Second World War, the number of pages for each poet averages seven or eight, thus permitting a wide selection of poets and poetry for the last half of the century. The book is a good source of well-known verse with a wide choice of poets.

AMERICAN POETRY
17th, 18th, 19th Centuries

An American Anthology, 1787–1900. *Edmund Clarence Stedman, ed.* **(1900) Houghton Mifflin. 878p.**

Anyone who wishes to find out what their grandparents or parents thought was the best in American poetry need only turn to this historical collection. As American as the flag, the choices were made by a banker and critic who wrote a history of the New York Stock Exchange. But Stedman was a literary figure, too, and gathered together the works of Poe and Whitman. Although he died in 1908, his idea of high quality poetry helped mold public opinion through the Second World War. Today his anthology is primarily a place to turn to for old favorites from Philip Freneau (b.1752) to Bryant, Longfellow, Whitman, all of whom published before 1900. Fifty-eight pages near the end contain short biographical sketches of all the poets. This is an extremely helpful feature, as many are now forgotten. For example, how many can recall the work of Francis Miles Finch, Mary Bradley, or Sarah Piatt? One suspects that the majority of the four hundred authors in the book are now little more than vague figures from a time past. But the anthology is invaluable for its social and historical implications and for any study of the history of American poetry.

Cowboy Poetry; a Gathering. *Hal Cannon, ed.* **(1985) Gibbs M. Smith. 201p.**

This pocket-sized collection, able to fit in a saddle bag, "begins with the classic poems that have proven their vitality by their longevity." The first entry is "The Cowboy's Soliloquy," which was first published in 1885 but "was undoubtedly sung and recited long before that." Notes accompany the verse, usually a line or two to a poem. About two-thirds of the book is devoted to contemporary poets. The folklorist/compiler hopes to set the record straight about the real life of the cowboy by puncturing its stereotyped picture. He allows the cowboys to speak for themselves "as they celebrate the huge sky, the rodeo, busting broncos, the cattle drive . . . the land, and the life and the times of the people who continue, spiritedly, to live that cowboy life." The book ends with a brief bibliography. There is neither an author nor a title index. The idea is marvelous, but its realization, especially in the modern period, is far from ideal. The collection often stumbles into sentimentality, with exactly the sort of stereotypical bravado the compiler has been trying to avoid. There are pleasant black and white drawings by Carrie Henrie.

101 Patriotic Poems. (1986) Contemporary Books. 138p., o.p.

No compiler is identified. No introduction or preface is supplied, and there is no table of contents, so it is difficult to see the plan, if any, of the poems' arrangement. One must, none the less, celebrate the effort, particularly as the well-known authors (from Patrick Henry to Martin Luther King) are balanced by those less celebrated. There are one hundred and one poems, beginning, suitably enough, with Shelley's "Tribute to America." The reader then moves on to Robert Bridges's "A Toast to Our Native Land" and from there to John Pierpont's "The Fourth of July." A number of the poets are English, with Sir Walter Scott's "Breathes There a Man" just preceding the final entry, Martin Luther King's "I Have a Dream" speech. Few of the poems are more than a few stanzas in length, and almost all have a recurring drumbeat rhythm. It is the stuff that children recite and memorize. At the end there is an index of authors and of titles.

Seventeenth-Century American Poetry. *Harrison T. Meserole, ed.* (1968) Doubleday. 540p., o.p.

Anyone who is familiar with the historical background of American poetry knows that a woman, Anne Bradstreet (c. 1612–1672), was our first great poet. Her verse "The Flesh and the Spirit" is an American classic. It is, of course, here along with twelve other outstanding poems. In the collection's chronological arrangement, she is followed by Michael Wigglesworth (1631–1705). His poem "A Song of Emptiness to Fill Up the Empty Pages Following" fairly well sets the tone for his work. It opens with the line "Vain, frail, short lived, and miserable Man." He, too, is a major poet, as is Edward Taylor. After these three follow the "Minor Writers" (fourteen, plus entries from The Bay Psalm Book) and "Other Representative Writers" (about three dozen). Thanks to this arrangement, the collection may be read in two ways. For the best writers of the age, simply stay with the three opening poets. For an overview of what it meant to be a poet in seventeenth-century America and what the concerns of the average individual were, turn to the body of the book.

Whichever way you choose, do not miss the splendid introduction. There are biographical sketches, and authors and titles of poems are indexed.

AMERICAN
20th Century

The American Poetry Anthology. *Daniel Halpern, ed.* (1975) Avon
Books. 506p., pap.

The editor of *Antaeus* and *The Antaeus Anthology* has a sure sense of
modernity, and it is never better displayed than in this collection of the
work of seventy-five poets, all of whom were born after 1934. While
many of the poets have more or less disappeared or are no longer that
representative of modern times, their voices were an excellent guide to
the period between the Korean and the Vietnam wars. There are amaz-
ingly different configurations of interests. Here one may find the
absurdist alongside the humorist and the realist. Most of the poets seem
rather naive. The sounds of youth and the preoccupations with trivial
experiences dominate. An exception may be the women, from Louise
Gluck to Diane Wakoski. They have interests that today seem much
broader in scope than some of their contemporary men. James Tate and
Charles Simic are among the survivors from this period, and their poetry
demonstrates why they were able to escape the 1960's. An important
collection about an important period in American history, this should be
in many libraries. Individual readers will prefer anthologies of a wider
scope.

American Poetry since 1970: Up Late. *Andrei Codrescu, ed.* (1987) **Four
Walls Eight Windows. 591p.**

An up-to-date collection, this volume allows the reader to compre-
hend the precise state of the art of poetry writing in America today. The
aim of the editor/poet is to set the record straight with regard to what he
terms "academic poetry," the poetry that is liked, and sometimes written,
by professors and taught in the colleges and universities across America.
In this anthology is an alternative kind of verse, informal and colloquial,
often in strange forms — poems written in short paragraphs of prose,
poems that are long catalogues, poems that range over the page like
overheard monologues. But, for all their trendy form, they are intelli-
gent, carefully written, and rewarding. They could, in fact, develop in

17

the reader an appreciation of new approaches to poetry. Most of these writers were born after 1945, with the exception of a few who were themselves strong influences on that generation. The variety is great, with over a hundred poets represented, most of them with several pages of poetry. It is an eye-opening collection.

The Best American Poetry — 1988. *John Ashbery, ed.* **(1988) Collier Books/Macmillan. 249p.**

This book performs a twofold function. It prints what it deems to be the best of American poetry published in the past year (in this case 1988), with remarks on the poems by the poets themselves. These comments are similar to ones poets make at poetry readings: they illuminate some aspect of the work or detail its inception. There is also some biographical information about each poet. Many of the finest poets in America are included: Joseph Brodsky, Donald Hall, James Merrill, Richard Wilbur, Seamus Heaney, and May Swenson. But there are seventy-five poets represented, many of whom were published in magazines, and most of them are completely unknown to the general reading public. Many of the contributors are women. In general the selective judgment of the editors is first rate; this is a fine way to acquaint oneself with the poetry published in America today.

The Bread Loaf Anthology of Contemporary American Poetry. *Robert Pack, Sydney Lea and Jay Parini, ed.* **(1985) University Press of New England. 348p., pap.**

"This book derives its title from the Bread Loaf Writers' Conference of Middlebury College in Vermont, which for sixty years has offered American poets a gathering place and . . . encouragement for the writing and reading of poetry." Beyond that necessary criterion for inclusion, a poet must have published at least two books since 1980. Most importantly, "none of these poems has yet been published in individual collections." The rigorous rules of inclusion eliminate amateurs, although here and there among the nearly 100 poets there are some less than persuasive voices. On the whole, though, who can argue with A. R. Ammons, John Ashbery (to begin the alphabet), or with Richard Wilbur and Charles Wright (to end it)? Men outnumber women about four to one. Each poet has an average of two to four entries, and they move from "Long Island" (Marvin Bell), to the "Abyss" (X. J. Kennedy), to Ellen Voigt's "Landscape, Dense With Trees." If one word were needed to summarize the poetry, it would be "professional," almost to a fault. This works well enough for the truly gifted, but it is a trifle dry for some others. Still, as a cross section of relatively modern American verse, it is a winner.

Contemporary American Poetry. *A. Poulin Jr., ed.* **(4th ed., 1985) Houghton Mifflin. 728p.**

Teacher and poet, Poulin offers here a collection of poets whom he believes every American student should know. The format is in the familiar university style, but it goes beyond a typical textbook and may be enjoyed by anyone, in or out of college. The fifty poets are offered in alphabetical order, and for each there is a selection of representative work. A full-page photograph of each of the poets precedes their dozen or so poems. There is an extensive section of "Notes on the poets" that provides some one hundred pages of biography, bibliography, and criticism. This is followed by an essay, "Contemporary American Poetry; the Radical Tradition," that in many texts would be the introduction. It is just fine here because it presupposes that by this point the student will have read many of the poems and at least be familiar with the ground the editor is covering. Almost all of the poets are widely published, and there are few exceptions to the high quality of their work.

The Contemporary American Poets; American Poetry since 1940. *Mark Strand, ed.* **(1969) World. 390p., pap.**

Poet and compiler, Strand observes, "It is one of the points of this anthology to demonstrate the variety of American poetry since 1940 and, in those cases where careers extend from that time, to demonstrate their development." Poets who published before 1940 are not included. Arrangement is alphabetical by poet, with A. R. Ammons and John Ashbery at the beginning and, some one hundred poets later, Charles Wright and James Wright. There are brief biographies and indexes of titles and first lines. Twenty years later, it is fascinating to look back to when this collection was published and see just how astute Strand was in his choices. Most of today's famous poets who were writing then are included. Some few simply disappeared in the 1970's and 1980's, but these are the exception. Strand is also to be commended for his wise choice of poems, some of which are by now minor classics or are well worth recalling.

Divided Light: Father & Son Poems; a Twentieth-Century American Anthology. *Jason Shinder, ed.* **(1983) Sheep Meadow Press. 293p., pap.**

Concentrated around the subject of fathers and sons, these poems are written by men about their relationships with their most significant male progenitors and progeny. The selection of poems is both astute and discriminating. The authors are of uniformly high caliber, and the poems are among the best of their work. All pieces were written in the twentieth century by Americans, and this narrow focus increases the depth of the exploration, since our distinctive society is plumbed for its insights into a particularly emotional topic. The material is arranged chronologically and features the work of Stanley Kunitz, Theodore Roethke, Robert Lowell, and Michael Harper, among many others. The variety in the handling of the subject matter is remarkable, moving from the beauty of Richard Wilbur's evocation of his father's artistic temperament, to Donald Hall's bittersweet reflection on the mortality conferred upon him by his baby boy. This anthology provides sharp insights into the artistically fertile ground of father and son relationships.

Ecstatic Occasions, Expedient Forms; 65 Leading Contemporary Poets Select and Comment on Their Poems. *David Lehman, ed.* **(1987) Collier Books/Macmillan. 256p.**

Deriving from a reasonable supposition that poems develop their particular forms because of impulses on the part of their creators, this volume pursues this premise by asking a number of contemporary poets to provide a poem along with a statement on the decisions they made as they wrote it. The result proves fascinating indeed to all those who are interested in the art and craft of poetry. The poets who contributed to this anthology include A. R. Ammons, John Ashbery, Amy Clampitt, Robert Creeley, Marilyn Hacker, Brad Leithauser, James Merrill, Louis Simpson, Mona Van Duyn, and Richard Wilbur, to name only some of the distinguished authors included. Their commentary on the poems tends to be brief, ranging from one half page to two pages in length, but reveals much about the poets' decisions and their creative process.

Fifty Years of American Poetry; Anniversary Volume for the Academy of American Poets. Introduction by Robert Penn Warren. (1984) Harry N. Abrams. 260p.

Here one celebrates fifty years of the Academy of American Poets, which should not be confused with the Poetry Society of America (which earlier celebrated its fiftieth anniversary with *The Golden Year*). Warren explains that one hundred and twenty-six poets are represented, each of whom is an award winner. "A glance at the table of contents will show that no one school, bailiwick, method, or category of poetry has dominated the interest of the Academy." True. Where else would one find Edgar Lee Masters and Ezra Pound award winners in the same year? In another fifty years one may ask who is Oliver St. John Gogarty, Edward Markham, or Kenneth Rexroth, but today they are well enough appreciated to be found in these pages. This is a profile of different approaches to verse, of truly different voices and opinions; an excellent choice for the individual reader who wants a broad impression of American poetry from 1924 to 1984.

The Generation of 2,000; Contemporary American Poets. *William Heyen, ed.* **(1984) Ontario Review Press. 364p., pap.**

"Contemporary," one learns from the introduction, refers to poets born between 1932 and 1949. The thirty-one poets are well established, and all have an audience reached, for the most part, through the little magazines. About one third are more widely published and are now well known to the general public, e.g., the late Raymond Carver, Wendell Berry, Louise Glück, Albert Goldbarth, Joyce Carol Oates, and Charles Simic. The one thing they share in common is excellence. Even the less well-known poets speak with authority, and they are a delight to read. This may be owing to the age constraints set by the compiler, but the fact remains that few of the poets are really weak. Each of the selections is preceded by a biographical sketch and a photograph. Of particular interest is the statement each poet offers about his or her poetry, often with quite specific notes about the poems that follow.

The Golden Year. *Melville Cane, John Farrar and Louise Nicholl, eds.* **(1960) Fine Editions Press. 368p.**

To celebrate its fiftieth anniversary, the Poetry Society of America invited members to submit no more than three poems for consideration. The result is this volume. It "includes at least one poem by every member submitting." There are over three hundred poets represented, but the collection is rather uneven. Witter Bynner, for example, is the only really well-known poet in letters "A" and "B." Louis Ginsberg is included, but not his somewhat better-known son; Robert Frost is represented by three poems (not his best), and numerous lesser-known figures find their way into the pages. The work resembles in no small way the Stedman *American Anthology*, which also pays tribute to poets who are better known to history than to current readers. This collection is of value to anyone wishing to discover poets of the years between the Second World War and 1960 but will be of marginal interest to others. (See also the similar volume, *Fifty Years of American Poetry*.)

A Green Place; Modern Poems. *William Jay Smith, comp.* (1982) Delacorte Press/Seymour Lawrence. 225p., o.p.

The well-known translator and editor William Jay Smith surveys the artistic scene and decides upon the more representative and better poets of the current half century. The choices are not that eccentric, and most of the poets included, as well as their poems, are good to excellent. One would have to go far to find a more inclusive anthology of truly modern poets. There are both the well known and some whom only Smith and a select few seem to read. More the pity, as many of the less celebrated figures have more imaginative verse. There are few disappointments, and much to celebrate. The artistic drawings by Jacques Hnizdovsky complement the poems.

The Harvard Book of Contemporary American Poetry. *Helen Vendler, ed.* (1985) Belknap Press. 440p.

A better title might be *The Helen Vendler Book of Contemporary American Poetry*, for she is so well known, particularly as an intellectual critic for *The New Yorker* and *The New York Review of Books*. She shares the distinction of being both a scholar and a popular poetry reviewer, an author and a fine teacher. Furthermore, she has a strong following among people who read poetry, not just among professors of the subject. Her choices, with the possible exception of a few younger poets, are hardly a surprise. She begins with the classic, short pieces of Wallace Stevens, moves on to Langston Hughes and Theodore Roethke, and some thirty poets later, she ends with Rita Dove, a questionable choice. Still, one can't help but admire Vendler's ability to pick winners before they are famous. There is no finer introduction to modern American poetry than this splendid collection.

In the American Tree. *Ron Silliman, ed.* (1986) National Poetry Foundation. 628p.

Much poetry is meant to be read aloud. Not here. "A latent tradition of poetics not centered on speech," is the course followed by the compiler. Furthermore, little attention is given to questions about excellence of composition. "It is now plain," Mr. Silliman explains, "that any debate over who is, or is not, a better writer, or what is, or is not, a more legitimate writing is, for the most part, a surrogate social struggle." The most important consideration does not regard quality, but the reader who is being addressed in the poem. "How does the writing participate in the constitution of this audience, and is it effective in doing so?" It is all a debate, of course, and the compiler is more than aware of the struggle. He divides the sixty or so modern poets geographically, i.e., West and then East, believing this accounts for "very different orientations toward such issues as form and prose style." A third part, "Second Front," is more thematic "and is intended to show how the concurrent discourse on poetics which has been so much a part of this debate relates to, and illuminates, the writing." Each contributor has a brief biographical sketch, helpful because few are that well known. Conversely, almost all are familiar to little magazine fans.

"Language" Poetries; an Anthology. *Douglas Messerli, ed.* (1987) New Directions. 184p.

The mysterious title of this book refers to a little known movement in poetry called "language poems." In his introduction, Douglas Messerli strains to provide an adequate definition and in doing so explores the history of the movement and suggests basically that these poets attempt to speak in dense and opaque terms rather than try to achieve lucidity or transparentness of expression. If the definition leaves the reader a bit bewildered, then the reading of the poems might help in showing exactly what these poets have achieved. Twenty poets are included, each represented by several works. One can't say that they will appeal to lovers of conventional poetry, but those who are interested in adventurous, modern forms will find them worth studying.

The Longman Anthology of Contemporary American Poetry, 1950–1980. *Stuart Friebert and David Young, eds.* **(1983) Longman. 592p.**

The compilers arrange the forty-eight American poets in this anthology in five sections, by their birthdates. Wallace Stevens and William Carlos Williams, for example, are grouped under the heading, "Two poets born in the nineteenth century." Then come "Nine poets born between 1900 and 1920" and so on to the last section, "Six poets born after 1940." As these are works to be read for class assignments, the compilers neatly represent each writer with approximately the same amount of material, two to three hundred lines of poetry. "We wanted to present enough work by each poet chosen to enable readers to get well acquainted with that poet's work." The format is attractive. Enough space is given to offer not only a biographical sketch of the writer (from one to two pages) but a good photograph as well. Basic titles of books by and articles about the poet are at the end of the selection, as is an occasional note. Unfortunately there are no indexes, and one must look to the table of contents for direction. On the whole the selection is very good, although somewhat scanty on poets born after 1940.

The Made Thing; an Anthology of Contemporary Southern Poetry. *Leon Stokesbury, ed.* **(1987) University of Arkansas Press. 326p.**

Here "contemporary" refers to poets who have published major works in the past thirty years. Here "Southern" means poets who "were either born and raised in the South or who have lived in the South at least since they began publishing their mature work." Beyond that, the only rule for inclusion or exclusion is quality as judged by the compiler. The seventy or so poets are arranged alphabetically with up to four poems each. A photograph and a brief biographical sketch open each selection. There are several points shared by the group beyond their point of origin. Most are teachers, and many have advanced degrees. Most are men. Most write about the historical South, and one is "struck by how much of the poetry is centered around a profound relationship to the natural world." Finally, "Southern poets are in general somewhat conservative in their approach to form." The most famous poets here are Wendell Berry, James Dickey, Donald Justice, Robert Penn Warren, and Charles Wright. But the real delight of the collection is to discover the numerous poets who deserve more recognition.

Modern American Poetry. *Louis Untermeyer, ed.* **(8th rev. ed., 1962) Harcourt, Brace. 701p., o.p.**

Louis Untermeyer was an anthologist other poets admired for the acuteness of his critical judgment. This volume, though only of average size, packs in more great American poems written from Walt Whitman up through the early 1960's than any comparable collection. The major poets are given very generous room for their work: Whitman has almost fifty pages; Emily Dickinson has almost fifty poems included; and Edwin Arlington Robinson has more than thirty poems. Robert Frost, Wallace Stevens, William Carlos Williams, and Elinor Wylie are also accorded a good deal of space. All of T. S. Eliot's "The Waste Land" is there, along with fine poems by Theodore Roethke, Elizabeth Bishop, Delmore Schwartz, Randall Jarrell, and Robert Lowell. Untermeyer's taste for good poems makes this volume a continual pleasure. It is an excellent place to start for those who have only a mild interest in poetry, for they will be met with the finest of poems by the most eminent writers. Also helpful are the rather lengthy biographical and critical introductions that precede each poet. This is a first-rate anthology.

The Morrow Anthology of Younger American Poets. *Dave Smith and David Bottoms, eds.* **(1985) Quill. 784p.**

Although some five years have gone by since this selection was published, most of the poets included are still relatively young. Diane Ackerman, for example, is such a poet, as are Albert Goldbarth, Michael Blumenthal, Robert Pinsky, William Matthews, and close to a hundred others. It should be mentioned that both poet/editors are included. Bottoms has only nine pages, while Smith has fourteen. All styles and types of poetry are included, but the particular emphasis is on the lyrical. Most of the writers born after 1940 are more involved with home life and with personal and economic difficulties than with metaphysical problems. In other words, there is little to shock or startle, but much to consider. There is some splendid verse that is as good as anything written during this century. See, for example, the aforementioned Ackerman and Goldbarth. Anthony Hecht has written an imaginative and informative introduction. He observes that daily activities are a major concern, with poets celebrating a librarian, a filmmaker, a lawyer, and even a sheepherder. The small photographs and brief biographies of each of the poets add to the book's appeal.

Naked Poetry; Recent American Poetry in Open Forms. *Stephen Berg & Robert Mesey, eds.* **(1969) Bobbs-Merrill. 392p., pap.**

Despite its racy title, this is a serious book concerned with new poetic forms — open forms or nontraditional verse. The names of the poets will all be familiar to readers of modern poetry: Kenneth Rexroth, Theodore Roethke, William Stafford, John Berryman, Robert Lowell, Denise Levertov, Allen Ginsberg, W. S. Merwin. Even Sylvia Plath is included. Each poet is introduced through a photograph and some biographical information, and then follows a long section of poetry, ranging from ten to forty pages or so. The poets are among the most powerful of their generation, and the selection is sensitive to the strengths of the individual artists. This volume offers the reader a clear insight into the new movement of poetry writing in the 1950's and 1960's. The search for new poetic forms and experimentation with the placement of poems on the page is well recorded. At the end of their selections of poetry, the authors include some notes on the new formal elements.

The New American Poetry, 1945–1960. *Donald M. Allen, ed.* **(1960) Grove Press. 454p., o.p.**

From 1945 to 1960 and after, Charles Olson, Allen Ginsberg, and Robert Duncan were among the major names in American poetry. They paralleled the periods of abstract and expressionistic art that was unique to America. They celebrated the new jazz, the new contemporary culture, and the new America that came out of the Second World War. The three, along with forty-one other poets and over two hundred poems, are by now less revolutionary and more a part of literary history, but their collective view of the world still influences much American thought. One is sad not to find Allen Ginsberg's "Howl" here, but there are few other oversights. There may be, in fact, too much Gregory Corso and not enough John Ashbery or Kenneth Koch. Be that as it may, this remains the standard anthology for anyone wishing to understand the period. Note, too, at the end of the volume the fascinating statements on poetry by the contributors, as well as biographical notes and a short bibliography that includes several little magazines and recordings.

New American Poets of the 80s. *Jack Myers and Roger Weingarten, eds.* **(1984) Wampeter Press. 435p., pap.**

Who are the new American poets of the 80's? Two of the sixty-five presented here are the compilers. The others are either well known (Russell Edson, Carolyn Forché, Tess Gallagher, Albert Goldbarth) or, not infrequently, rarely found these days in the little magazines or else-where. The selection process, made in the early 80's, proved to be extremely accurate in pinpointing some developing talents. For the most part, the poets, in alphabetical order with four or five poems each, were then between thirty and forty-five years of age. Each had to have produced at least one book. The compilers succeeded in their goal: there is hardly a poem in the work that is not worth considering. "We hope we have made our selections with an objective eye toward an eclecticism regarding styles, concerns, and forms." While "younger" is hardly applicable to many of the poets today, this anthology serves as a backdrop for their later, often more ambitious and polished, poetry.

The New Naked Poetry; Recent American Poetry in Open Forms. *Stephen Berg and Robert Mesey, eds.* (1976) Bobbs-Merrill. 478p., o.p.

This is a follow up of the same editors' *Naked Poetry*. Published seven years later, it follows the format of the earlier edition, i.e., the poet is represented by a dozen or so poems, and then there is a "Statement," of the poet's explanation of the work, or of his or her life, or of poetry in general. Statements are normally a page or two in length but may be no more than a single paragraph. Dead poets have largely been deleted from this revision. The twenty-six modern American voices in the book range from Gary Snyder and William Stafford to Denise Levertov and Adrienne Rich. Brief biographical sketches are given for each poet, as well as some fascinating photographs. (Some seven years later it is interesting to compare the faces with those in the earlier edition.) The "open form," about which the collection is built, is briefly explained, but here the editors ask the reader to return to the first edition for a fuller explanation. Briefly, "The metaphor is of the living and growing thing. The rhythm and shape of the flower cannot be made clear as separate from or meaning anything different." An excellent collection.

19 New American Poets of the Golden Gate. *Philip Dow, ed.* (1984) Harcourt Brace Jovanovich. 468p.

The alluring conception behind this book is to present a sample of the work of several poets writing in northern California today, letting them provide their own introductions to their lives and poetry. The result is a warm, informal introduction to the accomplishments of several lesser-known, and such quite famous, authors as Al Young, Robert Pinsky, and Susan Griffin. The standard of the work varies, but its intention to acquaint readers with contemporary voices and forms in poetry is fresh and serious. The writing is in no way provincial, and the concerns transcend state borders. Each author is represented by about a dozen poems that demonstrate his or her strengths in some detail. Handsome photographs of the writers further personalize the biographical introductions.

The Postmoderns; the New American Poetry Revised. *Donald Allen and George F. Butterick, eds.* **(1982) Grove Press. 436p., pap.**

Who are the postmoderns? According to the compiler the thirty-eight Americans here represented can claim that title because, first, they tend to be experimental and avoid the traditional, second, they emerged in the 1950's and came into their own in the 1960's and 1970's, and third, they were and are published in literary reviews and little magazines. Finally, but not least, "The body of them are writers who were given their wider recognition through the first edition of this anthology, titled plainly *The New American Poetry,* and published in 1960." (See *The New American Poetry.*) Arrangement is by the poets' birthdates. Charles Olson (b. 1910) is followed by William Everson, Robert Duncan, Lawrence Ferlinghetti, and Barbara Guest — all born before 1921. The poets born in the nineteen thirties end the collection, and they make up the greatest single group. Most are fairly well known and include Jerome Rothenberg, Michael McClure, Diane DiPrima, Amiri Baraka, Ed Sanders, and Ann Waldman. Each poet is represented with four or five poems. There are excellent biographical/bibliographical notes.

Preferences; 51 American Poets Choose Poems from Their Own Work and from the Past. *Richard Howard, ed.* **(1974) Viking Press. 323p., o.p.**

What fun! The appeal of this volume is multifarious: there are informal, clear photographs of all the poets; their poems are beautifully printed on large format pages; they revealingly select "in their own work and in the work of the past, a pair of poems . . . which they saw fit to put together." And then there is a substantial commentary on their choices by the distinguished writer and poet Richard Howard. He attempts to delve into the minds of the poets to explain their choices; he frequently quotes from interviews and essays that shed light on their decisions. He also comments on the essence of the two poems selected. In general, then, the reader has something of the pleasure of attending fifty poetry readings by distinguished authors offering their own kind of personal commentary. A. R. Ammons chose his own "Gravelly Run," along with Ralph Waldo Emerson's "The Snow-storm"; W. H. Auden chose "In Due Season," along with Thomas Campion's "What Faire Pompe"; Adrienne

Rich chose "The Afterwake" and Gerard Manley Hopkins's "Patience, Hard Thing!" The pleasures in this volume are hard to beat.

Singular Voices; American Poetry Today. *Stephen Berg, ed.* **(1985) Avon Books. 326p., o.p.**

The thirty poets are in alphabetical order, and at the time of publication were all living and most of them famous. There is only one poem by each poet, followed by criticism of that piece by the poet. "Faced with their own poems . . . the poets were driven to talk about the difficulties of creation and interpretation and just plain understanding, and to come up with fresh personal ways to guide the reader." There is a widely different approach by each of the writers, and, as the compiler claims, this is "an unpredictable cache of poems and essays." It is a wonderful place for both the beginner and the trained expert to dip into for ideas and criticism. Most of the poems take up a page or less, followed by two to four pages of critique. The volume ends with brief biographical sketches of the poets, among whom one will find Robert Bly, Hayden Carruth, James Dickey, Tess Gallagher, Louise Glück, Donald Hall, Maxine Kumin, Stanley Kunitz, Denise Levertov, Czeslaw Milosz, Louis Simpson, W. D. Snodgrass, William Stafford, Robert Penn Warren, and Richard Wilbur. Here is an ideal book for learning about poetry that is equally good as a bedside reader.

Strong Measures; Contemporary American Poetry in Traditional Forms. *Philip Dacey and David Jauss, eds.* **(1986) Harper & Row. 492p.**

This anthology works from the provocative premise that there are substantial, pertinent poems being written today in the verse forms of the past. The compilers have combed the best of contemporary poetry to ferret out these modern poems in traditional forms. The introduction is a long, thoughtful consideration of verse forms and their use by contemporary authors. Such devices as disguising the form, alternating between formal and free verse, and creating hybrid forms are considered. The poets whose works are featured range from John Berryman and Elizabeth Bishop to Amy Clampitt, X. J. Kennedy and Mona Van Duyn. Many of the poets are women, all are American. The compilers have fine taste in poetry, and all the poems make for rewarding reading. Almost two hundred poets are included, many of them represented by more than one poem. Here is a superb overview of some of the strong poetry written in America in recent decades.

The Voice That Is Great Within Us; American Poetry of the Twentieth Century. *Hayden Carruth, ed.* **(1970) Bantam Books. 722p., pap.**

One of America's leading poets put this collection together, and unlike many poet/compilers, he limits his own entries to five "short-shorts" he wrote while compiling the book. These brief works are "offered simply as a token ... of fellowship with all poets." For each of the one hundred thirty-six poets represented, there is a brief biographical sketch and list of major works. The poets are arranged chronologically, from 1900 to 1970. Robert Frost leads off with sixteen poems, about the average for major writers in this collection. Younger and minor poets have three or four pieces. No one is missed, and the selection from modern and contemporary American verse is among the best now available. Carruth employs three primary selection criteria: he reprints only works he thinks are the best, and not those that are merely famous; translations are excluded, as are excerpts from long or extensively annotated poems; and, finally, the choices are dictated "by my own feeling" of quality. The single drawback is the lack of either an author or title index.

See also ENGLISH AND AMERICAN POETRY: 20th CENTURY

AMERICAN
20th Century (Periodical)

The Antaeus Anthology. *Daniel Halpern, ed.* **(1986) Bantam Books. 615p., pap.**

Antaeus, a distinguished literary journal, has been published since 1969. This anthology is a gathering of some of the most remarkable poems published in the journal in the past twenty years. Among the extraordinary selections are verses that W. H. Auden wrote for the musical *Man of La Mancha*. These lyrics, based on the Don Quixote story but never performed, are printed here in their entirety. Many foreign poets are included in this volume: Paul Celan, Anna Akhmatova, Osip Mandelstam, and Czeslaw Milosz, to mention only a few. Some of the great American poets featured include John Berryman, Marianne Moore, "H. D." (Hilda Doolittle), and William Carlos Williams. English poets, are in abundance: Philip Larkin, Peter Porter, John Fowles, and Roy Fuller. This is an extraordinarily fine compilation of modern poems, made particularly rich by the interplay of English, American, and foreign voices. Because the taste of the editor is outstanding, the reader can be assured of finding poetry of the highest quality. Many new forms are on display, including poems written in paragraphs of prose. Individual poems are printed on separate pages, so they retain the dignified look they originally had in the journal.

Keener Sounds; Selected Poems from the Georgia Review. *Stanley W. Lindberg and Stephen Corey, eds.* **(1987) University of Georgia Press. 224p.**

One of America's outstanding literary reviews, the *Georgia Review* is edited by Lindberg. Published since 1947, the quarterly has gained distinction for its fiction and graphics. There are lengthy essays on poetry and usually fine selections of poetry. But while the poetry is worthy of consideration, it does not measure up to the fiction the review has published over the years. With that reservation, one must applaud the collection for offering one hundred fourteen new and older poets, for suggesting both new and older ways of approaching poetic subjects. John

Ashbery, Maxine Kumin, Howard Nemerov, and David Wagoner are certainly among America's strongest poetic voices; conversely, there are as many lesser-known poets with, all too often, lesser talents. There are some English poets, but most are American. The brief biographies of the contributors read like a roll call of modern poetry. This is an important anthology.

The New Yorker Book of Poems. *The New Yorker editors, comps.* **(1969) Viking Press; paperback edition published by William Morrow, 1974. 835p.**

Limited to entries from the pages of *The New Yorker,* this excellent collection covers poets who appeared there from the first issue in 1929 through 1969. There are nine hundred poems by almost every famous and minor poet of America, England, and Europe. The subject matter alone is a profile of the hopes and anxieties of the world at mid-century. Byron Buck can write about a "Song from a Two Desk Office," while W. H. Auden is equally serious about "Installing an American Kitchen in Lower Austria." At another level, Daniel Berrigan explains why "Somewhere the Equation Breaks Down," and Delmore Schwartz is eloquent "During December's Death." Less satisfactory is the arrangement, which the editors note "may strike the reader as an odd way." Indeed! The poems are printed alphabetically by title, although there is an author index. It is a pointless organization, but that hardly detracts from the brilliance of the volume. It is a book that can be by the bedside for a lifetime. Highly recommended for all.

The Ploughshares Poetry Reader. *Joyce Peseroff, ed.* **(1986) Ploughshares Books. 335p.**

Ploughshares is a little magazine with a big voice in contemporary American literature, publishing as it does some of the finest writers at work today. This anthology is a selection of the best poetry to appear in *Ploughshares* since its inception in 1971. The work of over a hundred poets appears here, many of them very familiar to readers of modern poetry: Denise Levertov, Philip Levine, Derek Mahon, Robert Lowell, James Merrill, W. D. Snodgrass, Mona Van Duyn, and Richard Wilbur, each represented by one to three poems. There are numerous lesser-known poets, all of whom are worth reading. The standard of writing here is very high; many of the poets are women. All the poems were written in English, and there is great variety; from an evocation of Noah's thoughts concerning the flood in "A Life-Giving," by Brad

Leithauser, to "Letters from a Father," documenting an elderly man's turning from the pain of old age to the pleasures of nature, by Mona Van Duyn.

The Poetry Anthology, 1912–1977. *Daryl Hine and Joseph Parisi, eds.* **(1978) Houghton Mifflin. 555p.**

Limited to work that appeared in *Poetry* magazine, here are samples from sixty-five years of modern poetry writing, beginning with Ezra Pound and ending with a somewhat less well-known but fine poet Sandra M. Gilbert. In between, under seven time divisions, we are presented with the work of almost everyone from A. R. Ammons to Louis Zukofsky. Even the lesser-known authors are carefully selected, not for their names, but for their contributions, to create a particularly strong record of what can be termed "new" voices, at least for the time. Ezra Pound, W. B. Yeats, and Vachel Lindsay have now joined the traditionalists, but such later entrants as John Ashbery and Frank O'Hara have a time to go before they can be completely understood or become a part of everyday culture. Note, too, that the introduction is a brief history of that great magazine, *Poetry,* and its founder, Harriet Monroe. One of the editors of the anthology, Daryl Hine, was editor of the journal from 1969 through 1977.

ANIMAL AND BIRD POETRY

Cat Will Rhyme with Hat; a Book of Poems. *Jean Chapman, ed.* (1986) Scribner's. 80p.

The copy on the book's jacket explains it all. This "rich and varied collection of poems will delight cat lovers, moving them both to laughter and to tears. The poems are grouped in eight sections, each celebrating an aspect of cat charm or behavior." The sections have such titles as "The Trouble with a Kitten," "I Am the Cat," and "Tip the Saucer of the Moon." The better known tributes are by such writers as T. S. Eliot, Ogden Nash, W. B. Yeats, and Wordsworth. Even the selective "anonymous" poems have a degree of charm. Those who are less than thrilled by a cat will still give honor to the eighth-century scribe who opens his work with the marvelous line, "I and Pangur Ban, my cat. . . ." The compiler is an Australian, young adult author who loves cats. The collection is for any person of any age who loves cats. Others may prefer to pass.

Fellow Mortals; an Anthology of Animal Verse. *Roy Fuller, comp.* (1981) Macdonald and Evans. 274p., o.p.

An English poet and novelist, Roy Fuller opens his tribute to animals with the "Creation of the Animals" from *Paradise Lost* and verses from Job and Isaiah in the King James version of the Bible. The arrangement after that is chronological, beginning with Henry Constable and, some one hundred poets and about twice as many poems later, ending with Ruth Pitter's "The Bat." There is a witty introduction and an index of first lines and extracts, but no other notes or guides. Fuller lets the poets speak for themselves. In his explanation of the collection, he makes several points. First, the chronological arrangement is because "I was interested in man's changing attitude to animals that the historical arrangement would be bound to reveal." Next, the cutoff for the birthdates of the poets is 1900, which, he says, "admits the modern sensibility, but does not allow it to dominate." That corresponds with the *raison d'être* of the book: "The growth of compassion for brute creation, as here revealed, must be accounted a considerable virtue, especially over a period when man has done much damage to his own kind. . . . It is man who has fallen, not the beasts."

The Penguin Book of Bird Poetry. *Peggy Munsterberg, ed.* **(1980) Allen Lane; published by Penguin Books, 1984. 361p.**

A peculiar feature sets this volume apart from almost all other anthologies. The subject is, of course, unusual, but even more so is the fact that almost a third of the book is devoted to an introduction. There may be a more thorough study of bird poetry elsewhere, but it is hard to believe. Ms. Munsterberg offers the reader not only the chronologically arranged poems, but a brilliant essay on how the bird has been celebrated by poets from the ninth century up to William Butler Yeats. Almost sixty poems at the close are from the anonymous oral tradition, without a time frame or an author, but familiar to many as nursery rhymes. The book ends with a selected bibliography (surely one of the most detailed for this subject anywhere), a glossary of bird names, an index of birds, an index of poets, and an index of first lines. The focus is on English poets, but the compiler points out that of the one hundred twenty species of birds treated in the poems, most can be found in America. Still, "if Americans have a complaint, it is not the question of names, it is the fact that among the species which we do not have are three of the most prominent birds in poetry." They are the cuckoo, the skylark, and the nightingale. In its poetic observations on birds, this anthology is truly unique and is recommended for both libraries and individuals.

ARABIC POETRY

Modern Arabic Poetry; an Anthology. *Salma Khadra Jayyusi, ed.* (1987) **Columbia University Press. 498p.**

Prepared under the Project for Translation from Arabic Literature, this is a valuable collection for anyone attempting to understand the Arab world, particularly so because the compiler, a distinguished poet and critic, is a leading expert on the Arab nations as well. While the focus is on poetry written in the twentieth century, primarily from the latter half of the century, the influence of earlier work is evident, as is the constant struggle for identity in, and reconciliation with, the modern world. If a window is opened for even the most avid poetry reader on a dark part of poetry, it is due in no small part to the superior system of translation. All of the poems are translated twice, the final version representing a consensus between the literal version and that creatively rendered by English-language poets. The list of the poet translators (each with a short biographical sketch at the end of the volume) includes John Heath-Stubbs, W. S. Merwin, Christopher Middleton, Anthony Thwaite, and Richard Wilbur. The introduction, which explains the content, form, and history of the poems, is a forty-page essay worth reading for its own merits.

Modern Poetry of the Arab World. *Abdullah al-Udhari, ed. and tr.* (1986) **Penguin Books. 154p., pap.**

Poet, teacher, translator, and editor, Abdullah al-Udhari is in an excellent position to present modern Arabic poetry to the West. He does not disappoint. Much, if not all, of the poetry is within the reach and understanding of the average reader. While the table of contents offers short biographical sketches of each of the twenty-two poets and the compiler's eight-page introduction is of some help, there are few notes. The poems must stand by themselves. This can be difficult when the secondary meaning of some verse, e.g., "Traffic Lights," by Mu'in Besseisso, or Mahmoud Darwish's "I have witnessed the massacre," is puzzling. At the same time, these two poems, as well as the hundred or so others, can be appreciated for the sheer beauty of movement, content, and style. "The strength of the Arab poet," the compiler writes, "is that he writes about the misery and tragedy of individuals who suffer. . . . The poet proclaims the individual and promotes Arab dignity." The translations are fluid, and the collection gives the outsider an excellent view of Arab thought and modern history. Indexes of titles and first lines are supplied.

ASIAN-AMERICAN POETRY

Breaking Silence; an Anthology of Contemporary Asian American Poets. *Joseph Bruchac, ed.* **(1983) Greenfield Review Press. 295p., o.p.**

The technological success of the Japanese, the remarkable business skills of Asians in America, and the power of their children to excel in schools have forced Americans to view Asians more favorably in a reappraisal of the exotic and sinister former stereotype. Drawing upon numerous little magazines, the editor (a little magazine publisher himself) offers the work of 50 poets, some of their poems being original to this collection. "My choices were subjective," Bruchac explains. "I picked the poems I liked best with an eye for variety and giving each poet enough space to give the reader a good taste of his or her work." The procedure for the first poet, Mei-Mei Berssenbrugge, is typical. Her entry opens with her picture and a brief biographical sketch, followed by a selection of her poetry. "Silence" is indeed now broken, and the murmurs to the explosions indicate a way of looking at life and at America rarely found elsewhere. It is a view that is as perceptive and imaginative as it is intelligent and disciplined. While few of the poets' names are that well known, their ideas and their dreams are known to all. Highly recommended for most libraries and for all people who enjoy poetry.

AUSTRALASIAN POETRY

An Anthology of Twentieth-Century New Zealand Poetry. *Vincent O'Sullivan, comp.* **(3d ed., 1987) Oxford University Press. 460p., pap.**

The compiler claims to have selected the poems for this volume on the basis of excellence. This may be the ideal, but when one is limiting the collection to a country the size of New Zealand (approximately one quarter the population of New York City), choices based on history and the natural development of the literature are inevitable and correct. There are not that many really outstanding poets when one is drawing from a base of about two million people, and the reader will probably fail to recognize more than two or three. Most of the poets are good, but not that good. Arrangement is chronological, with the vast number of entries coming from the late twentieth century. This anthology would be a good reference source in libraries and be of unquestioned interest to New Zealanders, but it is of quite limited value to others.

The Collins Book of Australian Poetry. *Rodney Hall, comp.* **(1981, 1984) Fontana/Collins. 460p., o.p.**

Suitably enough, the Australian saga opens with a Wonguri-Mandjigai song about the birth and death of the moon. The Aborigine's highly rhythmic, ritual poem is followed by some hundred and fifty "most alive of Australian poems." The work is in chronological order and ends in the mid 1980's. The compiler admits there have been literary influences on the poetry from the Pacific as well as from Britain and America, but he sees the Australian voice as distinctive. Any one poet's "poems interact and grow from one another. . . . If the poems have a secondary life, I would suggest it is not so much that of authorial ambition and achievement, as a special history of Australia." For example, Rhyll McMaster outlines the "Profiles of My Father" and also discourses on water tanks so suggestively as to give the outsider as potent a picture of the country as any travel book. The liveliness, the zest of most of the poetry is caught in the work of Henry Lawson, one of scores of poets who sing about the trials and the joys of early settlement. In "Will Yer Write It Down for Me?" he opens the story with "In the parlour of the shanty where the lives have all gone wrong" and ends it with "Takes his pen in tears and triumph, and he writes it down for them." The nineteenth-century poet's biography, along with those of all the entrants, is given in loving detail at the end of the volume. This is a marvelous collection.

The Penguin Book of New Zealand Verse. *Ian Wedde and Harvey McQueen, eds.* **(1985) Penguin Books. 575p., pap.**

This anthology begins with almost one hundred pages of Maori traditional poetry, drawn primarily from the nineteenth century and by memory from many centuries before that. There is a fine introduction to the Maori verse that does much to set the scene for what follows. Edward Tregear (1846–1931) is first in line of the credited poets, and he draws upon that same tradition for his art. The remaining eighty or so poets are presented in chronological order by date of birth, ending with Elizabeth Nannestad (born 1956). There is a select bibliography for each of the poets, but no biographical data is provided. And while there are a few notes, these are primarily for the Maori verse. As with other collections of this type, the real problem is the uneven talent of so many of the poets. At the same time, one must be grateful for the overview it offers the student and, of course, the sense of pride it affords the New Zealander.

Poetry in Australia. Vol. I: From the Ballads to Brennan, *T. Inglis Moore, comp.;* **Vol. II: Modern Australian Verse,** *Douglas Stewart, comp.* **(1965) University of California Press. O.p.**

In 1965, this was the definitive edition of Australian verse. The strength of the set is the first volume that has an exceptionally strong section of folk songs and ballads, as well as "bush ballads and popular verse." The volume ends with the end of the nineteenth and the beginning of the twentieth century. In addition to the ballads, there are some fifty credited poets. The pleasant surprises are the writers from "the colonial age," and a few of those writing in the nineties. All of them receive short biographical sketches, as do the poets in the second volume. In retrospect, the choices for the twentieth century are sometimes less than rewarding, although even the poorest give one a new appreciation of the land and its people. One notes the relative lack of introspective verse and the heavy debt owed the earlier ballads and verse. Both volumes are to be treasured for the popular, folksy entries that remind us that poetry first and foremost is something from and for the people. This was never more true than in this collection.

AUSTRIAN POETRY

Contemporary Austrian Poetry; an Anthology. *Beth Bjorklund, ed. and tr.* **(1986) Fairleigh Dickinson University Press. 328p.**

In his "Meditation at Seventy," senior poet Rudolf Henz admits to having been less than a social activist during his life. At the same time, he was committed to composing "book after book, line after line, for five decades." That might be the theme of the present collection, which covers almost the same amount of time for the fifty-five poets represented here. Representing a cross section of modern Austria, the assembled poets range in age from thirty-nine to eighty-seven. Probably not more than a handful are that well known outside of their own country. Initiated by h. c. artmann (a poet who frowns on upper case letters), the so-called "Vienna Group" is often found in English language journals. This and other equally fascinating movements are traced in the witty introduction by the translator and compiler.

BALLADS AND SONGS

American Folk Poetry; an Anthology. *Duncan Emrich, ed.* **(1974) Little, Brown. 831p.**

Year in and year out this is a favorite, much-consulted work at home and in the library. It is as basic as any collection of folk poetry can be. Although the editor points out that "folk poetry should not and cannot be judged on the aesthetic scales used to weigh the poetry of great literature," he suggests that it offers some strong challenges. The irony is that most of the poems are by the ubiquitous "anonymous." They are such a part of daily life that the original author has been long forgotten, a Homer without a name. Yes, Homer is brought to mind when one reads the magnificent section on "Wars and Other Disasters." The numerous pages dedicated to children's songs and verses do justice to anything in the literature. Combining song and verse, the eight separate sections are often subdivided. One imaginative subsection includes types of work: sailing, lumbering, coal mining. The massive volume, and it weighs several pounds, ends with a well-constructed bibliography and an index of titles and first lines. Highly recommended for anyone with the slightest curiosity about folk poetry, and a must for the library.

The American Songbag. *Carl Sandburg, comp.* **(1927) Harcourt, Brace. 495p., pap.**

There are songs (both words and music) galore in this collection by the well-known poet Carl Sandburg. He has divided the songs into "Dramas and Portraits," "The Ould Sod," "Minstrel Songs," "Tarnished Love Tales or Colonial and Revolutionary Antiques," "Frankie and Her Man," "Pioneer Memories," "Kentucky Blazing Star," and so forth. You will find such wonderful creations as "Foggy, Foggy Dew" and "The Erie Canal" among the two hundred and eighty songs, ballads, and ditties that Americans have been singing down the centuries. Many of these tunes and lyrics will be new to the reader, for most of them are by now obscure, but they should prove of interest to those who would like to pick them out on the piano or guitar. And it is delightul to come across a famous song like "Sweet Betsy from Pike" with all nine stanzas printed. Sandburg comments briefly before each of these songs, filling in its background and responding to its charms. With their personal tone, the notes make an appealing songbook even more attractive.

The Common Muse; an Anthology of Popular British Ballad Poetry, XVth-XXth Century. *Vivian de Sola Pinto and Allan Edwin Rodway, eds.* **(1957) Philosophical Library. 470p.**

Ballads are one of the most enduring and entertaining of all poetic forms, and this anthology is a collection of several hundred popular British ballads written from the fifteenth through the twentieth centuries. The organizing principle, after a long and scholarly introduction, is to divide the poems into general and amatory ballads. The former might be about history; social criticism; manners and fashion; soldiers, sailors, highwaymen, and poachers; portents and prodigies; crime and punishment; concluding with religion. The amatory section is divided into rural, urban, vocational, clerical, marital, and wise and foolish virgins. Those categories seem to encompass more or less everything an author would want to write about, and these ballads make for very varied and rewarding reading. They should please those who are interested in the history of poetry, as well as readers who are looking for entertaining, accessible poems with strong, lilting, musical underpinnings. Occasionally an author is identified, but most often the author is unknown.

English and Scottish Ballads (The Poetry Bookself). *Robert Graves, ed.* **(1957) William Heinemann. 163p., pap.**

A frontispiece of a facsimile page from The Roxburghe Ballads (an eighteenth-century collection of broadsheets), complete with a dramatic woodcut of St. George fighting a dragon, gives an accurate, historical feel to the poems. Ballads, according to a dictionary definition that Robert Graves includes in his long, scholarly introduction to this wonderful book, are "simple, spirited poems in short stanzas, in which a popular story is graphically told." The works in this collection date from the early fourteenth to the middle of the seventeenth century, the great age for the composition of ballads. Graves reports that ballads were sung to the music of a harp or viol to entertain people as they ate or drank. Their material came originally out of old, pagan witch cults, and many of the allusions can be traced to those occult roots. Ballads recounted the exploits of Robin Hood, a particularly popular figure whose adventures showed up in fifty different works, a few of them included in this collection. Other well-known ballads are "Lord Rendal" and "Barbara Allen." All these poems are beautifully wrought and a pleasure to read. They are here accessible to the ordinary reader and still provide the same enjoyment they afforded those long centuries ago.

English and Scottish Popular Ballads. *Helen Child Sargent and George Lyman Kittredge, eds.,* **from the collection of Francis James Child. (1904, 1932, reissued, 1947) Houghton Mifflin. 730p.**

Thanks to his systematic collection of folk ballads, Francis Child is remembered today as America's earliest advocate of the importance of these works. His largest undertaking was the eight-volume collection of *English and Scottish Ballads,* one of the most extensive in existence. This was revised and reedited by a contemporary, equally famous, professor at Harvard, and Child's daughter. The present volume represents each of the three hundred and five basic ballads in one or more versions. Short notes conclude the volume. (Scholars must turn to the original work for the exhaustive collations, elaborate bibliographies, notes, etc.) The introduction, although written almost one hundred years ago, remains one of the best overall histories of the ballad, in abbreviated form. This is by George Lyman Kittredge, a master of the well-turned phrase and one of Harvard's greatest teachers. "Mary Hamilton" is typical enough of how the material is handled. There is a brief explanation of the ballad's history, then two versions. While all of this may be too much for the average reader, the fact remains that it is still the one place to turn for the definitive rendition of a popular work.

The Faber Book of Ballads. *Matthew Hodgart, ed.* **(1965) Faber and Faber. 267p., pap.**

Easy to understand, thrilling to read, "a ballad is a song that comments on life by telling a story in a popular style," to quote the introduction to this comprehensive collection of ballads. The editor has divided ballads into various categories: "Traditional," "Robin Hood and Border Ballads," "Scots Eighteenth Century," "Folksong and Lyric," "Broadside Ballads," "Irish," and finally, "Australian and American." So, here you will find "John Henry" and "Barbara Allen," as well as "Sir Patrick Spens," "Edward," "Finnegan's Wake," and "Lord Randal." There is enormous variety in this collection, and the quality of the verse is very high indeed. Being outside the Great Tradition of English literature, they speak for "the people," and they continue, very powerfully, to speak to them as well. The introduction helpfully places the ballads within their historical contexts. Here they stand, accessible, emotional, literary experiences for anyone who can read.

Modern Ballads and Story Poems. *Charles Causley, ed.* **(1965) Franklin Watts; also published in Great Britain as Rising Early, 1964. 128p., o.p.**

The English poet Charles Causley limits "modern" to only some forty poems and ballads. The slim volume indicates the popularity of the form. Among the group is almost every well-known poet of the twentieth century: W. H. Auden, Robert Frost, John Betjeman, Ted Hughes, Edith Sitwell, Stevie Smith. What is fascinating about the selection is its focus. It takes a dim view of modern life, and while there are dashes of humor to relieve the tension, the topics move grimly from suffering and death to love and hatred. The compiler, in a fine introduction, fully explains his focus and his choices. He tells the reader to be watchful "for all kinds of ironic understatements." There is help not only by Mr. Causley, but by the poets themselves who sometimes explain the background of their work at the end of the poem. There are fine drawings by Anne Netherwood.

The Oxford Book of Ballads. *James Kinsley, ed.* **(1969) Oxford University Press. 711p., pap.**

In 1911 Sir Arthur Quiller-Couch published a similar work to this. Professor Kinsley has taken over the project, revised many of the ballads, and made additions. About half the ballads in the earlier edition have been dropped. The present volume includes about eighty-five with music to which the ballads are sung; almost fifty of these are new to Kinsley's edition. The entries are limited to traditional ballads of England and Scotland. They are "ballads which are related in theme or in mood." Here can be found riding ballads of the Scottish Border, Biblical ballads, tales of romance, among others. The compiler has rejected the printing of numerous versions of the same ballad and uses only the one he thinks is close to the oral tradition. All and all, this is the most authoritative collection of its type available.

The Oxford Book of English Traditional Verse. *Frederick Woods, ed.* **(1983) Oxford University Press. 424p.**

Complementing *The Oxford Book of Ballads*, this volume focuses on song lyrics that are part of the English oral tradition. Many of the lyrics, of course, are known and sung today. The scope is wide, and the compiler moves from the earliest English songs to a section of relatively contemporary verse familiar to anyone who appreciates the twentieth-century craze for folk songs. The "verse" is limited solely to song lyrics. The book is divided into such large subject headings as "The Pain of Love." The compiler leaves it to other collections to record sea chanties and familiar ballads and rhymes that are not traditional folk lyrics. While an argument persists over whether or not current or earlier versions of a song should be given, the compiler favors the latter; he also makes the point that "the words can be detached without damage" from the music. Lack of music may be considered a fault by some.

The Oxford Book of Sea Songs. *Roy Palmer, ed.* (1986) Oxford University Press. 343p.

About half of the approximately hundred and fifty songs in the collection have the primary music score. The others often state "sung to the tune of_____". "Sir Walter Raleigh Sailing in the Lowlands" is, for example, sung "To the tune of 'The Sailing in the Lowlands.' " This superior gathering of songs is "chiefly from England, but also from Ireland, Scotland, Wales, Canada, New Zealand, Australia, and America." They are arranged roughly in chronological order, which is often "dictated by the subject matter, a specific battle or shipwreck, for example, which took place on a particular date." Often at the conclusion of the entry, there is a detailed note supplying historical background information. There are also numerous footnotes explaining obscure words or phrases, as well as a separate glossary of nautical terms. The compiler's introduction discusses the history of the genre. He explains, too, why so often the music is lacking, remarking that "the words of a song without music are very like dry bones."

CANADIAN POETRY

Canadian Poetry in English (Canadian Literature Series). *Bliss Carman,*
Lorne Pierce, and V. B. Rhodenizer, eds. **(Rev. and enl. ed., 1954)**
Ryerson Press. 456p., o.p.

Covering Canadian poetry from the earliest times to slightly after the
Second World War, this collection offers almost two hundred poets, all
of whom wrote in English although not a few are from French back-
grounds. The collection is particularly strong in late nineteenth-century
and early twentieth-century work, and, as the compilers point out, it is
only a "reasonably critical" work. Verses are included that may not have
earned critical acclaim but are familiar to almost all Canadians. In ad-
dition, the original compiler, Bliss Carman, is a traditionalist who took a
dim view of modern trends in poetry. The result is a collection with wide
appeal for people who normally do not read poetry, or, at the most,
equate it with old time favorites that are recited in school and sometimes
at home. Thanks to the short biographical sketches before each of the
poet's work, one can glimpse many of the lesser-known writers from one
coast of Canada to the other. Carman is here, as is Pauline Johnson,
Duncan Scott, and numerous earlier favorites. The nineteenth century is
filled with male poets, but by the beginning of the twentieth such women
as Elizabeth Brewster and Miriam Waddington came into prominence,
usually for the best.

Modern Canadian Verse. *A. J. M. Smith, ed.* **(1967) Oxford University**
Press. 426p., o.p.

What sets this apart from other Canadian collections is that it is "in
English and French." Here is one of the few anthologies to take notice
of the major French-speaking poets in Canada, many of whom suffer
from not being translated into English. The French-language poems are
scattered throughout the volume. It is worth emphasizing that there are
no translations here; it is assumed that the reader has a command of the
French language. "Modern" in 1967 meant that all but a few of the poets
were living. By now, some have died, at least those in the first part of this

chronologically ordered book. The scope of the collection is explained briefly by the compiler: "This aims at variety, and it seeks to be representative — not of the average but of the best." There is no argument with this short explanation. One might have appreciated notes about the contributors, but it was decided to let the poets and the poems speak for themselves.

New American and Canadian Poetry. *John Gill, ed.* **(1971) Beacon Press. 280p., pap.**

Among the outstanding Canadian poets in this collection are Margaret Atwood, Irving Layton, and Patrick Lane. Americans include Marge Piercy, Dick Lourie and J. D. Reed. But few of the thirty or so poets are that well known. The compiler is a famous little magazine editor, and he has selected poets who are regulars in the little journals and not that frequently published in the larger literary magazines. The result is a limited success. The majority of poets and poems are well worth considering, but a few seem to be there primarily because they are personal enthusiasms of Gill. It is hard, however, to argue with a veteran editor's choices. What is interesting some twenty years later is how few of the "new" voices became veterans. Ironically, Atwood, among the best known of the names, is now a major novelist as well as a substantial poet. There are some striking photographs of the poets and longer than usual biographical notes.

The New Oxford Book of Canadian Verse in English. *Margaret Atwood, comp.* **(1982) Oxford University Press. 477p.**

Chosen by Margaret Atwood, the highly acclaimed Canadian novelist and poet, these verses cover the time of the earliest settlements in the sixteenth century to the present day. Many authors will be new to the general reader, but some like Earle Birney, Malcolm Lowry, and Michael Ondaatje, to say nothing of Robert Service, are better known. Atwood also includes many women in her collection, noting that Canada has had a higher proportion of fine female poets than either England or the United States. Many of the older works in this anthology are primarily of historical interest, conveying a picture of life in a newly settled land and the feelings that such an experience engenders. Later poems make a stronger aesthetic claim on our attention, and over half of the volume is devoted to modern works. Atwood provides an astute introduction in which she relates the poets from different generations to one another and to the reading public.

The Oxford Book of Canadian Verse in English and French. *A. J. M. Smith,* ed. **(1960) Oxford University Press. 445p., o.p.**

Including the works of almost one hundred poets who wrote in either English or French, this anthology begins its journey through Canadian literature in the early nineteenth century. Most of the poets will be new to general readers, but many of them are represented by at least two poems, giving the reader a sense of their general interests and how they treat their subjects. The French-language poems are not translated, so to fully appreciate this collection one must be able to read French. But even if the reader is limited to the poems written in English, there is still a great deal of material here. The editor points out, in a lengthy and perceptive introduction, that Canadian poetry has long been split by two quite contradictory goals: one is to communicate "whatever is unique or local in Canadian life," while the other is to register what Canadians have in common with people of other, more established cultural traditions. Both those aims can be seen in this anthology.

CHILDREN'S POETRY

Amazing Monsters; Verses to Thrill and Chill. *Robert Fisher, ed.* **(1982) Faber and Faber. 95p.**

This book is nothing if it is not fun. The poems are all about monsters of a most horrible variety, things that are slimy or are always behind you, dongs with luminous noses, or serpents that insist on singing. The names of some of the poets of these awful creatures will be familiar: Edward Lear, Lewis Carroll, Theodore Roethke, or J. R. R. Tolkien. Others are less well known. These poems seem ideal for reading aloud to children who want to be gently scared, but they are also a good deal of fun for adults who enjoy images of dreadful figures such as dragons, dinkeybirds, gruesomes, malfeasances, or even wendigos. The monsters are amusing as well as amazing, and the poems are generally of a fairly high caliber, as if that mattered when dealing with such unsettling topics as things that go bump in the night.

The Book of a Thousand Poems; a Family Treasury. *J. Murray Macbain, ed.* **(1983) Peter Bedrick Books. 630p.**

Another anthology of verse for young children, this differs from its competitors in several ways. First, the compiler includes the familiar with the not-so-familiar and laces it with poems of adventure. Second, the compilation is as much for the parent or teacher helping the child learn to speak and read as it is for the youngster who enjoys it. Macbain's thoughts on the use of poetry in the development of the child are set forth in the introduction. Third, there is a good section in the introduction on "suggestions for practical use" that demonstrates how the poems may be employed in the classroom. The collection itself is divided into thirteen topical sections. There is a classified list of subjects at the end of the volume, as well as indexes of first lines and authors. Essentially, the value of this anthology is to bring together in one place the classics of children's verse; it is good reference work for librarians.

Come Hither. *Walter de la Mare, comp.* **(3rd ed., 1957) Knopf. 777p., o.p.**

Many consider this the best introduction to English poetry for young people. As such, it is a standard item in many libraries and is familiar to parents and their children. The selection is excellent. The comments by the poet-compiler are to the point and easy to understand. The more-than-seven-hundred poems are as familiar as anything in the language, and the poets are all the old faithfuls. There is little truly modern English or American verse, *either English or American vintage,* but what is selected is truly representative. Most of the focus is on English poetry, particularly poets who appeal to children from age six through their teens. The subtitle is perfectly correct in its statement that this is "a collection of rhymes and poems for the young of all ages." The decorations by Warren Chappell are appropriate, although not overly imaginative. The format is bulky, but attractive.

The Faber Book of Children's Verse. *Janet Adam Smith, comp.* **(1953) Faber and Faber. 412p., pap.**

The selection here is incredible. My hat goes off to the compiler since she obviously thinks that children can read more sophisticated poetry than their parents! And, why not? If children are not challenged, then they will never have a sense of what they could respond to. And that is exactly what it takes to understand many of these poems: motivation and education. The editor has aimed her poetry at children from the ages of eight to fourteen. Some poems are sure to appeal to the younger set: some marvels and riddles, poems about fairies and nymphs, and such tales as the "Pied Piper of Hamelin," by Robert Browning. Much of the material is, however, for the older group of children, and a very bright group they had better be, if they are to comprehend these very advanced verses: John Keats's "On First Looking Into Chapman's Homer," Shelley's "Ozymandias," and Milton's "On the University Carrier." None the less, with warnings that these poems will bewilder and confuse most children, they are still an outstanding collection for gifted children and adults who are interested in fine poetry.

I Like You, If You Like Me; Poems of Friendship (Margaret K. McElderry Books). *Myra Cohn Livingston, ed.* **(1987) Macmillan. 143p.**

This volume is aimed at young people who are especially interested in the concept of friendship and would like to see how poets have charted this somewhat treacherous terrain. There are over ninety poems included, by poets from Wang Wei, writing in eighth-century China, to Shel Silverstein, who is writing today. These are likeable, simple poems, very lilting in some cases and sharply descriptive in others, and selected to appeal primarily to younger readers. The book is divided into such categories as "Lonesome: All Alone," "Would You Come and Be My Friend?" "The Friendly Beasts," and "One Good Friendship." This treatment is decidedly focused on adolescents and younger children who should appreciate poetry about a subject so close to their hearts.

Love Is like the Lion's Tooth; an Anthology of Love Poems. *Frances McCullough, ed*

See under LOVE POETRY

Messages; a Book of Poems. *Naomi Lewis, comp.* **(1985) Faber and Faber. 255p.**

Critic and writer Naomi Lewis draws upon contemporary poetry to offer young people (ages ten to fifteen) the best of the modern poets. The particular gift of the compiler is to select lesser-known poets from the twentieth century and earlier who will appeal to a young audience. Arrangement is by broad subjects that range from "A pen, a paintbrush, a guitar" to "Children's country" and "Difficult relations." Among the poets in the section on "A host of furious fancies" are Stevie Smith, Harold Monro, Louis MacNeice, and the compiler herself. Each part has about a dozen poems. There are indexes of authors and first lines.

The Moon Is Shining Bright as Day; an Anthology of Goodhumored Verse. *Ogden Nash, ed.* **(1953) J. B. Lippincott. 178p.**

One of America's greatest satirical poets, Ogden Nash proves to have been equally humorous and good natured. "When the suggestion was made that I assemble a collection of not-too-serious poems for boys and girls, I easily fell in with it. . . . As a man moves into his fifties [i.e., in 1953] he becomes increasingly aware of the reading that illuminated his childhood, and the temptation to pass a good thing along is irresistible. That is why there are few rare specimens in this collection, which has been gathered from the daisies rather than the orchids." The six sections have such wildly imaginative titles as "Has anybody seen my mouse" and "Yonder see the morning blink." Three indexes of titles, first lines, and authors bring the selection together for the user and librarian. But for the child such order is hardly required. The poems flow into one another. Every major and minor poet seems to be included, from Hilaire

Belloc to William Wordsworth. There are few blunders in choice of either poets or poetry. Nash is represented by a half dozen works, including his immortal "The Wapiti." It can be quoted in full: "There goes the Wapiti, Hippity-hoppity!" That fairly well sets the tone for the book, which can be read by the first reader or the sophisticated high school student, or by any adult with a sense of wonder and humor.

A New Treasury of Children's Poetry; Old Favorites and New Discoveries. *Joanna Cole, comp.* **(1984) Doubleday. 224p., pap.**

A children's author and winner of numerous "Notable Books" awards from the American Library Association, Joanna Cole knows well what poems young children like to read and have read to them. She begins with "First poems of childhood" and introduces the reader to such favorites as A. A. Milne's "Hoppity" and James Kirkup's unusual "Baby's drinking song." With that stage passed, she moves on to "People and portraits" and seven other sections that focus on things children enjoy. Here are animals, silly poems, play poetry, holidays, and a "Different way of seeing." For example, she introduces us to Charles Malam's "Steam shovel" and Mary O'Neill's "What is black?" The content is wildly varied. "I have not tried to make an objective collection, including all of the classic and contemporary poems that children ought to know. Instead I have chosen poetry that made me stop, feeling full of the brightness of the images or the joyousness of the rhythm or the recognition of a hidden feeling." The compiler's promises are more than fulfilled in this charming collection.

Once upon a Rhyme; 101 Poems for Young Children. *Sara Corrin and Stephen Corrin, eds.* **(1982) Faber and Faber. 157p.**

Here one finds both American and English poems, mainly modern, and ideally suited for children in grades one to seven. The poems are arranged under such catchy subjects as "Wind and weather," "Odd and funny," and "Viewpoints." This allows the reader to go from mood to mood, place to place. There are poems about animals, fabulous creatures, fireworks, locomotives. The poets range from the famous and nearly famous to the virtually unknown. All seem to have a good grasp of what entertains the child. There are black and white illustrations on almost every page, but here and there one finds garish color plates — all by artist Jill Bennett. This works well enough with lesser known works, but not when the illustrator is asked to pinch hit for Milne or Lear. The poetry is compiled for children, not for adults, and the book could be just the right one to buy a child.

The Oxford Book of Children's Verse. *Iona Opie and Peter Opie, eds.* (1973) Oxford University Press. 407p.

Celebrated scholars of children's literature, Iona and Peter Opie have assembled here "verses that have been written for children, or written with children prominently in mind, which either were cherished in their own day, or which have stood the test of time. Its object is thus to make available in one place the classics of children's poetry: that small satchelful of verse whose existence constitutes one of the pleasing advantages of being born to the English tongue." Most of the authors are British, but a few Americans are also in evidence. Here one can find Robert Southey's poem "The Old Man's Comforts and How He Gained Them," which Lewis Carroll parodied so triumphantly in "You are old, Father William." Several other superb Carroll poems are also reprinted. The anthology is arranged in chronological order, beginning with medieval poetry and works from the sixteenth century and concluding with twentieth-century verse. There are poems by John Bunyan, Isaac Watts, William Blake, Charles and Mary Lamb, and Robert Louis Stevenson, to name only a few of the famous authors. Many of the contributors are now unknown. This book is essential reading for families with small children. The poems should delight youngsters and provide as much pleasure for adults.

The Oxford Book of Children's Verse in America. *Donald Hall, ed.* (1985) Oxford University Press. 319p.

A fine companion to *The Oxford Book of Children's Verse,* which features English poems, and *The Oxford Nursery Rhyme Book,* this collection concentrates on poems for children written in America in the English language. But the editor does not end there: he also includes poems that were not intended particularly for children, and yet were avidly consumed by them. So, although this volume begins with two alphabets from *The New England Primer of 1727 and 1768* and carries on with Clement Moore's "A Visit from St. Nicholas," it also features Edgar Allan Poe's "Annabel Lee" and "The Raven," poems not usually thought of as youth-oriented. In the same way, many of Emily Dickinson's poems are reprinted here. But, the anthology is essentially indebted to poems from the pages of children's magazines over the past hundred and fifty years. There is a lot of Henry Wadsworth Longfellow, many poems by little-known poets, and from modern times we find Ogden Nash, Countee Cullen, Theodore Roethke, and X. J. Kennedy. Children should find this book extremely satisfying.

The Oxford Nursery Rhyme Book. *Iona Opie and Peter Opie, comps.* **(1955) Oxford University Press. 224p.**

There are over eight hundred rhymes and ditties in this volume, enough to entertain even the most truculent child or the most nostalgic adult. The compilers have included "infant jingles, riddles, catches, tongue-trippers, baby games, toe names, maxims, alphabets, counting rhymes, prayers, and lullabies." Here you will find "Jack Sprat," "Tommy Tucker," "Jack Horner," "Ding, Dong Bell," "Goosey Gander," and hundreds more. The contents are divided into helpful sections: "Baby Games and Lullabies," "First Favorites," "Little Songs," "People," "A Little Learning," "Awakening," "Wonders," "Riddles, Tricks, and Trippers," and "Ballads and Songs." Throughout, excellent, old wood-cuts illustrate the verses. Especially appealing are the ones for "The Tragical Death of A, Apple Pie; who was cut in pieces, and eaten by twenty-six gentlemen, with whom all little people ought to be very well acquainted." An alphabet follows. This book is delightful reading both for adults and for children and is unsurpassed as a resource book for parents or childminders.

Piping Down the Valley Wild; Poetry for the Young of All Ages. *Nancy Larrick, ed.* **(1968) Delacorte Press. 248p.**

The title, to be sure, is the first line in William Blake's famous "The Piper." The poem concludes with the fitting lines "And I write my happy songs/Every child may joy to hear." The sure sense of high quality makes this an outstanding collection for children. A. A. Milne is represented with "Puppy and I." Right after the child walks off with the puppy, Gwendolyn Brooks introduces us to "Pete at the Zoo." In the second of sixteen sections one meets Laura E. Richards and her "The Giraffe and the Woman," and a few pages on comes the unforgettable "Purple Cow." There are masses of animals pounding through these pages. When they are not on center stage, there is the sound of concrete mixers, and "Bam, bam, bam" a poem by Eve Merriam. One must not forget the clowns, gnomes, friendly witches, scarecrows, and, of course, Christopher Robin at "Buckingham Palace." All of the poems can be read aloud and were chosen precisely for that quality. This marvelous, imaginative collection is a total success.

Poems for Young Children. *Caroline Royds, comp.* **(1986) Doubleday. 45p.**

This is brief, delightful collection for pre-school and early grade-school children. There are forty-five poems, most of which are familiar. Here one finds Mother Goose and Robert Frost side by side with A. A. Milne and E. E. Cummings. There are pastel illustrations on every page and enough space around the poem so it stands out and can be easily read. Inga Moore's illustrations are excellent; they do as much for the work as the poems themselves. Every subject and mood is covered from tears and laughter to animals and the thrills of bed time. The poems are found in countless other similar anthologies, but the wise, limited choices and the marvelous layout make this an ideal book for young children — and certainly for parents reading to those children.

Poems to Read Aloud. *Edward Hodnett, ed.* **(Rev. ed., 1967) W. W. Norton. 390p., o.p.**

What makes a poem ideal to read aloud? Until the time of mass education and mass distribution of books and magazines in the late nineteenth century, almost all poems were delivered orally. At least this was the case with popular verses that hoped to gain more than a limited recognition at court or among the elite, and even here the poets and their followers prided themselves on memory and rhetorical skills. Things changed, and today, while poetry reading is no longer even as popular as it was in the late 1960's, it has a strong following at two or three levels. First, there are the poetry readings by established and aspiring poets. Second, a certain amount of memory is required for literature courses. And finally, a few people love to get together and rattle off poems which have a particular meaning for them and their friends. Of course, there are other reasons to value poetry readings, but with the general public in mind the compiler of this volume has brought together the best-loved poems in England and America. Shakespeare has the greatest number of entries, but other songs, sonnets, and readable verse by W. H. Auden, Thomas Campion, Emily Dickinson, John Donne, Rudyard Kipling, and William Wordsworth, to name a few, are here in abundance. They all contribute to a fine, specialized approach to poetry.

The Random House Book of Poetry for Children. *Jack Prelutsky, ed.*
(1983) Random House. 248p.

A poet himself, the compiler begins each of the numerous sections in
this volume with a poem written especially for it. In addition, there are
almost six hundred other poems, most of which are modern. Topics
range from dogs and cats to the seasons, home, children, nonsense,
wordplay, ghosts, and almost anything else of interest to the reader.
Furthermore, there are almost as many illustrations, usually quite small,
by Arnold Lobel, that fit in nicely with the poems. Most of the emphasis
is on fun, humor, and the delights of being a child in an adult world.
Some serious and thoughtful poems are included, such as Lillian Moore's
"Foghorns" and the work of Christopher Morley and Walter de la Mare.
Many of the entries are from such great artists as Shakespeare, William
Blake, and Emily Dickinson. There is a useful subject index. The col-
lection is one of the best available for elementary school children.

Read-Aloud Rhymes for the Very Young. *Jack Prelutsky, comp.* **(1986)**
Knopf. 98p.

In the familiar over-sized, picture-book format, the compiler, assisted
by illustrator Marc Brown, brings together nursery rhymes and poetry
for those aged five years and under. All of the poems are chosen to be
read aloud. Children "are great listening machines," and Prelutsky, also
the editor of *The Random House Book of Poetry* (annotated here), has col-
lected more than two hundred little poems to "feed little people with
little attention spans to help both grow." The poems are set against the
background of the colorful illustrations, and a child might enjoy looking
as much as listening and, eventually, reading. An index of titles, an index
of authors, and an index of first lines help the parent and librarian, but
the average child will need no assistance in going through this colorful
book. Most of the authors (the majority of whom are women), though
familiar to young people and parents, are not in the mainstream of
American poetry. Exceptions include Gwendolyn Brooks, Marchette
Chute, Nikki Giovanni, and Maxine Kumin.

Saturday's Children; Poems of Work. *Helen Plotz, comp.* **(1982)**
Greenwillow Books. 174p. o.p.

Divided into four sections, here is a successful effort to explain work
to children through poems. The compiler's succinct introduction nicely
covers the points she is illustrating through the selections. The divisions

include poetry about rural work, industrial labor, women's work, and working in general. There is a subsection on unemployment and another on child labor. There are two primary points about this unusual collection. First, there is a wide variety of poetry by outstanding poets. Among those represented are Anthony Hecht, May Sarton, Richard Wilbur, and Langston Hughes. While much of the emphasis is on modern poetry, there are representative voices, such as Robert Louis Stevenson, from earlier years. Second, the poetry is used to demonstrate sometimes willful misconceptions about work and to explain derogatory comments about working-class people.

Sprints and Distances; Sports in Poetry and the Poetry in Sport. *Lillian Morrison, comp.*

See under SPORTS POETRY

Story Poems, New and Old. *William Cole, ed.* **(1957) World. 255p., o.p.**

The remarkable thing about this collection of story poems for young people is that it eschews many of the familiar titles. What the compiler includes are the out-of-the-way poems that will have wide appeal for children and teen-agers. The selection is deliberate, as he believes that too many well-known story poems have been anthologized to the point where another similar collection is simply not needed. The ninety or so poems and ballads are literally stories in verse form, and when tried out on readers from the ages of ten to sixteen, all of them proved a great success. There is everything here from mystery and horror to love and tangled plots that would prove too unbelievable for movies, but are sure winners with poet and reader alike. The concentration is on English and American authors, and there are title and first line indexes of the poems. Black and white sketches by Walter Buehr which illustrate many of the narratives.

Straight On Till Morning; Poems of the Imaginary World. *Helen Hill, Agnes Perkins and Alethea Helbig, comps.* **(1977) Thomas Y. Crowell. 150p., o.p.**

A collection of nearly one hundred poems, nicely illustrated with black and white drawings by Ted Lewin, this anthology concentrates on the child's world of imagination. "Two things have been important in our choice of poems: content and style." The content is for a child of five to about twelve years of age, and the style "is as various as the people who wrote the poems." There are the standard subject divisions. This time the eight sections range from "Funny and fabulous friends" to "Once there was and was not. . . ." This is usual enough for children's collections, but what is unusual is the choice of poets. Few of them write exclusively for young people, and almost all are well known to adults. The list of authors is, in fact, a roll call of modern American poetry, with a bow to some equally famous English poets. Among those featured are: Hilaire Belloc, E. E. Cummings, Robert Frost, Nikki Giovanni, Donald Hall, Ted Hughes, Randall Jarrell, Kenneth Patchen, Theodore Roethke, May Swenson, and William Carlos Williams. This is an outstanding collection of poems.

Talking to the Sun; an Illustrated Anthology of Poems for Young People. *Kenneth Koch and Kate Farrell, eds.* **(1985) Metropolitan Museum of Art/Henry Holt. 112p.**

This oversized poetry anthology for children celebrates the pleasures in, and close ties between, art and poetry. The goal is achieved by illustrating each poem with a work from the Metropolitan Museum of Art. Most are paintings in full color, and range in size from a small insert to a full page. The makeup is extremely well thought out, and the whole is an invitation not only to the child, but to the adult. Koch, who is famous for his work with young people in various writing programs, explains that the poems were chosen first, and then the art was selected to go along with them. Some, although not all, of the poems are prefaced by a word or two to make the child think about the poem and the work of art. The book opens with an almost full-page picture of a Tiffany stained-glass window. The poem to accompany it is "Hymn to the Sun" by the African Fang people. Across the page is another African poem and a Russian painting of a sunset. The world view of poetry and art is carried throughout the collection's ten distinct sections. Here may be found the work of Robert Bly and Robert Frost, there, an American folksong or the Japanese poet Basho. The art is just as diverse. A remarkably imaginative book for children of all ages.

These Small Stones. *Norma Farber and Myra Cohn Livingston, comps.* **(1987) Harper & Row. 84p.**

Compiled for children in grades three to seven, the collection celebrates "small things of the real and imagined world." The slim volume is divided into six sections, each with about 10 short poems. "In My Hand" may concern a match, a jumping bean, marbles. A crab, a ladybug, or other little things make up the part about "On the Ground." In "In the Air" the readers find fireflies, birds, and even mosquitoes. And so it goes to the end, where there are useful indexes of first lines and titles. A subject index would have been helpful. The poets are wisely chosen, and while a few wrote only for children, the majority wrote for the child in everyone. Among these are Federico García Lorca, Emily Dickinson, Edward Lear, Pablo Neruda, Theodore Roethke, and other outstanding voices of the late nineteenth and twentieth centuries. Norma Farber died before the little book was published, but she is represented with two poems, as is her fellow editor. Thanks to the splendid selection and emphasis on easy to understand, shorter works, this is an ideal collection for both children and adults. Most of the verse begs to be read aloud.

This Delicious Day. *Paul B. Janeczko, comp.* **(1987) Orchard Books. 82p.**

Almost every year or so this compiler issues a new anthology for children and young people. This is one of his latest. As is his custom, there is no introduction, nor any word of explanation about its content or its purpose. In this case the title explains the scope. The sixty-five poems by almost as many poets are exclusively concerned with daily activity, primarily in the out-of-doors. The collection begins with Richard Snyder's "O I Have Dined on This Delicious Day," moves on to X. J. Kennedy's "A Certain Sandpiper," and winds down with Doris Hardie's "Song for Susannah: A Lullaby." Few of the poems are more than one or two stanzas, and all are within the easy understanding of a child. The poems are uniformly good, but no more than half a dozen would be of equal interest to adults. Happy exceptions are the work of X. J. Kennedy and a few other well-known writers such as Theodore Roethke and Philip Whalen. Mr. Janeczko is represented with a passable parody. A pleasant, but not altogether necessary book for children.

Untune the Sky; Poems of Music and Dance. *Helen Plotz, comp.* **(1957) Thomas Y. Crowell. 162p., o.p.**

Still another fine collection by the ubiquitous Helen Plotz, this, like her other anthologies, is directed to an audience of young people. William Carlos Williams sets the stage with verse from "The Desert Music." Two dozen other poems celebrate various musical instruments. As is her custom, the compiler includes writing from around the world, from all periods, and insists on the best works, whether they be by Plato, Po Chü-i, or a nursery rhyme. Psalm 100 is among the verses in the second section in "Singing Over the Earth," and W. H. Auden begins his famous poem "The Composer" with "One God Is God of Both." Dance is less frequently the subject of poems, but the compiler meets the challenge with fewer, but still quite good, poems, such as the delightful "I cannot dance upon my toes," by Emily Dickinson. As with her other collections, this is highly recommended for children and for anyone who delights in poetry and the arts.

Why Am I Grown So Cold? Poems of the Unknowable. *Myra Cohn Livingston, ed.* **(1982) Atheneum. 269p.**

In twelve sections, the compiler brings together one hundred and fifty poems to thrill and chill the child. Here are ghosts, devils, monsters, witches, and an aura of mystery. Ms. Livingston is widely known as an editor of poetry collections. Here she explains that "humankind has always been intrigued by the possible presence of ghosts and spirits. . . . Poetry abounds in tales of enchantment; its very words, rhythms, and sound create their own mystery." One may question the notion that "science has explanations for many phenomena, but it has yet to unravel many mysteries." Still, who is to argue with the poetic choices, serious or not, on the part of the compiler. She is to be congratulated for drawing upon the world's best poets, from Robert Frost and Thomas Hardy to Alexander Pushkin and Ezra Pound. This is the strength of an otherwise less-than-inspired reason for an anthology. One may debate what she thinks excites children, but who is to deny the strength of the poets and their work.

CHINESE POETRY

Among the Flowers; the Hua-Chien Chi. *Lois Fusek, tr.* **(1982) Columbia University Press. 240p.**

The translator explains that this is "a collection of five hundred *tz'u* lyrics compiled by Chao Ch'ung-tso (fl. mid-tenth century), a minor official of the later Shu dynasty (934–965). . . . The lyrics are dedicated mainly to the celebration of love. . . . The world depicted is the world of the courtesan and the singing girl, the beautiful 'flowers.' " Unfortunately, economics dictated a reproduction of the typewritten script, and there is nothing beautiful about the format. There is the usual, and in this case much appreciated, scholarly apparatus. While a trifle technical, the introduction sets the scene for the eighteen poets. What is known of them is given in biographical notes, and there is a useful glossary, bibliography, index of tune titles, and general index. It is difficult to evaluate the translations objectively. The sense of intent is nicely captured: although one suspects the loss of joy and the misery of the period, the *tz'u* are an attempt "to find, in beauty and pleasure, an end to pain." One regrets the absence of difficult-to-capture cultural supports. The lesson, as with anonymous early Egyptian poetry, is that love is a universal of time and place.

The Book of Songs; the Ancient Chinese Classic of Poetry. *Arthur Waley, tr.* **(1960) Grove Press. 358p., pap.**

Written, sung, and recited between 800 and 600 B.C., the two hundred and ninety songs were used for ceremonial purposes as well as for moral instruction. In this respect they are similar to the Japanese *Manyoshu* and the Greek *Anthology*, all of which is clearly explained in the introduction and in additional notes and appendices. Waley usually follows a song with a brief explanation, as well as with an occasional note. Much of this is not necessary. The songs rarely need any background information for the reader to appreciate them, particularly as they are divided into such subject areas as courtship, marriage, hunting, friendship. By now almost as famous as the verses he translated and explained, Waley's comments are great fun. For example, why are clothes and articles of personal adornment so often mentioned? Waley is not sure, but he suspects it is because clothes "may be regarded simply as an indication of personal status." He then proceeds to give an example or two of what he means, and while much of this is obvious, it is true that Waley comes close to being able to "recreate all the mental associations of people in China three thousand years ago."

The Columbia Book of Chinese Poetry; from Early Times to the Thirteenth Century. *Burton Watson, ed. and tr.* **(1984) Columbia University Press. 385p.**

Focusing on daily activity, "The book of Odes" sings of farming, building, love, war, and the natural interests of all people at all points in history. The odes probably were recited and later written down around 1000 to 600 B.C. These are the earliest entries of twelve sections that move through the principal dynasties of Chinese history to the 13th-century Yuan period. (After that, see the companion volume: *The Columbia Book of Later Chinese Poetry*). Poet Gary Snyder pays them the ultimate compliment: "The gathering of translations is the surest, the clearest, most comprehensive presentation of Chinese poetry yet. Burton Watson's life-long dedication to Chinese literature becomes a gift to us all." The antiquity, the remarkable continuity of Chinese poetry makes it impossible to do more than sample the virtually unbroken line of creativity. Limitations placed upon the selections in this volume are dutifully and clearly explained in the informative introduction. Watson is particularly helpful in his discussion of recurring themes and characteristics of the poems. And, when that is done, one is left with a marvelous reading experience. "The Chinese," the compiler explains, "have customarily looked upon poetry as the chief glory of their literary tradition." This anthology explains why.

The Columbia Book of Later Chinese Poetry. *Jonathan Chaves, ed. and tr.* **(1986) Columbia University Press. 490p.**

The companion volume to *The Columbia Book of Chinese Poetry,* this covers the period 1279 to 1911 (the Yuan, Ming, and the almost endless Ch'ing dynasties). Most of the focus is on the Ming period, and less on the shorter Yuan dynasty. The balance is perfect, not only between periods but in the choice of poets in terms of both quality and representativeness. The translations are equally excellent, and if one considers the ten scroll samples, typography, and general make-up, the book is a trib-

ute to the poets and the translator/compiler. An introduction explains
the various dynasties to the layperson. Before each of the sections of
poetry is a brief biographical sketch of the poet. The compiler says: "I
have omitted a number of major figures either because I could not find
an appropriate way to translate them effectively or because they were
simply not to my taste. On the other hand I have included some fairly
obscure poets who I think deserve to be better known." The formula is
close to perfect, particularly for the individual who may know little or
nothing of Chinese poetry — and certainly for the reference librarian
seeking translations of Chinese poets.

The Isle Full of Noises; Modern Chinese Poetry from Taiwan. *Dominic Cheung, ed. and tr.* **(1987) Columbia University Press. 265p.**

"The background of the development of modern Chinese poetry in
Taiwan is quite complicated," the compiler explains. "Poets bearing a
strong Chinese sentiment were writing in Japanese; other poets, strongly
committed to the Taiwanese identity, were writing in Japanese and Chi-
nese." This brief quote from a thirty-page, scholarly introduction helps
explain the title from, of course, "The Tempest," and particularly the
line which follows, "Sometimes a thousand twangling instruments will
hum about mine ears." Trying to sort out the instruments, the compiler
opens with Yang Mu (1940), gives a brief biographical sketch, places his
poetry on the island, and offers a generous sampling of his work. The
process is followed with some thirty other poets in chronological order.
An appendix includes names and titles of poems in Chinese, with Eng-
lish equivalents.

Waiting for the Unicorn; Poems and Lyrics of China's Last Dynasty, 1644–1911. *Irving Yucheng Lo and William Schultz, eds.* **(1986) Indiana University Press. (1986) 425p.**

The Ch'ing Dynasty (the last Chinese dynasty) includes a wide diver-
sity in politics, art, and poetry. Considering the length of the reign of the
Manchus, it is little wonder there is so much difference from age to age,
poet to poet. At the same time, there are no new genres, but more
dominant modes of thought and aesthetics. And, as the editors observe,
there is a great degree of historical mindedness and "preference for
dealing with the concrete, as evidenced by the growth of realism and
popularity of both narrative and . . . poems on objects." Arranged chron-
ologically, the almost seventy-five poets wrote from the mid-1660's to the
turn of the twentieth century. Each is represented with anywhere from

four to a dozen poems. To help set the stage, there is a biographical background sketch for each, which not only tells about the poet, but about the period, content, and style. (There are some delightful examples of calligraphy, usually accompanying a scroll painting or drawing.) The translations are good to excellent. The scores of translators are dutifully given credit after the selected bibliography. Liang Ch'i-ch'ao wrote: "Trying to stay the departing spring is of no avail." True, but at least a gallant effort is made to show the essence of numerous springs. The success of the effort is impressive.

Zen Poems of China & Japan; the Crane's Bill. *Lucien Stryk, Takashi Ikemoto, and Taigan Takayama, trs.* **(1973) Grove Press. 143p., pap.**

This slim volume offers the layperson a fine introduction to Chinese and Japanese poetry. While the focus is on Zen, the style and content is more broadly Asiatic, and the selections will give the Western reader an excellent notion of thought in that part of the world. Beyond this, the hundred and fifty translated poems are moving in themselves. Few are difficult to comprehend, although they may be considerably more subtle than a first reading would indicate. The verse is divided into three broad subject categories: "Enlightenment," "Death," and "General." There is a well-written introduction that will help the general reader understand the history of Zen as well as its essentials and how it is related to Zen poetry. The foreword and preface also explain the four basic moods of Zen: sabi, wabi, aware, and yugen. These are nicely defined, and the examples given for each render them relatively clear. There are notes at the end of the volume that enlighten the reader about basic cultural situations, foreign terms, etc. As there is a note for virtually each poem, the poetry is always lucid.

DEATH POETRY

Death in Literature. *Robert F. Weir, ed.* **(1980) Columbia University Press. 451p.**

Unlike the *Oxford Book of Death,* which it closely resembles, this is confined to the subject as it is represented in literature. The amount of duplication is less than one might think, and anyone who turns to one will want to use the other. They nicely complement each other. Here the selections range from 2300 B.C. to A.D. 1979, and a variety of cultures are tapped. Literature of India, China, Japan, Greece, Nigeria, Lebanon, Russia, Germany, England, France, Spain, Ireland, and the United States provide material. Each of the eleven sections has a separate introduction of two to four pages. "Many of these introductions contain brief descriptions of literary works which are used to illustrate a sectional theme and supplement the selections." In addition, there are often brief remarks about individual pieces. The emphasis falls much more on excerpts from prose than on poetry. In fact, the poetry is limited to rather obvious choices from such poets as Donne, Milton, and Dylan Thomas. This, too, is the case with the *Oxford Book of Death,* so one might conclude that there is still room for another anthology devoted entirely to poetry about death. A small point—the names of the numerous translators are not given after the work, and one has to turn to the acknowledgments to discover a vital piece of information.

The Oxford Book of Death. *D. J. Enright, ed.* **(1987) Oxford University Press. 352p.**

Poet, novelist, and critic, D. J. Enright makes an obvious point early in his brief introduction: "In this line . . . the compiler could easily and even pleasurably persist in his task until death should part the one from the other." This unusual collection is thus conceived as a book for everyone. Ironically, death seems to be a theme where writers show "themselves more lively" than in many other situations. The anthology is divided into fourteen complementary sections, from definitions of death to views and attitudes about it. Side by side with graveyards and funerals, one finds the subjects of resurrection and immortality, as well as the hereafter. Fittingly, the collection concludes with a section of "Epitaphs, Requiems and Last Words." About half of the book is devoted to poetry, the other half to prose. In the "Definitions" section, for example, one finds a page-long introduction by Enright—a practice he follows throughout the volume. A poem by Shelley follows, and several exemplary passages from longer works by the Venerable Bede, Stevie Smith, and others. The bits and pieces sometimes seem like long quotations from a commonplace book. The last lines in the anthology are the last words of Goronwy Rees: "What shall I do next?" After this marvelous collection it is hard to think of anyone doing anything more brilliant on the subject.

DISABILITY POEMS

Toward Solomon's Mountain; the Experience of Disability in Poetry.
Joseph L. Baird and Deborah S. Workman, eds. (1986) **Temple University Press. 151p.**

The editors ask a rhetorical question: "Why, one might ask, why an entire volume of poetry devoted to this particular subject," i.e., to the experience of disability. The thirty-five poets, most of whom suffer some type of health problem, answer the question in several ways. The most captivating is with a tone of black humor and its disregard for traditional tears and moaning. There is great self detachment and a wide variety of approaches to encounters with ill health. Neil Marcus, for example, offers "Zotz," a shorthand method of writing. It is an expression that is heroic and humorous. While few of the poets' names will be known to readers, the topics are familiar to anyone. The high level of writing, the hard won conquest of pain is related in cool lines and phrases. The thematic index gives one a good idea of subject matter. The first section covers aging, with five poems. Longer sections are devoted to alienation, anger, day-to-day realities, irony, and synthesis. Although this is a special book for a special reader, it reaches out as well to a general audience.

DUTCH POETRY

Dutch Interior; Postwar Poetry of the Netherlands and Flanders. *James S. Holmes and William Jay Smith, eds.* **(1984) Columbia University Press. 326p.**

Recalling the genre paintings of the seventeenth century, here the Dutch interiors are equally rich, complete with the same hidden ironies, messages, and interpretations. For example, Adriaan Morriën begins "Gastronomy" with: "She is the finest banquet you could eat:/ from top to toe fried liver, beefsteak, kidneys,/ sweet & sour like a none-too-large gherkin." Then there is Gerrit Komrij, another of the forty-five voices here, whose poem "An Afternoon" resembles a Jan Steen interior. What is quite remarkable is that all of the poets began publishing after the mid-1940's; as the introduction points out, "There was no truly modern poetry in Dutch." But there was, and is, a tremendous *avant garde* that had the courage to draw upon old themes while avoiding the familiar prosodic forms. This is experimental poetry whose song should be better known outside of the Netherlands and Flanders. Arrangement is by "Prelude to Experiment" (five poets); "The Fifties" (fifteen poets); "The Sixties"; and "The Seventies: Neo-reality and a Return to Form." There are able translations, a bibliography, and excellent notes on the poets.

ENGLISH POETRY
Comprehensive Collections

English Lyric Poems, 1500–1900. *C. Day Lewis, ed.* **(1961) Appleton-Century-Crofts. 249p., pap.**

This anthology covers a long time span: 1500–1900. The table of contents divides the selections into: songs, story lyrics, lyrical poems, and devotional lyrics. Within the sections, the poems are arranged chronologically. This is quite a lovely organizing scheme, since the poems can be read with others of their genre, as well as with other works by the same author and his compeers. Thus, in the "Song" section, many of Shakespeare's poems are followed by those of Thomas Campion and Robert Herrick. The section entitled "Story Lyrics" includes over two dozen anonymous folk songs and ballads. Among the "Lyrical Poems" are works by Emily Brontë, Blake, Thomas Hardy, and W. B. Yeats. Most poets are represented by up to three of their works; it is the rare poet who is accorded more space, but this provides a good overview of some of the finest poems written in Great Britain and Ireland in the four centuries surveyed.

Everyman's Book of English Verse. *John Wain, ed.* **(1981) J. M. Dent. 672p.**

Everyman is an English series that pioneered pocket-book sized reprints of the classics. The present anthology is from the same publisher. Here, alas, the number of pages matches its weight; there is simply too much of everything, with little or no real focus. The compiler is a well-known author and critic whose introduction is skillfully written and indicates an unusual sensibility. Of his selection, he says, "It is an act of homage," adding, "an utterance of thanksgiving for the richness and beauty of English poetry." He catalogues what is different about his choices. First, there "is a mass of lesser-known verse . . . including the anonymous, the scurrilous, the randy and the rollicking." Fine, but this is better done in other collections that are limited to humor and satire. Second, Victorian nonsense poets are included. But this is not unusual. Third, bits are taken out of long poems. One can take strong exception to that editorial choice. The collection opens with the Anglo-Saxons, which the editor thinks unusual. It is, in fact, common in most collections of this type. It then moves chronologically to end with Seamus Heaney and Brian Patten. There are over five hundred numbered entries and about one third that many poets. Indexes of authors, titles, and first lines are provided. As far as it goes, this is a standard, much too bulky, collection of standard English verse. Good enough, but there are other better, more focused collections.

The Faber Book of Reflective Verse. *Geoffrey Grigson, ed.* **(1984) Faber and Faber. 238p.**

Geoffrey Grigson declares at the beginning of this book that he hopes readers will not be upset at finding a good many familiar verses in this collection of works that are " 'poetical' in the sense of being solemn, peaceful, musical, and correspondent to the solemn and peaceful mood rather than the excited or ecstatic mood. . . ." Since it seems clear that many lovers of poetry relish particularly the insights they gain from writing that is reflective in nature, then this volume should find its strong admirers. The poems are arranged in no clearly discernable order, but seem to be placed next to others of similar subject matter. The solemn topics revolve around the seasons, death, sleep, ignominy, failure, and, in the words of Samuel Johnson, "the vanity of human wishes" (the poem that corresponds to that heading being inexplicably omitted). Authors represented herein include Matthew Arnold, William Cowper, John Donne, Shakespeare, Tennyson, and Wordsworth. Very few modern poets show up, and again one wonders why. Surely solemnity has not disappeared from the poetic vocabulary. The most recent authors cited are Louis MacNeice and W. H. Auden. This is surely the most appropriate anthology to turn to when you are in a melancholy mood and wish to intensify it.

Fifteen Poets; Chaucer to Arnold. (1941) Oxford University Press. 503p.

The best explanation of content and purpose is found in the three paragraph preface: this collection "contains a substantial sample — about 1,000 lines by each poet — of the best work of the great masters of English poetry from Chaucer to Matthew Arnold. . . . The selections are preceded by short essays of appreciation by various hands, and by summaries of the poets' lives." This is almost to hide the glory of the collection. Who, then, does the introductions? W. H. Auden offers four pages on Byron; F. L. Lucas has six pages of tribute to Wordsworth; C. S. Lewis salutes Edmund Spenser; and E. C. Blunden comments on the skills of Shelley. Even those who are not well known, those who may be less at home with poetry than others, manage to offer original ideas about the poet and his poems. It is a unique collection with many insights, and it does, as the preface hopes, "serve as a link between the normal type of anthology, in which a large number of poets are each represented by a small amount of verse, and the Complete Works of the poets." A helpful feature is a glossary of names that explains who everyone is in the poems from Adriane to Zoroaster. Unfortunately, there are no indexes of authors, first lines, or poems; one must work through the table of contents.

First Lines; Poems Written in Youth, from Herbert to Heaney. *Jon Stallworthy, ed.* **(1987) Carcanet. 119p., pap.**

Inspired by the question of when or why or how does a writer begin to write poems, the editor compiled some of the first efforts of well-known poets. They make for fascinating reading. Each author is briefly introduced, and the circumstances surrounding his first work are sketched. The poems follow in a spacious, attractive layout. Here we find George Herbert's sonnets written to his mother while he was at Cambridge University. He was only sixteen years old at the time. William Chatterton, who died at the age of eighteen had, of necessity, to get an early start, and his poem "Sly Dick," a satirical work, was written when he was only eleven. Blake composed a song that was reputedly written when he was only thirteen years old, but the editor queries that age, for the work does indeed appear to bear the marks of greater maturity. Elizabeth Barrett Browning's first lines also date from the age of thirteen, and Edgar Allan Poe's poem "To Helen" was composed when he was either fifteen or sixteen. This is altogether an astonishing volume! Some of the modern authors whose earliest work is included are Sir John Betjeman, Louis MacNeice, W. H. Auden, Dylan Thomas, Sylvia Plath, and Philip Larkin. Engrossing as the poems themselves are, the informative notes that precede them, offering documentation and biographical context, make the works even more fascinating.

Golden Treasury of the Best Songs and Lyrical Poems in the English Language. *Francis Palgrave, comp.* **(1929) Oxford University Press. 555p.**

Working with Tennyson, to whom he dedicated the first edition in 1861, Palgrave set the course for acceptable English poetry through the rest of the nineteenth and well into the twentieth century. Even today the original selection, despite numerous modifications and additions, is better known to laypersons than almost any other anthology. There are better ones. Many are more comprehensive and offer necessary guidance in terms of meaning and style, but Palgrave (as the collection usually is called) dominates. The notable omissions in the 1861 edition long ago were added, particularly the seventeenth-century poets. Palgrave still is honored for being among the first to appreciate the delights of Wordsworth, and if he gave too much space to Tennyson he had the courage to include "anonymous," which at that time had been considered less than acceptable in many homes. Today Palgrave is a figure who has earned a place in every library in America.

Golden Treasury of the Best Songs & Lyrical Poems in the English Language. *Francis Turner Palgrave, comp. With a fifth book selected by John Press.* **(5th ed., 1964) Oxford University Press. 615p., pap.**

This deservedly famous anthology claims to be different from the others in that it aims "to include in it all the best original Lyric pieces and Songs in our language . . . and none beside the best." What is, therefore, effectively excluded is narrative verse and didactic poetry. The poems are arranged chronologically by period. Book One includes works from Sir Thomas Wyatt to Shakespeare; Book Two, George Herbert to Milton; Book Three, Thomas Gray to Burns; and so forth. The final book is selected by John Press, who brings in the work of the latter part of the nineteenth and the twentieth centuries. The result of such a concentration on lyrical writing is that the poems tend to be passionate and deeply personal. The editors succeed in reprinting only the work of the best poets, so the collection is filled with riches. On any page, readers will find poems to engage them on many levels: intellectual, emotional, and aesthetic. This volume should appeal to readers who wish for a large collection of well-known and excellent poems. As noted in the previous annotation, if readers need notes to help them understand poetry, they must needs turn elsewhere.

A Little Treasury of British Poetry. *Oscar Williams, ed.* **(1951) Scribner's. 874p., o.p.**

Set between the little treasuries of American and modern poetry, this follows the same format as its cousins. It is bulky, pocket sized, and concludes with small photographs of the poets. The arrangement is chronological and in two parts—poets from 1500 to 1900 and poets from 1900 to 1950. Coverage, as in the other anthologies, is excellent in that all of the major, and not a few minor, poets are represented by characteristic, usually well-known poems. As might be expected, more space is given to Shakespeare than anyone else, but Williams strikes a sound balance between the figures and their work. One might confidently read this from cover to cover and end up an expert on British poetry, even without benefit of notes or commentary by the compiler. Williams believes in letting the poems speak for themselves, and he offers no help — besides a well-written introduction — to either the beginner or expert. He does point out his natural bias: "two fifths of the pages herein [are devoted] to the verse of the past fifty years. . . . This anthology is being published for living readers." And with that he justifies what may or may not be a good choice, but his own.

The New Oxford Book of English Verse, 1250–1950. *Helen Gardner, ed.* (1972) Oxford University Press. 974p.

A huge expanse of time is covered in this anthology; it takes in the full range of English, nondramatic poetry written primarily by British authors. This sensitive, discerning volume opens with an anonymous poem "Cuckoo Song," with its famous beginning, "Summer is y-comen in,/ Loude sing, cuckoo!" and ends with poetry by Dylan Thomas. In between, all the major poets are given ample space to display some of their most glorious works. Gardner allots Blake eight pages, Pope twelve, and John Donne eighteen, but Edmund Spenser has been allowed thirty so some of his long poems can be printed. The same is true for T. S. Eliot, whose "The Love Song of J. Alfred Prufrock," "The Waste Land," and "Little Gidding" are printed in full, along with a few short poems. The poets are arranged chronologically by their date of birth. Among the scores of poets included, several are women, most notably Aphra Behn, Emily Brontë, Elizabeth Barrett Browning, Christina Rossetti, Kathleen Raine, and Stevie Smith.

The Oxford Anthology of English Literature. Vols. I–II (see note at end). *Frank Kermode and John Hollander, general eds.* (1973) Oxford University Press.

By anyone's reckoning, these would be judged massive volumes. Their purpose, in the words of their editors, is "to provide students with a selective canon of the entire range of English literature from the beginnings to recent time. . . ." This, assuredly, is what they accomplish. The poems are organized in chronological stages, and they are amply introduced. "Beowulf," for example, is given eight pages of introductory comment. Furthermore, there are many helpful notes to aid the reader.

Many plays written in verse are reprinted in full, including, in the medieval section, *The Wakefield Second Shepherd's Play,* a mystery play on religious themes, and *Everyman,* a morality play. The editors have printed the music for those ballads they chose to include — a delightful addition. There is a great deal of Edmund Spenser's *The Faerie Queen,* and dozens of poems by Shakespeare, John Donne, Ben Jonson, and Pope. Later, in the second volume, Blake and the Romantic poets are much in evidence, followed by Thomas Hardy, W. B. Yeats, D. H. Lawrence, and T. S. Eliot. The volume concludes with works by Philip Larkin, Ted Hughes, and Geoffrey Hill. Once again, as with the *Norton Anthology of English Literature,* reading this seriously is comparable to taking a University course in English literature.

NOTE: This work is also published as six paperback volumes: Medieval English Literature, *J. B. Trapp, ed.;* The Literature of Renaissance England, *John Hollander and Frank Kermode, eds.;* The Restoration and the Eighteenth Century, *Martin Price, ed.;* Romantic Poetry and Prose, *Harold Bloom and Lionel Trilling, eds.;* Victorian Prose and Poetry, *Lionel Trilling and Harold Bloom, eds.;* Modern British Literature, *Frank Kermode and John Hollander, eds.*

The Oxford Book of English Verse, 1250–1918. *Sir Arthur Quiller-Couch, ed.* (New ed., rev. and enl., 1939) Oxford University Press. 1083p., o.p.

The editor's ambitious task here was to gather into two volumes the best of English verse from the thirteenth century through the First World War. He begins firmly within the British Isles, but toward the end of his project he includes a good deal of American poetry. Many of the great poems are included in this anthology, but they are all of a lyrical or epigrammatic nature. No epic works are included, and there are few shortened versions of long poems. For the most part, each author is given a relatively small space in which to make an impression on the reader. Occasionally authors, like Edmund Spenser, for instance, are given more. Others so favored are Michael Drayton, Shakespeare, and Milton. Since this anthology has so long a period to explore, most authors are represented cursorily, although there are generous selections from Wordsworth, Keats, and Shelley. In general, this is a worthwhile anthology of fine poetry.

The Oxford Book of Short Poems. *P. J. Kavanagh and James Michie, eds.* (1985) Oxford University Press. 307p., pap.

The short poems that the title refers to are very short—less than fourteen lines. The two poets set out to explore "what poets and poems have been overlooked or treated ungenerously, and what short poems, even if they have been anthologized, have had their effect muffled by their longer companions." Although arranged chronologically from the thirteenth century to the present, the compilers admit to certain imbalances in their selection. First, the eighteenth century put great emphasis on long poems, and there are few short ones of note from that great era. Second, the tones alter, sometimes drastically, from period to period. "The vernacular, unembarrassed directness of the earliest lyrics drifts . . . into the tight grip of reason, reasonableness and sounds." Third, confidence in the short poem is restored in the twentieth century through the genius of the great masters: Thomas Hardy, W. B. Yeats, and Robert Frost. The pleasure in the collection resides in the variety of moods, subjects and tones. Consider, for example, Thomas Beedome (d. 1641) and his four-line tribute to Sir Francis Drake: "Drake, who the world hast conquered like a scroll,/Who saw'st the Arctic and Antarctic Pole,/If men were silent, stars would make thee known:/Phoebus forgets not his companion." The compilers call this "sudden perfection," and fortunately there is much more of the same in this unique, fine collection.

Seven Centuries of Poetry; Chaucer to Dylan Thomas. *A. N. Jeffares, ed.* (1955) Longmans, Green. 463p.

This work signified a struggle against specialization. As the compiler explained: "We now have an emphasis upon the value of examining several writers in some detail. A greater depth of knowledge and more original power of criticism" are needed. To that end, the anthology begins with anonymous Old English poems and moves through the centuries to conclude with Dylan Thomas. The selection is limited exclusively to English poets. Within that limitation, the scope is broad; the compiler has succeeded in overcoming the difficulty of narrowness. Unfortunately, after a five-page introduction, there are no notes, no explanations, no biographical sketches, nothing but the well-known poets and their work. While no one can fault the collection itself, there is some doubt that a work of this kind is of any real value to anyone who can find better, more complete, and more informative collections of English poetry.

Six Centuries of Verse. *Anthony Thwaite, ed.* **(1984) Thames Methuen. 290p., pap.**

Based on a television series about English poetry, the "six centuries" in the title refer to the period from Chaucer to the late twentieth century. And that is how the book is divided. There are fourteen time periods, with Chaucer, Shakespeare, Milton, and Wordsworth given separate sections. Other poets are grouped under such headings as "Romantics and Realists, 1790–1920." "This book is an attempt to give a guided tour of English poetry . . . rather than a literary history or a straightforward anthology, although it has elements of both." Written as a companion to a television series, it is no accident that the text has more illustrations than usual. It is all for the good. For example, in the "Medieval to Elizabethan, 1400–1600" section one finds reproductions of contemporary woodcuts or paintings (in black and white) on almost every page. The text of the television series is fitted nicely before and after each of the poems. The result is an illustrated, friendly introduction to the basics of poetry for students and laypersons alike. Biographical and bibliographical notes round out a fine approach.

The Treasury of English Poetry. *Mark Caldwell and Walter Kendrick, eds.* **(1984) Doubleday. 734p., o.p.**

This is not the largest nor the most bulky of numerous collections of this type, but it has a definite advantage over others. The compilers try to print the poems in their entirety, and not in part as is too often the case in other anthologies of such wide scope. Also, all of the Old English poems are translated into modern English for the student and the general reader of the collection. "Our selections are ample enough to portray the unique qualities of the more than a hundred English, Irish, Scottish, and Welsh poets we include." The work has the most famous and best loved of English poems in their complete form. The only real exceptions are Milton's *Paradise Lost* and Chaucer's *Canterbury Tales*. Unfortunately, while the brief introduction is useful, there are no supporting notes or any specific information about the poets, a major drawback in a compilation primarily for students. Conversely, the excellent selection and the decision to include numerous lesser-known poems gives this a dimension that makes it well worth considering.

ENGLISH POETRY
c. 450–1500—Old English, Middle English

An Anthology of Old English Poetry. *Charles W. Kennedy, tr.* **(1960) Oxford University Press. 174p., pap.**

Divided into nine categories, generically rather than chronologically, the collection opens with elegies and dramatic lyrics, moves on to "Beowulf" and closes with historical battle poems. The translator remarks, "It has been my endeavor to translate selections into a modern verse faithful to the Old English text, and, as far as linguistic changes permit, suggestive of the alliterative rhythms of the Anglo-Saxon originals." As these poems were all in the oral tradition or in written form before the Norman Conquest they are, literally, in a foreign language. Just how much so is spelled out nicely in the brief, yet scholarly and well-written, introduction. Anyone not familiar with the verse should begin here and then move gradually into the collection. One may take exception to some of the translations, particularly the famous poem "The Wanderer," but in other sections, most evidently "Beowulf," the translation is exceptional. As the translator points out, "In this body of Old English poetry much is excellent; a part is timeless." As such, this is a special collection that should be treasured by anyone who loves poetry.

Medieval English Lyrics; a Critical Anthology. *R. T. Davies, ed.* **(1964) Northwestern University Press. 384p.**

Beginning in the mid-12th century and ending with Thomas Wyatt's "What I Once Was" in the early sixteenth century, here are nearly two hundred poems that reflect thought, aesthetics, politics, and, in general, the history of medieval times. The compiler has chosen to reprint the verses in modernized spelling and punctuation. Also, he has supplied each poem with a title of his own invention. This, he notes, "will probably offend everybody," but there is no need for an apology. The spirit of the sometimes fugitive verse is captured, and where there is need for additional explanation, it is appropriately given in footnotes. There are also notes near the end of the work. The introduction gives a full account of how the poems were translated, changed, and otherwise edited. Despite the care given to spelling changes, reading these poems may be difficult for anyone but the student or dedicated layperson, particularly in the earliest works. At the same time, the verse is so delightful, so expressive of what for many is a black hole in the history of poetry, that it is well worth the effort.

The Oxford Book of Late Medieval Verse and Prose. *Douglas Gray, ed.* **(1985) Clarendon Press. 586p.**

There are twenty sections in this volume, beginning with a combination of prose and poetry drawn from early chronicles. These offer glimpses of life at the end of the fifteenth and start of the sixteenth century. Next come representative letters, and from then on there is a counterpoint of prose and poetry by an individual author (John Lydgate to John Skelton) and subject sections that include both forms. The concluding hundred or so pages include extensive commentaries, a glossary, and the standard indexes. There are many kinds of writing, many opinions, many styles, and many skills. It is hardly a work to encourage browsing by laypersons, but those who are curious, along with scholars and students, will find much here to enliven the time and impart a sense of what it meant to move from the medieval period to the "modern" stage.

ENGLISH POETRY
1500–1700—Early Modern

The Anchor Anthology of Sixteenth-Century Verse. *Richard S. Sylvester, ed.* **(1974) Doubleday. 624p.**

What is unique here is that the editor has chosen to present a selection of English sixteenth-century verse largely in its original spelling and with its original punctuation. Another unusual feature is the inclusion of both major and minor poets, for all of whom complete poems are printed, an editorial decision based on the fact that the book will be primarily for classroom use. This having been said, the collection can be enjoyed by anyone with the patience and the interest to read the poets who loomed largest in the century, Thomas Wyatt, Thomas Campion, and Henry Howard, Earl of Surrey. It should be noted that Shakespeare's sonnets are not included, but there is a general sampling of those poets the editor calls "The Sonneteers"—from Thomas Watson and Thomas Lodge to Bartholomew Griffin and, of course, Anonymous. John Skelton is the only cleric among the poets, and, in his effort to reconcile the present and the past, he is one of the more fascinating writers among the twenty-five poets represented. The introduction offers a brilliant entry into the world of the sixteenth-century poet. A short commentary about each of the poets, a bibliography, and an index are provided.

Cavalier Poets; Selected Poems. *Thomas Clayton, ed.* **(1978) Oxford University Press. 364p., pap.**

Never was a group of poets more suitably named. The Cavaliers were the legendary lyric voices of the court of King Charles I. Before his untimely execution, they surrounded him with some of the best verse in the English language. Robert Herrick, for example, opens this marvelous collection with "The Argument of His Book." He sets the stage for the other three: Thomas Carew, John Suckling, and Richard Lovelace. Herrick begins with the now famous lines, "I sing of brooks, of blossoms, birds, and bowers;/Of April, May, of June, and July flowers." And Lovelace draws the anthology to a conclusion with the end of Charles, the end of an age, and the end of the poets: "Sir, now unravelled is the

Golden Fleece." In between is what the jacket copy for once correctly describes as "quintessentially romantic, graceful, courtly, and sometimes roguish verse." There is a scholarly introduction; footnotes to help explain allusions, personalities, and historical events; a chronological table; a good bibliography; as well as a glossary and index. A work like this does more to explain the glory and delights of poetry than almost anything else in the English language. A must for all libraries, and for many individual bookshelves.

Elizabethan Lyrics. *Norman Ault, ed.* **(3d ed., 1949) William Sloane Associates; paperback edition published by G. P. Putnam's, 1960. 560p.**

In close to six hundred and fifty poems, the editor dramatically illustrates why the Elizabethan lyric was and, to a lesser extent, remains so popular. As they were written to be recited, sung, and thoroughly enjoyed by the populace, they are a far cry from the metaphysical and philosophical poems of the same period. Recognizing their unique contribution to popular culture, the editor arranges them according to the date when each poem first became known to the public. "The plan renders it possible to follow step by step the development of the lyric, and its many fashions and phases, throughout the period." What makes these verses so lovely and bewitching is their essential beauty and, quite often, their high sense of humor. Written to be sung, intoned, or spoken, they sparkle with the life of the times. Fortunately for the average reader, the editor has employed modern spelling and modern punctuation. From time to time, where the original spelling is needed for a sense of rhythm and meaning, there are explanatory notes. "Forget not yet . . ." opens the volume. It is a suitable beginning — and an end. Anyone who takes the time to read in this collection will "forget not yet."

Jacobean and Caroline Poetry; an Anthology. *T. G. S. Cain, ed.* **(1981) Methuen. 334p.**

The poetry of 1600–1660 is the subject of many college courses, and "the primary aim of this anthology is to offer an annotated selection substantial enough for it to be used as the only primary text in a course on early seventeenth-century poetry." Arrangement is chronological, and the first of two parts consists of substantial selections from ten leading poets of the period, including Michael Drayton, John Donne, Andrew Marvell, and Henry Vaughan. The second shorter section covers minor poets, although the compiler insists this is really "a miscellany in which poems have been chosen either for intrinsic merit or in a very few cases for the light they shed on intellectual attitudes of the period." For the student, each of the major poets is introduced by a one-page essay, but there are no essays for the second part; such notes as there are focus primarily on the ten poets. Recommendations for further reading and an index of first lines concludes the volume.

Metaphysical Lyrics & Poems of the Seventeenth Century; Donne to Butler. *Herbert J. Grierson, ed.* (1921) Oxford University Press. 302p.

This is a close second to Hugh Kenner's collection entitled *Seventeenth Century Poetry: The Schools of Donne & Jonson.* It suffers from being somewhat outdated. Published in 1921, it lacks the benefits of later scholarship. The number of choices is not so great, and the arrangement by three broad subject headings, rather than by poets, is awkward. It also lacks an author index. In spite of that, the volume has positive features. First and foremost, compared to Kenner the others, the introduction is more informative and certainly more graciously written. The notes, too, are fuller and respond to the shortcomings of some readers' historical knowledge. And while there are fewer poems than in Kenner, they are more representative and are ones likely to have meaning for the average student or layperson. Finally, but not least significant, the format, and particularly the type face, beautifully suit the subject.

The Metaphysical Poets. *Helen Gardner, ed.* (1957) Penguin Books; reprinted by Oxford University Press, 1961. 310p.

Kenner, Grierson, and Gardner — all, with certain authorial inclusions and exclusions, edited versions of the metaphysical poets. Gardner differs from the other compilers in that she moves beyond the usually accepted seventeenth-century time limit to include such previous and subsequent poets as Milton and Sir Walter Ralegh. In her biographical notes she carefully explains why these others qualify as metaphysical poets outside the seventeenth-century. With occasional modifications, the original spelling is maintained. There are too few explanatory footnotes and only a selective reading list. The felicitous introduction is not as far reaching as Grierson's, but in terms of clarity and definitions it is an improvement over both her rivals. Except for the broader scope, the selection pretty well follows the standard choices found in the other two works.

The Oxford Book of Seventeenth Century Verse. *H. J. C. Grierson and G. Bullough, eds.* **(1934) Oxford University Press. 974p.**

This heavy volume pays homage to the masters of seventeenth-century English verse. John Donne is accorded sixty pages or so, Ben Jonson and Robert Herrick over thirty pages each, Dryden fifty pages, and Milton a whopping one hundred. Interspersed among these great writers are scores of lesser ones. So readers can steep themselves in the work of the masters, as well as acquaint themselves with such other fine writers of the period as Andrew Marvell. It is interesting to see their work alongside that of the dominating figures of the age. The selections tend to be of the highest order. There are hundreds of short, lyric poems, as well as extended extracts from such long works as Milton's "Paradise Lost." In general, this anthology is an excellent introduction to this exciting, passionate age.

The Oxford Book of Sixteenth Century Verse. *E. K. Chambers, comp.* **(1932) Oxford University Press. 905p.**

With the end of medieval poetry and the beginning of the sixteenth century, who is on the doorstep waiting for the new age? "The Nutbrown Maid," of course, and she suitably begins this standard anthology. After a few more ballads, one is introduced to John Skelton, "the only authentic voice that comes to us from the first quarter of the sixteenth century." Authentic or not (the point is controversial), until the Elizabethan age much verse was written, to be charitable, by "minor" poets who were little more than court hangers-on in quest of patronage. Reading the short, informative introduction, one sees why Elizabethan poetry is so popular, even today. It is "characteristically light hearted," and shows a "thorough going zest in earthy things." There was a sober side to it as well, and room, too, for the disillusionment of Greville and "the quietism of Dyer." Within the nine hundred pages is a glutton's sampling of all sides of the sixteenth century. Note that the spelling, capitalization, and punctuation are modernized.

Seventeenth Century Poetry; the Schools of Donne and Jonson. *Hugh Kenner, ed.* **(1964) Holt, Rinehart and Winston. 460p., o.p.**

Traditionalists seem particularly fond of the age of Donne and Jonson, and the distinguished editor is no exception. It is the age of gossip and metaphysics, two related aspects of the human spirit. "For more generally," Kenner explains, "it was a time of great active intelligence, intelligence working its way down into the very capillaries of a poem; and it ended when, by the time of the Restoration, the nature of the intellective process itself had been revalued." Opening with a generous sampling of Donne (1572–1631), Kenner moves on to the Donne circle, i.e., Lord Herbert of Cherbury, Aurelian Townshend, Richard Corbett, and Henry King. Then come the one whom he dubs "the divine poet", George Herbert (1593–1633), and his successors, Richard Crashaw, Henry Vaughan, and Thomas Traherne. Then Cavalier poets take center stage with Robert Herrick and Thomas Carew. The collection ends with the Restoration of Charles II and the poetry of Andrew Marvell. Since this is primarily a student's anthology, the editor chooses to retain original spellings, and while there are some footnotes, there are really not enough to clarify the more obscure poems for the modern reader. Each poet has the usual biographical/historical introduction. The selection is generally good, if traditional. This works nicely for most of the poets, but not for all, particularly Richard Lovelace. (See *Cavalier Poets; Selected Poems* for better choices in this period.)

Seventeenth-Century Verse and Prose. Vol. I: 1600–1660; Vol. II: 1160–1700. *Helen C. White, Ruth C. Wallerstein, and Ricardo Quintana, eds.* **(1951, 1952) Macmillan. O.p.**

Dividing the seventeenth century between Charles I and Cromwell in Vol. I and the Restoration into the Stuart reign in Vol. II, the authors follow traditional lines. There are several unusual points. First, the scope is much broader than general collections of this type, particularly since a good half is prose. Second, the scholarly introductions that open each volume and precede the different sections are written with the student and layperson in mind. They make a difficult period, a group of sometimes abstruse writers, easier to appreciate. Third, the choices for each of the authors is more extensive than usually found in similar compilations. And then there are the usual aids from an index of authors, to an index of titles and first lines. Note, too, the useful bibliography in each of the volumes. Although the work is intended for college courses, it is an ideal reference work for medium to large libraries and a fine introduction to the seventeenth century for both beginner and expert.

Silver Poets of the Sixteenth Century (Everyman's Library). *Gerald Bullett, ed.* **(1947) J. M. Dent. 428p.**

The Everyman Library editions are famous for bringing prose and poetry to the ubiquitous everyman at a reasonable price. While the list is not growing as quickly as it did in earlier years, and while the cost of a volume has gone up dramatically, the present work is an excellent illustration of the series — as well, of course, as being a fine collection of sixteenth-century poetry. The editor sets the stage: "The word silver in the title of this volume, where minor might perhaps have been expected . . . marks the critical survey of English poetry." Wyatt, Sidney, Ralegh, Davies, the Earl of Surrey are represented with three subject areas each, and there are the usual glossary, index to first lines, and background material on Elizabethan thought and publishing. (Best of all, in this day of giant volumes, the slim work fits nicely into the hand, if not always the small pocket). Typically, one finds for Wyatt sonnets, translation from Petrarch, songs, and satires. The drawback is the complete absence of notes. The uninformed may be at sea, literally, when it comes to appreciating the imagery and figures in Ralegh's "The Ocean's Love to Cynthia."

ENGLISH POETRY
18th Century

**The Late Augustans; Longer Poems of the Later Eighteenth Century
(The Poetry Bookshelf).** *Donald Davie, ed.* **(1958) Macmillan. 130p., o.p.**

The very slim little volume offers a small number of poets — eight to
be exact, with one extended poem for each. The exception is Oliver
Goldsmith who is represented by two works, "The Deserted Village" and
the lesser known "Retaliation." He is surrounded by William Shenstone,
Samuel Johnson, Thomas Gray, Christopher Smart, John Langhorne,
William Cowper, and Wordsworth. There is a thirty-three-page intro-
duction and twenty-five pages of notes. Clearly this is a work for the
student, although, as with so many of these texts, it can be read and
enjoyed by the interested layperson. Covering a span of sixty years, from
about 1740 to 1800, the collection puts the lie to the notion that liter-
ature came to a halt with the death of Pope in 1744 and only began again
with Wordsworth and Samuel Taylor Coleridge. The lengthy poems are
many things, but they are neither dull nor prosaic.

The New Oxford Book of Eighteenth Century Verse. *Roger Lonsdale,
ed.* **(1984) Oxford University Press. 870p.**

The beauty of this collection lies in its wide-netted culling of all sorts
of poetry from the eighteenth century. While such great and well-known
poets as Pope, Blake, Burns, and Thomas Gray are given ample space,
dozens of less well-known poets are also included. Among these, several
are women whose way into anthologies was all too often firmly blocked.
So, many discoveries await the reader. One, surely, is the wide-ranging
subject matter of the verse. Another, since the voices here are so diverse,
is a clear sense of exactly what life and writing in the eighteenth century
were really like. In his learned introduction, Roger Lonsdale contrasts
the stated ideals of eighteenth century poetic verse — "lucidity, elegance,
refinement" — with the broader sense of the period's fuller, more varied
artistic output.

ENGLISH POETRY
19th Century

British Poetry 1880–1920; Edwardian Voices. *Paul L. Wiley and Harold Orel, eds.* **(1969) Appleton-Century-Crofts. 681p., o.p.**

This heavy volume concentrates on a specific moment in British poetry; it begins with the end of the Victorian era (and includes Thomas Hardy and A. E. Housman), and it ends at the conclusion of the First World War. Authors of Hardy's caliber are accorded almost thirty pages, and readers can get a fine sense of their achievements in verse. In the second section, "The Decadent Movement," there are poems by Oscar Wilde, Arthur Symons, Ernest Dowson, and William Henley, none of them among the great writers of English verse. Robert Louis Stevenson and Rudyard Kipling are featured. This more or less indicates the arrangement of the rest of the book: several mediocre voices along with fine poets. Among the other excellent writers who are given considerable space are Gerard Manley Hopkins, W. B. Yeats, Rupert Brooke, D. H. Lawrence, Sigfried Sassoon, and Wilfred Owen. The great poets' treatment of the First World War makes for memorable verse.

A Choice of English Romantic Poetry. *Stephen Spender, ed.* **(1947) Dial Press. 384p.**

Often called a romantic poet himself, Stephen Spender is in a splendid position to choose from the best of the English romantics. And he does. His choices are limited to a few familiar major figures — Blake, Wordsworth, Samuel Taylor Coleridge, Byron, Shelley, Keats, Tennyson, and Emily Brontë — with brief sections on minor figures. None of these was exclusively a romantic poet, and Spender's contribution is to guide the reader from one poem to another within the boundaries of the romantic landscape. He makes the point, too, that there is a great difference between the romanticism of the early nineteenth century and of other periods. "The Romantics," he explains, "emphasize one aspect of imagination: inventive fantasy. They lack the imaginative power which has a firm grasp of objectivity and of systems of thought." Spender is correct in saying some readers may be upset at his choosing segments of long poems, although the passages are complete in themselves. At the same time he has selected what he terms the "best plums" of romantic poetry.

English Romantic Poetry and Prose. *Russell Noyes, ed.* (1956) Oxford University Press. 1,324p.

A huge, comprehensive volume, this, in the words of its editor, is "useful for the selections of fifty-four representative English Romantic writers." The reader is also supplied with a helpful introductory essay devoted to major aspects of English romanticism, including its historical and literary roots, its overriding emotional postures, and its concomitant philosophies. The anthology begins with writers from the early eighteenth century, including Thomas Gray, William Cowper, Burns, Blake, Wordsworth, Samuel Taylor Coleridge, Byron, Shelley, and Keats. There are extensive selections from these greatest exponents of English romanticism. Anyone interested in this celebrated movement could not hope for a more helpful, generous, sampling of its intense, lyrical poetry. This volume presents its finest achievements.

Everyman's Book of Victorian Verse. *J. R. Watson, ed.* (1982) J. M. Dent. 373p.

The subject of verse written during the reign of Queen Victoria is divided here into Early Victorian (1837–1851), Mid-Victorian (1851–1867), High Victorian (1867–1885), and Fin de Siecle (1885–1901). This arrangement allows the reader to see how the Victorian style developed and finally drew to a close. The editor has selected what he found to be the most interesting and timeless poems written in this era, and he has included work by little-known poets as well as by the famous ones. The editor, a scholar of the Victorian age, wishes to reawaken the public's appreciation for Victorian verse, and in this anthology, he goes a long way to doing so. There are many discoveries to be made: Anne Brontë's lovely, lyrical poems, along with those of her sister Emily; Robert Browning's considerable achievements in narrative verse; Tennyson's poems; and later the works of Gerard Manley Hopkins and Thomas Hardy. There are scores of lesser-known poets whose moving work should also absorb the reader.

The New Oxford Book of Victorian Verse. *Christopher Ricks, ed.* **(1987) Oxford University Press. 654p.**

Christopher Ricks, the eminent critic, explores in his introduction the meaning the connotations of the word "Victorian." He traces its image of flawed creativity to the early deaths of the three great writers of the second generation of Romantic poets, Byron, Shelley, and Keats. The Victorians, nevertheless, had their own literary geniuses, and Ricks presents them in all their glory, awarding Tennyson and Robert Browning over forty pages each, and selecting many poems by Emily Brontë, William Barnes, and Elizabeth Barrett Browning. Other poets given considerable compass are Christina Rossetti, Gerard Manley Hopkins, Lewis Carroll, Rudyard Kipling, and Thomas Hardy. Lesser-known poets are included along with these authors, although they are given less space. In general, this anthology provides a broad, accurate, and absorbing picture of the precise accomplishments and limitations of the often-maligned Victorian poets. And it offers readers several entire, long masterpieces: Christina Rossetti's "Goblin Market," Lewis Carroll's "The Hunting of the Snark," and Edward Fitzgerald's "Rubaiyat of Omar Khayyam."

The Oxford Book of Nineteenth-Century English Verse. *John Hayward, ed.* **(1964; reprinted, with corrections, 1965) Oxford University Press. 970p., o.p.**

Among these six hundred poems by more than eighty-five poets who lived and wrote in the nineteenth century can be found many of the masterpieces of English Romantic verse. Here, all the writers are in fact British, and all the great ones are in evidence: Blake, Wordsworth, Samuel Taylor Coleridge, Byron, Shelley, and Keats. Later writers include Tennyson and Robert Browning, as well as Christina Rossetti and Thomas Hardy. All of these major authors are accorded a great deal of space, some more than fifty pages in which to demonstrate their talent and their range. The editor has chosen wisely among the vast number of poems of each writer, and this volume is a pleasure to read for anyone with a taste for English Romantic poetry. There are excerpts from such long works as Byron's "Childe Harold's Pilgrimage" and Wordsworth's "The Prelude," all of "The Hunting of the Snark," by Lewis Carroll, and "The Rime of the Ancient Mariner," by Samuel Taylor Coleridge, and hundreds of lyrical poems. Admirers of the Brontë sisters will find examples of the verse of Charlotte and Emily.

The Poorhouse Fugitives; Self-Taught Poets and Poetry in Victorian Britain. *Brian Maidment, ed.* **(1987) Carcanet. 374p.**

One must have an understanding of, or at least an interest in, the development of England during the Industrial Revolution to appreciate fully this unusual collection of poems by self-taught English artisans. It is true the compiler includes extensive notes and gives background information before each of the six sections and subsections, but even with that, the reader needs to be concerned with, say, "poems of social indignation" or the city of Manchester or the ideals of the Chartists. Made even more difficult by a variety of dialects, the collection is not for the general reader. Nevertheless, the compiler is to be applauded for a truly outstanding profile of Victorian writers who may be labelled poets of humble birth, uneducated poets, industrial poets, regional poets, or even "auto-didacts." Little or none of the poetry will be recognized, because the editor has tried to avoid well-known anthology pieces and local favorites. Instead he concentrates on works that have "never been reprinted since their original publication." For example, under the heading "Chartist Lyrics" one finds five poets giving us such poems as "When the world is burning" or "The song of the low." Of particular value is the prose section with the self-explanatory title "The Difficulties of Appearing in Print."

ENGLISH POETRY
20th Century

Modern British Poetry. *Louis Untermeyer, ed.* **(7th rev. ed., 1962)
Harcourt, Brace. 500p., o.p.**

By the 1960's Louis Untermeyer had split his *Modern American & British Poetry* into two distinct volumes. As with all of his collections, here one finds a bias toward the traditional and the conservative, but always excellent, poetry. There are few, if any, of the wilder voices in English poetry, particularly those that came up after the Second World War. At the same time the tried and true, from C. Day Lewis to W. H. Auden and Stephen Spender are given considerable space to reveal their unique talents. And there is the joy of the collection. There may not be that many poets, but their representative poems indicate their various moods, styles, and stages of development. As a result one can find almost any favorite, well-known poem by well-known British poets. In an informative preface, the compiler not only gives a bit of background on each poet, but places him or her in the history and development of the English scene. More complete information on the life of the poets is given generously before each of their sections.

The Oxford Book of Twentieth-Century English Verse. *Philip Larkin, ed.* **(1973) Oxford University Press. 641p.**

Philip Larkin is widely viewed as one of the most perceptive voices in contemporary British poetry, if not indeed in the English-speaking world. His choice of English verse is, therefore, fascinating to see. He confines himself to poets who wrote and/or lived in Britain for a significant part of their careers, so there are few American writers in this very English collection of verse. Larkin first devotes a great deal of space to a poet he holds in the highest esteem, Thomas Hardy, allowing him a full twenty-five pages. Kipling, W. B. Yeats, T. S. Eliot, and W. H. Auden are also given copious space in which to demonstrate the scope of their talent. Virtually all of the other poets are given much less room, but the selection of their poems is made with great care and taste. Larkin includes only six pages of his own poems, so modest and so devoted is he to presenting a wide variety of modern voices, many of whom are less well known and many of whom are women. Over two hundred poets are introduced to the reader, all of them worth reading. A fine sense of the active, dedicated, twentieth-century English poet is resoundingly established.

Portraits of Poets. *Sebastian Barker, ed.* **(1986) Carcanet. 124p., pap.**

Limited to the English "senior poets of our time," i.e., born between 1897 and 1939, this is a combination of brilliant individual photo-portraits of the writers and representative, previously published poems. Possibly an important figure was missed by Barker, but he is hard to identify. Some of the longer works are excerpted, but primarily the whole poem is printed. What the reader has is a photographic album and an anthology of poetry in one book. Both the photographs and the poems are first rate. The camera work is formal, but highly imaginative. The pictures are particularly impressive because they are taken where the poet is most at home, whether that be in a study or in a locale related to a particular poem. There is as much variety in the photographs as there are attitudes among the poets. The result is a brilliant portrait gallery of many of England's leading poets.

ENGLISH AND AMERICAN POETRY
Comprehensive Collections

The Brand-X Anthology of Poetry: Burnt Norton Edition. *William Zaranka, ed.* **(1981) Apple-Wood Books. 358p., o.p.**

Despite the title and the compiler's effort "to present an alternative to the traditional literary corpse," this collection follows traditional lines. Arrangement is chronological, beginning with Chaucer and moving through the Renaissance, the Cavalier poets, the eighteenth century and so on, ending primarily with Americans born after 1930. What makes this effort different, but not all that different, are comments along the way by Zaranka, a professor at The University of Denver. Unfortunately, he is prone to punning and writing in a style that worked well enough for Ezra Pound's brand of pedagogy, but is a repetitive reminder of "Brand-X" types of crankiness. He calls the Middle Ages, for example, "The Middle-Aged" and opens this section with a characteristic phrase: "no survey of Middle-Aged literature could call itself complete without at least some mention of the great Hell's Anglo-Anne Sexton poet." Fortunately, the choice of numerous poets and poetry overcomes this foolishness, and the result is a passable collection of use to libraries. Individuals should look elsewhere.

Burning with a Vision; Poetry of Science and the Fantastic. *Robert Frazier, ed.* **(1984) Owlswick Press. 139p.**

Science and the fantastic: a fascinating topic for poetry! Here we have poems on such subjects as "Computative Oak," by Ruth Berman, "Cytogenetics Lab," by Lucille Day, "The Pterodactyl," by Philip Jose Farmer, and "The Aging of Clones," by Andrew Joron and Robert Frazier. These poems, written in a variety of contemporary styles — some traditional forms, some prose poems, others in open forms — are not as impenetrable as they first may sound. And they are certainly up to date in their concerns. This is the place to look for a bisection of art with science. Most of the poets are little known to the general public, but some names are familiar: Diane Ackerman, Loren Eiseley, Ursula K. Le Guin, and D. M. Thomas, for example. But, as the editor states in the introduction, "In this volume, you will encounter poetry that speaks directly of science; that deals with it in an indirect manner; that employs its language for uncommon effect on a common situation . . ." and where else are you likely to find that in abundance? This is new poetic territory. It must be said, however, that the quality of the poetry varies.

The Harper Anthology of Poetry. *John Frederick Nims, ed.* (1981) Harper & Row. 842p.

This volume has the look of a textbook in English and American poetry: it is thick, each poet is briefly introduced, there are brief definitions of obscure words and voluminous notes on the more esoteric poems. This approach will prove very helpful to general readers who wish to extend their knowledge of poetry. The editor discusses his enchantment with poetry in the introduction, and that sentiment is present throughout the volume and proves to be contagious. The collection begins with anonymous poems written before 1400, runs through the time of Chaucer, John Skelton, Edmund Spenser, Shakespeare, Donne, Robert Herrick, Milton, and onward. After the Romantic poets, we find Emily Dickinson, Thomas Hardy, Robert Frost, Wallace Stevens, William Carlos Williams, and then the contemporary poets. All in all, the works of more than two hundred poets are on display. This is a very civilized anthology: the selection of poems is extremely tasteful, with the most important works in English represented. The contemporary poets are allocated ample space to lay serious claim to a reader's attention.

A Little Treasury of Modern Poetry, English and American. *Oscar Williams, ed.* (3d ed., 1970) Scribner's. 937p., o.p.

This pocket-sized collection is as familiar to the average reader as any work in this guide. Williams had an uncanny skill for intelligently selecting precisely the type of poet and poetry that appeals to the average reader — as well, of course, as to students of Poetry 101 in hundreds of colleges and universities. The anthology is a standard for library browsing and reference. It is not hard to see why it is so popular. The format is easy to handle, and the pages are loaded with the familiar, tried and true. As one might expect, "modern" begins with Thomas Hardy and a selection of about a dozen of his poems. This is the average number for the major writers, with half again as many for the lesser figures. American and English authors are mixed together in chronological order. It is hard to name one major poet who was writing up to the time of the last edition who is not represented. The introduction, notes, and related aspects of the book make it a fine companion for one and all.

100 Poems by 100 Poets; an Anthology. *Harold Pinter, Geoffrey Godbert, and Anthony Astbury, comps.* **(1986) Grove Press. 176p.**

Playwright Harold Pinter explains that "this book took final shape on a train journey to Cornwall. Anthony Astbury, Geoffrey Godbert and myself . . . consider each poem here to be representative of the poet's finest work." On the twelve-hour train trip, the three argued fiercely about what was to be included since they were limiting themselves to one poem per poet. Entries are not necessarily the most famous works. The distinguished jury decided to reprint all poems in full, to include only those written in English, and to exclude living poets. The latter decision may have been a consideration of copyright, but Pinter claims it was made "since we needed to make our choice from the total corpus of each poet's work." The poets are arranged in alphabetical order, ranging chronologically from John Skelton (1460–1529) to Sylvia Plath. It is an awe-inspiring gathering. Almost every poet belongs to the "classics" roll call, but not all of the poems; there are numerous, marvelous surprises. This is a nearly perfect collection for anyone who loves poetry.

The Oxford Book of Narrative Verse. *Iona Opie and Peter Opie, eds.* **(1983) Oxford University Press. 407p.**

Narrative poems have a particular charm: they combine the delights of verse with the plots of fiction. All too often, anthologists are unable to include narrative poems in their collections because of their length. This volume adjusts the balance and prints dozens of narrative poems, most of them in their entirety, beginning with some of the tales of Geoffrey Chaucer and concluding with a poem by W. H. Auden. Some of the choices of the astute editors are predictable, for example, Pope's "The Rape of the Lock," and Samuel Taylor Coleridge's "The Rime of the Ancient Mariner." Others are lesser-known works, such as Christina Rossetti's "Goblin Market" and William Plomer's "Atheling Grange: or, the Apotheosis of Lotte Nussbaum." All these works comprise an important part of the poetic tradition in England and America, and they deserve to be readily available to readers. They are particularly good for reading aloud, and some of the works, such as Dryden's "Cymon and Iphigenia" or Burns's "Tam o'Shanter" could provide a taste that whets the appetite for more of the author's works. Humor can also be found in this collection, e.g., Lewis Carroll's "The Hunting of the Snark," as well as a great deal of drama. This is a most absorbing collection.

Poets of the English Language. Vols. I–V. *W. H. Auden and Norman Holmes Pearson, eds.* (1950) Viking Press. Vols. I–III, V: o.p.; Vol. IV, "Romantic Poets," pap.

This is one of the most famous collections of the twentieth century. Working with a Yale professor, Auden wrote the introductions to each volume. Pearson's initial selection of poems were reviewed and approved by Auden. The publisher has divided what is normally a single-volume work into five separate, pocket-sized books. In terms of format and convenience, much can be said for the decision. The problem for libraries may be, of course, keeping the five together. For the layperson the separate volumes are a definite plus. One can pick up English poetry at five distinctive points, beginning with the medieval and Renaissance poets and ending with the Victorians and Edwardians. The selections of American and British verse from 1400 to 1914 hold numerous surprises; there is pleasure in finding the unusual choice. If Matthew Arnold and Walt Whitman are well represented, so are Herman Melville, Coventry Patmore, and Lionel Johnson — all in the fifth and final volume. Arrangement throughout is chronological, and each volume is indexed with biographical notes. A "Calendar of British and American Poetry" opens each book, in which parallel historical dates are given in relation to the poems. The special delight of the collection is in Auden's astute, personal involvement. His intellectual appraisals and explanations establish the poets and poems as only a great poet could. The volumes should be treasured for Auden's far-reaching, polished literary introductions. Highly recommended for libraries and for individuals.

Quest for Reality; an Anthology of Short Poems in English. *Yvor Winters and Kenneth Fields, eds.* (1969) Swallow Press. 200p.

Most of the nearly two hundred poems by forty-eight poets share three things. First, they are short — a half to two pages in length. Second, only the sixteenth and seventeenth centuries are included, with a few nineteenth-century entries, followed by numerous poets from the twentieth-century American scene. Third, their selection is based on "a high degree of concentration which aims at understanding and revealing the particular subject as fully as possible." The eccentric criteria allow for few real surprises before the twentieth century. After that, when one turns to Edgar Bowers, Catherine Davis, Alan Stephens, Helen

Pinkerton, and Charles Gullans (all born in the late 1920's), there is a suspicion that Winters trusted more to highly personal taste than to concerned judgment. While a useful library source for hard-to-find modern poets, the volume is of quite limited value to laypersons.

The Rattle Bag; an Anthology of Poetry. *Seamus Heaney and Ted Hughes, comps.* **(1982) Faber and Faber. 498p., pap.**

Compiled by two of the best poets writing in English today, "this anthology amassed itself like a cairn." The familiar are in the same mixed, or rattle, bag as the poems from the by-ways. At the same time, the focus is on the average reader, young or old, who is looking to experts for guidance to the best in American and British poetry since Ben Jonson. There is a dash of European, Latin American, and other poetry, but the primary emphasis remains on English and American verse. Both compilers show a strong preference for twentieth-century work. It is arranged, as the title suggests, in no particular order. Poems are in alphabetical order by title or first line because any other arrangement "would have robbed the order of the poems of an unexpectedness. . . . To have done it thematically would have made it feel too much like a textbook. To have done it chronologically would have left whole centuries unrepresented." There is a brief glossary and a listing of poets and their poems. The introduction is exactly two short paragraphs; the compilers preferred the anthology to speak for itself. And it does. When published it received high acclaim as "a standard which other anthologies will find it difficult to equal." There is no argument with that evaluation.

Sometime the Cow Kick Your Head; the Biennial of Light Verse & Witty Poems (Light Year '88/89). *Robert Wallace, ed.* **Bits Press. 1988. 235p.**

Good light verse is a perennial delight, and good light verse of contemporary vintage is often hard to find. Is it being written, and, if so, where can it be found? That difficult question is addressed in this series of annuals/biennials by an editor who clearly relishes his task of accumulating the best entertaining, witty, amusing, and frolicsome verse currently being written. Gavin Ewart, the British poet, opens this collection with a gloomy view of "Country Matters" that begins, "The badgers are boring, the trees are so trivial,/they both have me snoring — for I am convivial." It is not a perspective of which Wordsworth would have approved. Most of the poets will be new to readers, although, along with the acclaimed Ewart, there are Roy Blount, Jr., John Updike, Donald

Hall, William Stafford, and the always witty X. J. Kennedy. Women are generously represented, with, among many others, famous poets like May Swenson and Marge Piercy. After an introduction that discourses upon the state of the art of light verse, the poems are arranged along thematic lines. This is a collection to revel in, to read out loud to friends, and generally to smile and chuckle over. The quality of the verse is high, and the humor never palls. The enigmatic title, by the way, derives from a poem by Andrew J. Grossman that starts, "Sometime the cow kick your head/Sometimes she just moo/Even the cow don't know/What she going to do." You, if you are smart, will find a copy of this superior anthology. Recommended for all libraries.

The Sonnet; an Anthology. *Robert M. Bender and Charles L. Squier, eds.* (1987) Washington Square Press. 428p., pap.

Prepared as a textbook for college classes, this is "a comprehensive anthology of British and American sonnets from the Renaissance to the present." The editors first bring on stage Thomas Wyatt (1503–1542), the earliest of the English Renaissance poets. There is the usual, expected brief background information on the poet and his poetry, and then a half dozen works selected from his more typical, well-known verse. The pattern is carried right through to the modern period. There is an index of authors, titles, and first lines, and a brief (perhaps too brief) explanation of the sonnet and its place in history. It is hard to think of a poet composing in the English language who is left out. Conversely, there are too many minor voices, and probably too much is attempted for one volume. While the selection is good, the volume disappoints in its failure to offer many surprises in the development of the form. Still, as a basic, representative text it is hard to beat.

A Treasury of Great Poems, English and American. *Louis Untermeyer, ed.* (Rev. and enl. ed., 1955) Simon and Schuster. 1,286p., o.p.

This is a huge volume that auspiciously begins with personal remarks by poets about poetry. It is evident from the start that the well-known editor is someone who cares deeply about the subject to which he is introducing the reader. The anthology opens with selections from the Bible. Treating the Bible as literature, the "Song of Songs" is included, along with selections from "The Book of Job" and other passages from the Old and New Testament that are of interest to students of literature. The anthology then proceeds chronologically through "Foundations of English Spirit," featuring the works of Chaucer, "The Popular Ballad,"

"Early Songs of Unknown Authorship," and so on, through the fifteenth and sixteenth centuries. There are long sections devoted to Shakespeare's sonnets and passages from his plays, many poems from John Donne, Robert Herrick, George Herbert, Milton, Andrew Marvell, Blake, and the Romantic poets. In the section "Challenge to Tradition," American poets begin to appear: Walt Whitman, Herman Melville, Emily Dickinson. Finally, in the twentieth century, there are selections from A. E. Housman, Edwin Arlington Robinson, Robert Frost, and Marianne Moore, concluding with the work of Robert Lowell, May Swenson, and Richard Wilbur. This is a very readable, very accessible, excellent collection. Each author has a biographical introduction, and throughout the book there are running, perceptive comments on the essence of the various poems and their place in the literary scene.

Tygers of Wrath; Poems of Hate, Anger, and Invective. *X. J. Kennedy, ed.* (1981) University of Georgia Press. 282p.

The epigraph that adorns this book is taken from Blake's *Proverbs of Hell:* "The tygers of wrath are wiser/than the horses of instruction." It is clear that X. J. Kennedy is taking his project seriously. Wrath, hatred, anger, and invective are in full supply here, vividly portrayed by authors both old and modern. Many more men are in evidence, which may say something either about the sexes or about their writing habits. The poems are divided by subject: "In Praise of Hate," "Nearest but Not Dearest," "Sexual Skirmishes," "Personal Animosities," "Collective Detestations," "Nobles, Statesmen, Prelates, and Top Brass," "Poets, Critics and Scholars," "Offending Race of Humankind," and "Damned Abstractions." There are enough subject categories for any poet to work out his bile. And, for readers with darker sides to their personalities, these poems can provide some group support. The poets are largely first rate: T. S. Eliot, William Carlos Williams, Pope, Sylvia Plath, John Donne, Philip Larkin, Emily Dickinson, to name a few. This is a foully engrossing volume of verse.

ENGLISH AND AMERICAN POETRY
Popular Culture

Best Loved Story Poems. *Walter E. Thwing, ed.* **(1941) Garden City. 754p., o.p.**

It's all here, from "The Shooting of Dan McGrew" to "Horatius at the Bridge" and "The Owl and the Pussy-Cat." Now these may not always be the work of "great poets" as the compiler claims, but they certainly are familiar. The criteria, besides familiarity, that are used for selection are twofold. The poems must originate in America or England, and they have to be contemporary with, or after, Shakespeare. A glance at the eleven bold subject areas indicates that most of the glory is from the late nineteenth and early twentieth centuries, before MTV and rock and the modern song poem. Even the subject divisions are related to the natural bravado of a day past, e.g., "Courage and Adventure," "Faith and Repentance," and "History and Legend." Fittingly enough, this last subject area opens with Tennyson's "The Revenge," and shuts down with Robert Browning's "Incident of the French Camp." This is not the type of anthology many people will have around, but it is a grand choice for libraries. It has the old favorites, it has the beloved themes, and it offers a shadow of days long past.

The Faber Popular Reciter. *Kingsley Amis, ed.* **(1978) Faber and Faber. 256p.**

Breathes there a reader so young, who never to herself hath said — "No more reciting!" With due respect to Sir Walter Scott and hundreds of others, Amis has collected a number of poems and verses that are standard material for recitation, primarily in the primary through high school grades. Most of them are so well known as to be the objects of parodies, and almost all are less than appropriate for the average collection of excellent poetry. Here the focus is entirely on verse, no matter how banal, no matter how bad, that the school child must learn by heart. True, from page to page one does find evocations of anguish, love, hate, and something more than the constant, repetitive rhythm of the words, but this is not as frequent as that familiar beat. Kipling's "Boots-boots-

boots-boots-movin' up an' down" is a typical entry. In the introduction, Amis, an English novelist, points out how all of these verses bring back memories, some delightful, others chilling. Today, for better or for worse, few school children master any of these poems, and Amis believes they are missing a great experience. No matter, the old favorites are all here, and it is a grand collection for that reason alone.

The Family Album of Favorite Poems. *P. Edward Ernest, ed.* (1959) **Grosset & Dunlap. 538p.**

The title speaks for itself, particularly as there is no introduction to better gauge the potential audience. The few line drawings depicting typical scenes of family life set off the sixteen sections of traditional poetry. Actually, with the exception of some shining lights (from Robert Browning and John Donne to T. S. Eliot and W. B. Yeats), most of the poets are now little read except in anthologies of this type. Here, however, the compiler has gathered together numerous old "chestnuts" that may be recited by secondary school students or asked for in libraries. Favorites such as Edgar A. Guest's "Just Folks" will never win a prize as great poetry, but at one time it was on the lips of millions of people as the ideal type of poem for the ideal family. The titles of the sections pretty well set the tone: "Life Is Real, Life Is Earnest"; "Mother nature, father time"; and "The Children's Hour." There are useful indexes of authors, first lines, and titles.

The Family Book of Best Loved Poems. *David L. George, ed.* (1952) **Doubleday. 485p., pap.**

The purpose, scope, and audience is clearly stated in the first sentence of the introduction. The compiler wishes "to provide for all members of the family a satisfying collection of poems which have long endeared themselves to every American home." Some lesser-known works are introduced, too, but "in all cases the sentiment of the poem rather than the fame of the poet has been the deciding factor in determining its selection." Here sentiment is neatly arranged in sections from "Love" to "Faith and Inspiration" to "Frontier Days." The menu is so well known as to need little or no explanation, and there are few, if any, surprises. Poets are limited to English and American voices, primarily of the late nineteenth and early twentieth centuries. The tried and true receive the most space. Whether it is Elizabeth Barrett Browning or Robert Browning, whether it is Longfellow or Tennyson, one will find most of their well-known verses included. But since sentiment is the evaluative guide, there are some less than satisfying poems by writers now forgotten. The collection promises familiar verse for the family, but it may be mildly faulted for considering all families equally innocent and unsophisticated.

The Family Book of Verse. *Lewis Gannett, ed.* **(1961) Harper & Row. 351p., o.p.**

This anthology was compiled by a former book critic of *The New York Herald Tribune* and was meant to serve the purpose of helping families share poetry by reading it aloud to one another. In his warmhearted introduction, the editor describes his early morning poetry sessions with his father when he was a child. He expresses the hope that parents will continue, even in an age dominated by television, to read poetry to their children. The verses included in this volume are fine for that purpose. They are organized into sections according to major emotions or topics: ecstasy, love, mysteries, childhood. For the most part, the poets included are first rate: Keats, Emily Dickinson, Robert Browning, and Robert Frost are among those prominently featured. This would be a fine book for developing a younger person's interest in literature.

The Gambit Book of Popular Verse. *Geoffrey Grigson, ed.* **(1971) Gambit; also published in Great Britain as The Faber Book of Popular Verse. 376p.**

In his introduction, Geoffrey Grigson defines popular verse as that which is "not 'literary,' it is not egoistic or private, or . . . obscure." He mentions as well that its appeal is immediate. His book is divided into thematic sections: "Childhood, Some Children's Rhymes, and Game Rhymes"; "The Season"; "Living Things"; "Nonsense and Mystification"; "Love"; and so forth. The poems, which are mostly anonymous, satisfied a large public in the past and are just as appealing today. There are riddles in verse that should delight youngsters, as well as adults who relish puzzles. Perhaps some of the most enjoyable moments are when one comes unexpectedly across lyrics to tunes one knows: "The Foggy, Foggy Dew," for example, or "I Know Where I'm Going."

One Hundred and One Famous Poems. *Ray J. Cook, comp.* **(Rev. ed., 1958) Reilly & Lee; reprinted by Contemporary Books, 1981. 186p., o.p.**

Suitably enough, this well-known, much publicized collection of popular poetry opens with Longfellow's "The Builders." This tribute to the joys of capitalism and individualism runs like a theme throughout the whole work. The volume ends with a prose supplement that includes the

"Gettysburg Address," "The Ten Commandments," the "Magna Carta," Patrick Henry's speech "The War Inevitable," and "The Declaration of Independence." It celebrates the glories of nationalism and the singular pleasures of what William Watson calls "the things that are more excellent." And those things are what the editor describes in a three-paragraph preface: "There are souls, in these noise-tired times, that turn aside into unfrequented lanes, where the deep woods have harbored the fragrances of many a blossoming season. . . . It is the purpose of this little volume to enrich, ennoble, encourage." No one can argue with the sentiment, but sentimentality is another thing. The book is unfortunately, sentimental to a fault, although, to be sure, there are some excellent poems, each accompanied by a photograph of the poet. It is historically interesting, but that is about all anyone can say for this collection.

Poetry Worth Remembering; an Anthology of Poetry. *Roy W. Watson, comp.* **(1986) Brunswick. 274p.**

Depending on individual taste any poem is worth remembering. How, then, does the compiler decide what he thinks is memorable? A nine-line preface offers little help. "The purpose of this book is to show the beauty, the depth of thought and creativity of both men and women in their poetic writings . . . this book explores, along with other meanings, the realities of life and the mysteries of death." In other words, it is a collection of traditional, middle-of-the-esthetic-road, verse — in no apparent arrangement. There is an index of poets and a table of contents arranged alphabetically by title. Many of the poems are from collections published at the turn of the century. This anthology is useful primarily for featuring many little-known poets. (The basic writers are found in abundance in other better-edited and better-organized collections.) Here, for example, is Phillips Brooks, Maimee Lee Brown, and George W. Bungay, along with Horatius Bonar and Noah Barker. The only readily recognizable poets in the "B's" are Robert Browning and William Cullen Bryant. Surprisingly, this collection was published in 1986 not 1906!

The World's Best Loved Poems. *James Gilchrist Lawson, comp.* **(1927) Harper & Row. 455p.**

Considering the fact that this was published over sixty years ago, it is not a criticism to say that the collection concentrates on popular verse that is often more sentimental than worthy, more filled with moral and religious lessons than with vivid portraits of individuals or situations.

Sensibility, if not always sense, rules the compiler's choices. The collection is an effort "to gather into one volume the choicest of the world's most helpful short religious and popular poems. . . . Many of the pieces were selected not from the standpoint of highest literary merit, but because of their appeal to the human heart." The arrangement is by subject, beginning with "Autumn" and working through the alphabet to "Worry." There are indexes of first lines, titles, and authors to bring some order to the compiler's selection. Particularly striking is the index of authors; few are known today. This is a reference work for the library where hard-to-find, little-known poets are a problem to locate.

ENGLISH AND AMERICAN POETRY
20th Century

Chief Modern Poets of Britain and America. *Gerald DeWitt Sanders, John Herbert Nelson, and M. L. Rosenthal, eds.* (5th ed., 1970) Macmillan. 480p., pap.

"Modern" refers to the twentieth century in this case, up to the publication date of the fifth edition, i.e., 1970. The few exceptions are Emily Dickinson, Gerard Manley Hopkins, and those who "came into their own in our age." The poets are arranged chronologically in each of the two parts; Sylvia Plath is the last poet in the American section; ironically enough the final poet in the English section is Ted Hughes. There is a considerably larger representation of poets from before the Second World War than after, but there are, fortunately, enough other compilations of modern poetry so that the average reader or the average library need not worry about this lack of poets from the last half of the 1900's. On a more positive note the collection is excellent because it includes a large selection of poems from each of the poets, it considers poets such as Edgar Lee Masters and Carl Sandburg with care, and does not simply dismiss them as once popular, and finally, but not least, there are useful biographical and bibliographical notes.

The Direction of Poetry; an Anthology of Rhymed and Metered Verse Written in the English Language since 1975. *Robert Richman, ed.* (1988) Houghton Mifflin. 168p.

Tradition is the key word in this anthology. While all of the poems are modern — and nothing here was written before 1975 — they all share the traditional form of rhyme and meter. The seventy-six poets are of various ages, but the majority are young and not that well known. They come primarily from America and Britain, but others call Australia, Canada, and the West Indies home. As the compiler says, this collection "celebrates the work of a particular group of poets — the most important group to have emerged in the last fifteen years." One may argue with the characterization of "most important," but there is no argument with the quality of the selection. This seems particularly evident among such

106

older poets as Elizabeth Bishop, John Fuller, and X. J. Kennedy. Somehow their training and their experience make the work of the senior members more memorable. At the same time, the fascination of the collection lies in sampling the traditional forms through the eyes of the truly young, less well-known writers. This is a collection that will have wide appeal.

English and American Surrealist Poetry. *Edward B. Germain, ed.* **(1978) Penguin Books. 348p., o.p.**

The strange dreamlike quality of surrealism is here captured in verse. The many poems celebrate the delights of surrealism in film, art, and artistic living. The fantastic imagery is everywhere, and many of the poems must be read several times for meaning — if, indeed, there is any meaning at all, other than the poet and the poem. The combinations and juxtapositions may not be every reader's idea of good poetry, but it is, at the very least, challenging. For a good explanation of surrealism and poetry see Mr. Germain's introduction. People, he explains, who dismiss surrealism outright are missing an important step, taking the work at its literal meaning. "If the poet writes: A horse galloped on a tomato, that is exactly what he means." And here he illustrates his point with a poem by David Gascoyne. Not all of the poets and poetry are quite so difficult. There is the work of Dylan Thomas, for example, who may be in unfamiliar company, but is there. Most of the surrealists gave up writing before the Second World War. The anthology is a reminder of a fascinating long-gone age.

The Faber Book of Modern Verse. *Michael Roberts, ed.* **(4th ed., revised by Peter Porter, 1982) Faber and Faber. 416p., pap.**

This is a compelling anthology of modern verse. There are ample selections from many of the great modern poets, and the choice of their works is outstanding. Furthermore the range of the poets covered is liberal: American as well as English authors are included, and many contemporary poets are among those worthy of representing the modern canon. Among the present-day poets whose verse is printed alongside the works of Gerard Manley Hopkins, W. B. Yeats, T. S. Eliot, Ezra Pound, and Marianne Moore are Geoffrey Hill, Ted Hughes, John Ashbery, and Seamus Heaney. The reader can turn to this volume to look seriously at the various, difficult, and marvelous accomplishments of poets in the modern age, for much of their very best work is on display here. A few omissions however seem strange: there is no sign of Robert

Frost, and of the twenty-four contemporary poets added by the current editor, only one is a woman — Sylvia Plath.

The Faber Book of Twentieth Century Verse. *John Heath-Stubbs and David Wright, eds.* **(3d ed., 1975) Faber and Faber. 348p.**

No matter what its title, of the scores of poetry anthologies, the majority in part, or in full, embrace the twentieth century. There is no shortage, then, of twentieth-century verse collections. Why, then, another compilation? As this one has gone into several editions and sold rather well, there must be an explanation. It is not the arrangement, which is the perfunctory A to Z by author. It is not the wide selection of individual poems. There are normally no more than two to four for each of about one hundred and twenty-five poets. (And there are some questionable choices of scope. W. H. Auden has five poems, Philip Larkin one, and Robert Graves seven, outnumbered only by Ezra Pound). It may be the unusual choice of minor poets. For example, in how many collections does one find Lascelles Abercrombie or Anne Finch matched poem for poem with Ted Hughes and Sylvia Plath? Still, all the major twentieth-century figures are in evidence. So, in general, the collection is about as diverse as any. The varied styles and preoccupations of the writers establish "the expression of the common imaginative experience of the age."

Modern American & British Poetry. *Louis Untermeyer, ed., in consultation with Karl Shapiro and Richard Wilbur.* **(Rev., shorter ed., 1955) Harcourt, Brace. 697p., o.p.**

Karl Shapiro and Richard Wilbur each have eight or nine poems in this standard collection. They have a discerning hand, too, in the other selections for this edition, which was considerably updated from earlier ones. There are many more first-rate, modern (up to 1950) poets in both the British and American sections. Guided by the two younger poets, Louis Untermeyer, the father of numerous collections, was wise enough to delete some earlier, less inspired poetry. At any rate, the 1955 edition remains very basic, in that all major, and many minor poets, are included. This selection truly is representative of the twentieth century, including works by Emily Dickinson and Gerard Manley Hopkins who really came to be appreciated only in this century. The choices are exceptionally fine. Here one finds the best of American poets Robert Lowell, James Merrill, Randall Jarrell, Robert Frost, and, from the British side, W. H. Auden, Louis MacNeice, Stephen Spender, to name a few. One can readily pick up countless volumes to carry the reader from 1950 to the present day.

New Poets of England and America. *Donald Hall, Robert Pack and Louis Simpson, eds.* **(1957) Meridian Books. 351p., o.p.**

Selected by what were then three young poets (all widely published today), this includes almost all famous American and English poets writing from the 1930's to the mid 1950's. But the emphasis is on "new," so the regulars from Pound to Cummings are not included. Instead the reader is given representative samplings of some of the best work of Robert Lowell, Richard Wilbur, Kingsley Amis, to name a few. The pattern was to be followed again in the even better *New Poets of England and America; Second Selection.* In both anthologies, the work is divided into two sections: English and American; in both anthologies, the English seem to fare better, if not in the amount of space, then in the quality of the verse. But only in this earlier edition can one find a marvelous, sometimes sarcastic introduction by Robert Frost. Both works are indispensable for an understanding of modern poetry.

New Poets of England and America. *Donald Hall and Robert Pack, eds.* **(Second selection, 1962) World. 384p., o.p.**

Anyone over forty years of age was not considered for this project, for that was the definition of "new" in 1962 when the well-known collection was published. Based on the earlier successful edition, it is neatly divided into two sections. Hall edited the English side and opens with: "People are writing some very good poems in England these days. Not many American critics will admit it." He goes on to support his argument with Kingsley Amis, Thom Gunn, Geoffrey Hill, Ted Hughes, Philip Larkin, and about two dozen other worthies. There are only one or two women in the group, a group which over the years has gratified most readers. Robert Pack edited the American side with James Dickey, Anthony Hecht, John Hollander, Philip Levine, among others. In retrospect, the English poets do look superior to the Americans. One would venture to guess that more English poets are better known to readers than are the Americans. Suitably enough, some of the best Americans are such women as Sylvia Plath, Denise Levertov, Adrienne Rich, and Anne Sexton. There are short biographical notes, but no first line, subject, or title indexes.

The Oxford Book of Contemporary Verse, 1945–1980. *D. J. Enright, comp.* **(1980) Oxford University Press. 299p., o.p.**

Poet and critic, D. J. Enright selects who he considers to be the leading English, American, and Commonwealth poets for the period from 1945 to 1980. Arrangement is chronological by birth date, with Stevie Smith (b. 1902) leading off the group of about forty-five poets. Douglas Dunn (b. 1942) is the last to be included. About five lines of biographical data are given for each of the poets in the Table of Contents, and there are indexes of first lines and authors. In making his selection, Enright says he went out of his way to achieve geographical representation. Other principles of selection are explained in the thirteen-page introduction. Half a dozen or a dozen poems are given for each of the authors. The value of the choices is obvious, since a decade later almost all of the poets are still highly regarded, still often quoted. Some, such as Stevie Smith and Philip Larkin, are dead, but most are still alive. Among these are the compiler himself, Kingsley Amis, Roy Fuller, Seamus Heaney, Ted Hughes, and Richard Wilbur. While women are included, they are in the minority. Still, the poems are among the best written by contemporary poets up to 1980, and the introduction, a short essay on the delights of poetry, should not be missed.

The Oxford Book of Modern Verse, 1892–1935. *William Butler Yeats, ed.* **(1936) Oxford University Press. 454p., o.p.**

The great Irish poet William Butler Yeats was asked in 1936 to choose the best poetry from his generation, and this volume is the result of his search. A few poets have been excluded because they would not give their permission to be anthologized (e.g., Robert Graves and Laura Riding), and others were scantily represented because their fees were too high (e.g., Ezra Pound), but for the most part the selection is startlingly good. The poems by T. S. Eliot that Yeats chose are impeccable, what is included from Ezra Pound is also of the first rank, and it is particularly interesting, of course, to see what Yeats selected from his own vast oeuvre. Many of the other poets are little known today, but their writing bears inspection, for it reveals the convention from which the most modern poets revolted. Among other well-known authors whose work is included are Thomas Hardy, C. Day Lewis, W. H. Auden, and Louis MacNeice. The poets are frequently represented by more than one work, so the reader is able to grasp something of the range of their poetry. Yeats supplies an introduction in which he details the many strands that went into the making of modern poetry.

The Poetry Anthology, 1912–1977. *Daryl Hine and Joseph Parisi, eds.*

See under AMERICAN POETRY: 20TH CENTURY (PERIODICAL)

FINNISH POETRY

Salt of Pleasure: Twentieth-Century Finnish Poetry. *Aili Jarvenpa, tr.* **(1983) New Rivers Press. 240p., pap.**

Thanks to numerous black-and-white photographs (by Oliver and Robert Jarvenpa) that set the mood, crystal clear translations, and a brief sketch of each poet, this is an easy, delightful collection to read. There probably is not one person in a thousand who would recognize more than one or two of the poets, at least if they are not Finnish Americans, as is the translator/compiler. The twenty-six poets "have been selected as representative of the best in twentieth century Finnish poetry." Eino Leino (1878–1926) begins with "Äijö's Song": "He was Äijö, born alone/ began alone/died alone,/sat on the edge of the cloud,/watched the world go by." A lyric poet of considerable influence, his style and intellectual interests are reflected by many of the others. If there is any universal theme it is, as the introduction notes, "the reflective melancholy." There is a surprising lack of Russian influence and of war poetry in the collection. The quality of the work is high, and anyone who appreciates nature will find pleasure in these pages.

FRENCH POETRY

The Defiant Muse; French Feminist Poems from the Middle Ages to the Present. *Donna C. Stanton, ed.*

See under WOMEN'S POETRY AND FEMINIST POETRY

The Poetry of Surrealism; an Anthology. *Michael Benedikt, ed. and tr.* **(1974) Little, Brown. 375p., pap.**

This is similar to the *Random House Book of Twentieth-Century French Poetry,* but its focus and emphasis differ. Benedikt, as the title indicates, is involved only with modern French poets who have something to do with surrealism. Here, the elusive quality of the surreal is explored in the introduction, but it comes down to a single, simple statement: "Man is in a crisis." The compiler then calls upon some fifteen poets to elucidate. In the Random House collection there are twice that number of voices, a third again as many pages, and original French as well as the English translations. A number of poets and poems duplicate what is found in Benedikt. And while the compiler is a fine translator, his translations are not always as satisfactory as those found in the Random House work. So, for an individual, either book would suffice; for libraries, the Random House collection might be preferable, with its separate scope, a separate focus, and translations and poetry not found in the other.

Proensa; an Anthology of Troubadour Poetry. *Paul Blackburn, comp. and tr.; George Economou, ed.* **(1986) Paragon House. 325p.**

Troubadours were singer-poets who performed throughout the south of France in medieval times. Their poems date from the twelfth through the thirteenth centuries, and they sang of courtly and profane love. Paul Blackburn elected to make the poetry sing again, to a modern, English-speaking audience, and so he translated the poets in a richly passionate and contemporary style. He preserves the essence of the old verses, but gives them fresher structures and graceful, English phrasing. The result is that these aged poems are easy to read and empathize with, as they

113

render the emotions of a long, lost society comprehensibly to a modern audience. Thus, the troubles of Bertran de Born, writing in the late twelfth century, with the performance demands of his Count, seem easy to understand. Blackburn's translations, which took over ten years to complete, serve the cause of this ancient Provençal poetry by allowing modern readers to appreciate its artistic excellence and variety.

The Random House Book of Twentieth-Century French Poetry. *Paul Auster, ed.* **(1982) Random House. 638p., pap.**

While Auster successfully conveys the glory of French verse, he fails on one count. The book is much too large. While the reference value of such bulk is fine for a library (and, as such, highly recommended), it is a bad choice for the individual who may wish to read in comfort. The number of poets is appropriate, but there are too many selections from lesser known, less-talented people. With that, one must commend Auster for insisting on a bilingual edition and excellent translators. For example, the volume opens, as it should, with Apollinaire. "Zone" is in French on the left hand side. The translation into English on the other side is by Samuel Beckett. And within this single poet's work, one also finds translations by Richard Wilbur, Dudley Fitts, W. S. Merwin, and others. The cast of translators is as impressive as the translations and, in some of the later poets' work, even better than the original. There are adequate notes on the poets and a list of translators, but despite the size of the volume no alphabetical listings of poems, poets, or first lines. Auster's own translations and his introduction support his reputation.

The Women Troubadours. *Meg Bogin, ed.* **(1980)**

See under WOMEN'S POETRY AND FEMINIST POETRY

GAY AND LESBIAN POETRY

Gay & Lesbian Poetry in Our Time; an Anthology. *Carl Morse and Joan Larkin, eds.* **(1988) St. Martin's Press. 463p.**

Here are more than ninety poets and over two hundred poems that testify to the gay and lesbian movement, primarily in the United States. Although the volume is large, the compilers limited their choices to poetry written after 1950. For the most part, the selection is good, and the work represents a fair cross-section of the movement's advocates. As of 1988, it is the best collection of its type. From page to page, one moves from psychological and mystical preoccupations to the everyday problems and delights of the poets. The writers are among the best, from W. H. Auden and James Baldwin to Adrienne Rich and Allen Ginsburg. The alphabetical arrangement of poets scatters the better-known among the less common. A definite attraction is the offering of leading poets from the black, native American, Asian-American, and Hispanic communities. There are some excellent photographs of the poets. As one might expect, AIDS plays a role in many of the poems, but none excels that of Thom Gunn's "Lament" for a lost friend.

The Penguin Book of Homosexual Verse. *Stephen Coote, ed.* **(1983) Penguin Books. 410p., pap.**

Published five years prior to *Gay & Lesbian Poetry* (annotated here), this includes many of the same poets and poetry, but the selection is more historical, going back to Homer, Sappho, and Pindar. As the compiler points out, the collection "ranges in time and place from classical Athens to contemporary New York." Furthermore, not all of the poets celebrate the gay life. In fact "in tone and content [the poems range] from celebration to satire." The editor offers a brief, yet thorough, well-written introduction to the history of homosexual poetry and love. Gay and homosexual are used interchangeably, although "homosexual was chosen for the title because it can be employed relatively neutrally." Most of the poems are written in the Western tradition, and there are numerous translations, with due credit to the translators. Approximately half of the poems are from the late nineteenth and twentieth centuries, and the majority of poets are represented by one or two poems. The exceptions, with at least a half dozen entries each, are C. P. Cavafy, A. E. Housman, Shakespeare, and epigrams from the Greek Anthology.

GERMAN POETRY

An Anthology of World Poetry. *Mark Van Doren, ed.*

See under WORLD POETRY.

The Defiant Muse; German Feminist Poems from the Middle Ages to the Present. *Susan L. Cocalis, ed.*

See under WOMEN'S POETRY AND FEMINIST POETRY

The Oxford Book of Verse in English Translation. *Charles Tomlinson, ed.*

See under WORLD POETRY

GREEK POETRY

Voices of Modern Greece. *Edmund Keeley and Philip Sherrard, trs. and eds.* **(1981) Princeton University Press. 204p.**

The voices are five major Greek poets, Constantine P. Cavafy (1863–1933), Angelos Sikelianos (1884–1951), George Seferis (1900–1971), Odysseus Elytis (b. 1911), and Nikos Gatsos (b. 1914). The translations, by the compilers, seem to capture the meaning and usually the spirit of the verse. Only here and there do the poems seem a bit flat, a trifle too hampered by literal translation. Of some help are the notes that establish the background of the works and pinpoint individuals mentioned in the poems. There is also a section that gives the biographies of each poet. An index of first lines completes the volume. Numerous poems were published earlier, and this is a splendid opportunity to have them gathered into a single volume, together with an author's later work. The selection is, in the words of the editors, "composed of translations of what seem to us to come over most successfully into English and at the same time to be representative of the best poetry of the original poets." A worthy goal and one they successfully achieved.

HEBREW AND YIDDISH POETRY

American Yiddish Poetry. *Benjamin Harshaw and Barbara Harshaw,*
eds. **(1986) University of California Press. 815p.**

In this bilingual anthology the compilers rightfully set out to save
seven Yiddish poets from neglect or oblivion. These are Americans who
wrote in the twentieth century, who published in Yiddish newspapers
and magazines, whose verse appeared in books long out of print. Most
were born at the close of the nineteenth century, and the majority are
now dead. They had a major influence on Jewish thought in America,
and some of them went beyond the community to speak to the world.
Most of them, however, gained little recognition outside their immediate
circle. And they deserve an audience that will weigh their individual and
collective contributions. There are excellent translations, notes, brief in-
troductions, and, not least significant, a sixty-five-page introductory es-
say, "American Poetry in Yiddish."

Israeli Poetry; a Contemporary Anthology. *Warren Bargad and Stanley*
F. Chyet, comps. and trs. **(1986) Indiana University Press. 273p.**

Hebrew, in the words of these editors, was assuredly "never a dead
language." It has always been used for religious purposes and sometimes
for secular literary ones as well. Since the founding of the State of Israel,
there has been a flowering of creative writing in Hebrew. The poetry
that has been collected in this anthology treats the past forty years of
literary achievement in Israel. The contributors are arranged chrono-
logically, and each of the eleven poets is accorded a good deal of space.
Perhaps the most famous of the authors is Yehuda Amichai, but all of
them are outstanding. Two are women. Each poet is introduced through
generous biographical notes. The forms of the works vary; there are
traditional forms, prose poems, and open forms. These are excellent
poems, but they would be more accessible with notes explaining some of
the foreign words.

Modern Hebrew Poetry. *Bernhard Frank, ed. and tr.* **(1980) University of Iowa Press. 176p.**

Compared to *Voices within the Ark, the Modern Jewish Poets,* which came out the same year, this is about one sixth the size and limited only to Hebrew poetry. Most of the poets are in both volumes. The poems however, are not the same, and where the individual or library has one, the other will be wanted. If a choice must be made, this collection has generally superior translations. And yet, it is worth emphasizing, the scope is so much narrower that comparison is hardly fair. There are some sixty poets present. The greatest number of entries are for Israel Efrat, Yehudah Amikhai, and Itamar Ya'oz-kest. Pinkhas Sadeh has a single poem. The introduction contains a history of modern Hebrew poetry, with its place in the Hebrew tradition.

The Penguin Book of Modern Yiddish Verse. *Irving Howe, Ruth R. Wisse, and Khone Shmeruk, eds.* **(1987) Viking Press. 719p.**

A bilingual anthology, this is particularly useful for those who read Yiddish; it also a fascinating anthology for English readers who are interested in Yiddish culture. While it covers a variety of Yiddish verse written in the past hundred years, it features the works of such major poets as Jacob Glatstein, Moyshe-Leyb Halpern, and Abraham Sutzkever. The translations are by such fine writers as Cynthia Ozick and John Hollander. A learned introduction by the editors details the sociopolitical context in which the poems were created, and biographical notes introduce each of the writers. This book is an eye-opener for readers with only a vague knowledge of Yiddish cultural achievements. The poems evoke a vivid sense of life in the European and American ghettos, intense religious experiences, celebrations of the family, and sophisticated ruminations on art. The variety of poets is great, and their responses to their own and surrounding communities are highly individual and compelling.

A Treasury of Jewish Poetry. *Nathan Ausubel and Maryann Ausubel, eds.* **(1957) Crown. 471p., o.p.**

Both secular and religious Jewish poetry is included in this standard, although by now somewhat dated, anthology. The material moves from the Biblical period to the modern, and while the focus is on Jewish poets, their themes do not necessarily concern Jewish subjects. This wide scope allows the compilers to say in the introduction that the content is much broader than in similar collections. "Jewish poetry consists of all poetry created by Jews." On the whole, the choices from this wide field are excellent, and most of the outstanding poets of all times are included. Post Second World War writers, possibly for lack of space, are not as well represented as they might be, but this is made up for by the emphasis on poets throughout the ages. There are biographical sketches of each of the authors, and an index of titles and first lines. The introduction is a model of scholarship, as are the numerous translations throughout the whole volume.

Voices within the Ark; the Modern Jewish Poets. *Howard Schwartz and Anthony Rudolf, eds.* **(1980) Avon Books. 1210p., pap.**

The problem is familiar and can be stated as a question: If one limits a collection of verse to "modern" poets and then imposes a further, narrower limitation, is it possible to find that many good voices? Here the focus is on "modern Jewish" poets and the net is cast wide to include those writing in Hebrew (over seventy-five), Yiddish (another forty or so), English, and "other languages." The latter two categories take up almost eight hundred pages. Poets are arranged alphabetically under each category, and for each there is a reasonably detailed biographical sketch. The translations seem excellent. Each section has separate, perceptive introductions that are models of their kind, providing the setting for the poetry. It is difficult to find a Jewish poet writing between 1920 and 1980 who is not included. To return to the opening question, more selectivity is needed. There are absolutely marvelous poems in this volume, but the majority are, to say the least, minor. The major poets are found in greater depth in other collections. It is, nevertheless, a must for libraries and for individuals because of its target audience.

HISPANIC AMERICAN POETRY

Contemporary Chicana Poetry; a Critical Approach to an Emerging Literature. *Marta Ester Sánchez, ed.* **(1985) University of California Press. 375p., pap.**

There is a great deal of prose in this volume, since it is an attempt to introduce its readership to an emerging poetry. At the outset, in "Setting the Context," the editor discusses the precarious topics of gender, ethnicity, and silence in Chicana poetry today. She then goes on to explore the work of Alma Villanueva, Lorna Dee Cervantes, Lucha Corpi, and Bernice Zamora. Along the way, many poems by each of these writers are quoted, and the appendix includes still more poems. The analyses are sophisticated and require a good deal of knowledge about poetic techniques and explication. But the introduction to societal codes and norms will prove helpful to those who want an understanding of contemporary Chicana poetry. And the poems themselves are a striking choice from a group of poets who are not heard from very often by the general reading public. All of these poets are women, and they represent a fairly wide range of Chicana writing today.

The Defiant Muse; Hispanic Feminist Poems from the Middle Ages to the Present. *Angel Flores and Kate Flores, eds.*

See under WOMEN'S POETRY AND FEMINIST POETRY

Fiesta in Aztlan; Anthology of Chicano Poetry. *Toni Empringham, ed.* **(1981) Capra Press. 128p., o.p.**

In only three bilingual sections, the poets celebrate the life of the Chicano. "La Familia" has eight poems, from Teresa Acosta's "My mother pieced quilts" to Margarita Reyes's "The old man who is gone now." The next section is called "The Streets of the Barrio" and is by far the finest in the collection. Here eight poets tell what it is like to live in their own community. Luis Rodriguez sums it up in prose: "Here in the barrios we can open up, be ourselves, and be funny in a Chicano sort of way. . . . True there is death and violence here, but there is much more life." "El Mundo," the final section, is the longest and its fifteen poets consider everything from a "Dopefiends Trip" to "The Spanish Girls" and "Visions of Mexico While at a Writing Symposium in Port Townsend, Washington." There are biographical sketches of the poets, and a splendid introduction by the compiler who also translated the poetry. He explains the title: Chicanos "live in Aztlan, the name given by the Aztecs to their place of origin, the land to the north, which they left to found their great empire near Mexico City. For Chicanos, Aztlan represents their homeland."

Inventing a Word; an Anthology of Twentieth-Century Puerto Rican Poetry. *Julio Marzán, ed.* **(1980) Columbia University Press. 183p.**

This bilingual edition includes twenty-three poets who represent "a continuation into the twentieth century of two poetic traditions — each with distinct attitudes toward language, culture, and politics that have competitively co-existed in Puerto Rican literature since the emergence of Puerto Rican consciousness in the nineteenth century." One would be hard pressed to find a better history of that development than in the articulate, scholarly introduction by the compiler. The poems, ably translated by the same compiler, represent a variety of styles. Final choice, as is often the case with translations, is based on which of the poems can be understood in English. "To be sure, deciding on this basis resulted in some notable omissions, especially of the purist and avant-garde poetry. . . . These omitted poems sounded either old fashioned or generally unexciting in translation." There are brief biographical notes, but no index.

HOLIDAY POETRY

The Naked Astronaut; Poems on Birth and Birthdays. *René Graziani, ed.* **(1983) Faber and Faber. 380p., o.p.**

The quest for a subject that has not already been the theme of a poetry anthology drives editors to compile guides such as this one. Sometimes they do quite nicely. This is a case in point. "To the best of my knowledge, the subject of birth and birthdays has not been anthologized before." Here is a pleasing collection, divided by broad subjects from "Birth and Good Wishes" to "Variations." The first has the greatest number of poems, closely followed by "Poet's Anniversaries," where Walt Whitman writes about his seventy-first year and Howard Nemerov celebrates his fifteenth birthday. In general, the poets and the poems are outstanding and would be so in any collection, no matter what its theme. There are an index of first lines and a brief glossary.

O Frabjous Day: Poetry for Holidays and Special Occasions. *Myra Cohn Livingston, ed.* **(1977) Atheneum. 205p.**

Each basic American holiday is celebrated with a half dozen poems by almost as many poets. Most of the entries are from the moderns, i.e., those born no later than the end of the nineteenth century. And most of the poets are standard voices from T. S. Eliot to Ted Berrigan and William Carlos Williams. The compiler is to be congratulated on three counts. First, there are some exceptional voices from other lands, other times, and these include a Chinese ninth-century poet and the noble Roman Sedulius Scottus. Second, while centered on American culture, there are holidays — particularly Halloween, Easter, and birthdays — where the English and others are brought into the collection. Third, the selection itself represents an unusual, imaginative grasp of the meaning of our holidays, and while much of this is suitable for children, it can be enjoyed as well by adults. The holidays include, other than those previously mentioned, New Year, Valentine's Day, Lincoln's and Washington's birthdays, Memorial Day, Fourth of July, Columbus Day, Thanksgiving, Christmas, and other religious holidays. An odd section:

Assassination Poems, which includes poetry about the death of John F. Kennedy, Lincoln, Malcolm X, etc. There are brief notes on a few of the poems, followed by indexes of authors, titles, first lines, and translators.

Our Holidays in Poetry. *Mildred P. Harrington and Josephine H. Thomas, comps.* **(1929) H. W. Wilson. 479p.**

Some sixty years ago, this book was first published. It has been a hit ever since. Teachers, librarians, students, and parents all love it because of the three hundred fifty poems that enhance the experiences of various holidays. The poems are listed alphabetically by title under eight headings: Abraham Lincoln, George Washington, Easter, Arbor Day, Mother's Day, Memorial Day, Thanksgiving, and Christmas. About forty poems are given for each event. Published in a period when holidays were significant, there is no effort to commemorate sports, local customs, or commercial kinds of diversions. The poems are old-fashioned and safe. Quality varies considerably, although no one could ever accuse the compilers of being inconsistent about tying poems to holidays. Annette Wynne's "The Pilgrims Came," for example, is side by side with several Psalms, Robert Herrick, and Robert Bridges. In the index of authors the first entry is Henry Abbey with "What Do We Plant When We Plant the Tree," followed directly by Joseph Addison. Quite jolly, without pretension, the collection serves its purpose well and faithfully. It is likely to be around for at least sixty more years.

The Oxford Book of Christmas Poems. *Michael Harrison and Christopher Stuart-Clark, eds.* **(1983) Oxford University Press. 160p.**

This is a splendid anthology for young people and adults. Any collection with such a title needs no introduction, and the compilers agree. They open immediately with the poems and some one hundred and sixty pages later close with an index of titles and first lines. The poems are arranged under four major subject headings: "The sky turns dark, the years grow old;" "This was the moment when before turned into after;" "Glad Christmas comes, and every hearth makes room to bid him welcome now;" "Open you the east door and let the New Year in." All of the headings, of course, are from poems — normally the first in each section. There are colorful illustrations throughout the slim volume, and while almost all of the poems will appeal to adults, the line drawings seem particularly suited to younger readers. Most of the poets are well known, having found fame in the latter part of the nineteenth or in the twentieth century, and almost all are exclusively English and American voices.

There are a few traditional poems, although the majority are by such people as Louis MacNeice, W. H. Auden, Spike Milligan, and John Betjeman.

Poems of Christmas. *Myra Cohn Livingston, ed.* **(1980) Atheneum. 172p.**

The well-known anthologist turns her hand to Christmas and produces a good selection of poems for ten-year-olds to teenagers. Many of the verses will be equally attractive to adults. There are eight subject sections with about one hundred poets from various eras. The majority are American and English, and there is a strong influence of late nineteenth- and early twentieth-century voices. While W. H. Auden, Gwendolyn Brooks, T. S. Eliot, Robert Frost, and W. B. Yeats are strong entries, one wonders about some of the company they keep — Clement Clarke Moore and Edwin Morgan, to name only two of dozens of poets whose only apparent claim to prominence lay in writing about holidays. Nevertheless, it works well enough. The modest and mediocre fit nicely into the pattern of the theme, and the handful of genuine poetic voices are a pleasant change. The book is compiled primarily for children and to illustrate the joys of a single holiday. Indexes of titles, authors, and first lines, are provided.

HUMOROUS AND NONSENSE VERSE

A Century of Humorous Verse, 1850–1950 (Everyman's Library).
Roger Lancelyn Green, ed. **(1959) E. P. Dutton. 289p.**

There are enough selections in this anthology to tickle anyone's funny bone, but what might be the best of the lot are located in the appendixes at the end of the book. There, all but buried, is a superb, plentiful collection of limericks by known and unknown authors, along with some wonderful rootless rhymes and stray verses. Otherwise, in the core of the book, one can find lively and amusing examples of comic verse written by Kipling, Lewis Carroll, Edward Lear, and Ogden Nash, to mention the most famous. There are also scores of currently unknown poets who are, as often as not, quite adept at satire, parody, and nonsense. Also included are the delightful poems "The Ballad of Private Chadd," by A. A. Milne, "Aunt Tabitha," by Oliver Wendell Holmes, and "The Bath," by G. K. Chesterton. This book is most entertaining to dip into for small, comic breaks in the day; it helps provide therapeutic moments of helpless laughter.

The Faber Book of Comic Verse. *Michael Roberts and Janet Adam Smith,*
eds. **(Rev. ed., 1974; paperback ed., 1978) Faber and Faber. 400p.**

This volume concentrates on nonsense, parody, and satire and covers a span of four centuries of comic writing. It arranges the material chronologically and, within time periods, topically. Therefore, it is easy to spot such highlights as hilarious epitaphs and epigrams. In addition, there is a fairly good selection from such top writers as Edward Lear, and Lewis Carroll. The book is regrettably weighed down by much undistinguished verse — neither very funny nor very fine — and its coverage of modern comic poetry is sparse. It provides, nevertheless, a sense of the range of humorous and satirical verse in English and includes such popular forms as the limerick and many works by the productive anonymous writers of the sixteenth through the twentieth centuries. Most poets are represented by just one or two poems.

The Faber Book of Epigrams and Epitaphs. *Geoffrey Grigson, ed.* **(1977) Faber and Faber. 291p., o.p.**

Reading too many of these poems at one sitting could put you off epigrams for life, but if taken in judicious doses these are really succulent, small morsels. Epigrams and epitaphs have a long, distinguished history, dating back to ancient Greece and Rome. Epigrams tend to be short, sharp poems that praise or disparage someone or some thing; epitaphs comment, sometimes grimly or amusingly, on the dead. This collection, with its lucid introduction by Geoffrey Grigson, sets forth the epigrams and epitaphs of such major writers as Martial, Blake, Robert Herrick, Pope, and Emily Dickinson, alongside dozens of anonymous writers. Many of these poems are funny, lightly humorous, or rude and wounding, others are clearly philosophical. Whatever the reader's taste or temperament, there will be poems here to suit — poems of outrage, poems of spite, poems of acclaim, poems of gratitude. Also included is John Gay's wonderful epitaph for himself, summing up everything a sardonic spirit has to say about life.

The Faber Book of Nonsense Verse. *Geoffrey Grigson, ed.* **(1979) Faber and Faber. 352p.**

In his introduction, Geoffrey Grigson explores the meanings of nonsense verse, and concludes, "Whatever the kind or the mixture, the nonsense poem — if it works — refreshes us by surprise, by invention, or by commenting, in what is said or how it is said, on sense taking itself too seriously or being pompous, or in fashion." There are some real surprises here: the original "Pop Goes the Weasel," which was a popular song in the Victorian era, and many wonderful limericks. The great stars of this collection are, predictably, Lewis Carroll and Edward Lear. The former has dozens of his nonsense poems reprinted, including the long and celebrated "The Hunting of the Snark." You will also find "Jabberwocky," "The White Knight's Ballad," and "Father William" among the many entries. Edward Lear's "The Owl and the Pussycat" and "The Dong with a Luminous Nose" are included. Among the more remarkable modern poets found here are Stevie Smith and T. S. Eliot. The overall quality of the book varies: many of the poems are undistinguished, but most of them are amusing. The anonymous verses are printed in roughly chronological order.

The Faber Book of Parodies. *Simon Brett, ed.* **(1984) Faber and Faber. 383p., pap.**

At least half of this collection is prose, but there is more than enough poetry to justify its inclusion in a collection of poetry anthologies. Arrangement is alphabetical by the author being parodied. Usually there are one or two parodies for each of the writers. The book opens, for example, with a parody on Douglas Adams's "The Scriptwriter's Guide to Galaxy" by Andrew Marshall and David Renwick. Ronald Mason, John Flood, and Russell Davies poke affectionate fun at three of W. H. Auden's poems, and Ezra Pound is among those who poke fun at W. B. Yeats. Who are the writers most likely to be parodied? If the number of listings is any guide, Shakespeare comes first, followed by Swinburne, Tennyson, and Wordsworth. Most of the take-offs tend, incidentally, to concern English writers, by about nine to one. Among the Americans present are Ernest Hemingway (with parodies by Raymond Chandler and Henry Hetherington), Damon Runyon, J. D. Salinger, and Mickey Spillane. A good number of the parodies are by equally famous writers, from Robert Benchley and Kenneth Tynan to Ezra Pound and Lewis Carroll. One learns some surprising things, e.g., Carroll's famous verse "Father William" was inspired by a deadly serious poem with similar lines from the pen of Robert Southey.

The Fireside Book of Humorous Poetry. *William Cole, ed.* **(1959) Simon and Schuster. 522p., o.p.**

This heavy volume of humorous poetry is a mixed bag: some of the verses are largely forgettable and others are excellent. The poems are thematically arranged: "The Other Animals," "Eccentrics and Individualists," "Edibles, Potables and Smokeables," and "Juveniles," are the first four sections, and there are fifteen others. The best poets, whose work keeps recurring throughout the anthology, are W. S. Gilbert, with some of the excellent lyrics from his operettas, Lewis Carroll, with, most notably, "The Walrus and the Carpenter," and Ogden Nash with many entries. Some superior segments of the book are those about animals and the section of witty verse forms such as epigrams and clerihews. Other authors who are well represented are Hilaire Belloc and Dorothy Parker. There should be some humor here for every reader's taste, but unfortunately the finest writers are surrounded by too many mediocre ones.

The New Oxford Book of English Light Verse. *Kingsley Amis, ed.* **(1978) Oxford University Press. 347p.**

Compiled by the celebrated writer Kingsley Amis, this volume of comical, wry, and satirical poetry is arranged in chronological order, from Shakespeare to the present day, and includes both the work of acknowledged poets and savory contributions from anonymous authors. (If Virginia Woolf was right in claiming that Anonymous usually was a woman, then women are well represented in this collection. Otherwise, they are in very short supply.) The standard of the light verse is high, with substantial sections devoted to the work of Byron, Lewis Carroll, and Philip Larkin. The limericks Amis has chosen are bawdy and extremely funny. The spirit soars with this collection; the verse is unreservedly delightful. In a thoughtful introduction, Amis defines "light verse" and makes clear his differences with W. H. Auden, the previous compiler of this volume. Auden's selections tended to have a more revolutionary intent, Amis's are resoundingly apolitical. His purpose is to provide the kind of verse that people love to read, and he has gathered together an outstanding collection of just that kind of poetry.

A Nonsense Anthology. *Carolyn Wells, comp.* **(1930) Scribner's; paperback edition published by Dover, 1958. 300p., pap.**

"On a topographical map of literature," writes the compiler in her introduction, "nonsense would be represented by a small and sparsely settled country, neglected by the average tourist." Well, that was probably true back in 1930, but by 1989 there have been at least a dozen popular collections of nonsense and humorous verse published. This anthology has the distinction of being one of the first and is still one of the best. Here one finds the familiar, venerable poets from Lewis Carroll and "Jabberwocky" to Edward Lear and his "Limericks." Of the seventy or so poets, the majority are English. Happy exceptions include Gelett Burgess, with "The Purple Cow" and seven other equally delightful poems. Many of the experts at fun are well-known serious poets, but some are remembered today only for their nonsense verse, Francis Stokes's "Blue Moonshine" and George Canning's "The Old Gentleman." There are indexes of authors, first lines, and titles. The arrangement is by such rather arbitrary categories as "High Sentiments" and "Resounding Trivialities," but the verse ought not to require any order at all.

The Norton Book of Light Verse. *Russell Baker, ed.* **(1986) W. W. Norton. 447p.**

Chosen by the exemplary satirist Russell Baker, more than four hundred entertaining poems are here arranged thematically, covering such topics as "Twentieth Century Blues," "Some Fun with the Mother Tongue," "Love," and "Words to Live By." The definition of light verse is broad enough to include bleakly sardonic, wisely bemused, and blithely humorous works. A delectable selection, the volume features excellent poems by first-rate writers, as well as good deal of delicious fluff. Unfortunately, the editor also prints lyrics from songs, and although undoubtedly clever, their infectious music is sadly lacking. (Noel Coward and Cole Porter are the most obviously abused; others, like W. S. Gilbert, survive the translation of mere words into print.) English and American, male and female, well-known and minor poets from the nineteenth and twentieth centuries are in evidence. This is a superior survey, one every library should own.

The Oxford Book of American Light Verse. *William Harmon, ed.* **(1979) Oxford University Press. 540p.**

From Colonial times to the present, the compiler assembles a group of masters of light, humorous verse. Among those included are Ogden Nash, X. J. Kennedy, Walt Whitman, and many anonymous and little-known poets. Among the best are those who were unintentionally humorous. These are so bad that they are good. Examples range from The Rev. Thomas Holley Chivers to the Julia A. Moore, the "Sweet Singer of Michigan." Compared to Kingsley Amis's *New Oxford Book of English Light Verse* (annotated here), this is a bit tame. The difference between the two is most marked in subject matter. The English tend to consider class, intellectual games, and politics a fair target, while Americans put greater emphasis on common daily activities. Given that distinction, the American light verse book is to be recommended for its frequently witty, sometimes satirical, and even ribald approach to life.

The Oxford Book of Light Verse. *W. H. Auden, ed.* **(1938) Oxford University Press. 552p., pap.**

Similarly to the more ambitious *Poets of the English Language,* this volume has the distinction and interest of having been compiled by W. H. Auden. The choices illustrate the poet's infatuation with style and shades of satire. The order of the poems is chronological, and "the impossibility of adequately modernizing poems of the Middle English period has made it necessary to reproduce in their original forms all poems up to the early sixteenth century." After that the poems are modernized in spelling and punctuation. Many of the early entries are anonymous ballads, but by the time of Chaucer, there is a spattering of named authors. Auden unfortunately chose not to include any of his own better nonsense verses, but all the other fine writers are here, from Edward Lear and Lewis Carroll to John Betjeman, who winds down the collection. Light verse is not easy to describe or delimit, but Auden explains it neatly in his brief introduction. His choices support his considered definition, and one should remember that "light" does not necessarily mean popular or pleasing. There are numerous examples of ready wit, such as Sassoon's devastating "The General" or the more famous "Verses on the Death of Dr. Swift Written by Himself: Nov. 1731" that were equally suitable when he died some fifteen years later.

The Oxford Book of Satirical Verse. *Geoffrey Grigson, comp.* **(1980) Oxford University Press. 454p., pap.**

Ernest Hemingway is not associated with poetry, but here he is represented with one satirical scatological verse of six short lines. Pope, Dryden, and Swift, who knew a bit more about satirical comment, are given seven to twelve times as much space, as are such later poets as Byron and Hilaire Belloc. The eighty or so masters of the art are disparate in time and in fame, but they share one common trait: the ability to swing a punitive, often scathing, blow at the ego. The juxtaposition of the varying talents is unceasingly fascinating. Failures or successes at conventional verse, these writers are all articulate in satire, even if they have only one entry as in the case of Hemingway, Kingsley Amis, Clive James, and, yes, Philip Larkin. Perhaps the weakness of an otherwise fine collection is the failure to give over space to the moderns, such as Larkin, who really deserve more than one entry. Modest Geoffrey Grigson fails to include any of his own fine poetry, and he does little service to American writers. He clearly favors the English. The chronological arrangement (from the fifteenth through the twentieth centuries) has its points, but would it not have been better to arrange the poems by broad subject? The brief introduction contains an excellent definition of "satire."

Parodies; an Anthology from Chaucer to Beerbohm — and After. *Dwight Macdonald, ed.* **(1960) Modern Library. 575p., pap.**

An outstanding social and literary critic, Macdonald loved parody. "I enjoy it as an intuitive kind of literary criticism. . . . It is Method acting, since a successful parodist must live himself, imaginatively, into his parodee. . . . I like its bookish flavor because I like books, and parody is a kind of literary shop talk." The parodists move through literary history, from Chaucer to Jane Austen to Cyril Connolly. The authors parodied are sometimes also the parodists, but this is unusual. Macdonald acknowledges that parody ages faster than any other literary genre because the reader must be familiar with the material being parodied. Twentieth-century readers may be particularly deficient with respect to literary references. In addition, "the objections to breadth in parody are that it is not sporting to hunt with a machine gun. . . . Most of what passes for parody is actually so broad as to be mere burlesque." The compiler fortunately avoids both what can no longer be understood or appreciated and the broad, meaningless parody. Probably more than two thirds of the collection is poetry, but there is such noteworthy prose as Baron Corvo's "Reviews of Unwritten Books" and E. B. White's "Across the Street and into the Grill," the latter a takeoff on Ernest Hemingway. There are four logical sections, followed by an excellent appendix in which Macdonald gives a fuller explanation of the parody form.

Sometime the Cow Kick Your Head; the Biennial of Light Verse & Witty Poems. *Robert Wallace, ed.*

See under ENGLISH AND AMERICAN POETRY

HUNGARIAN POETRY

The Face of Creation; Contemporary Hungarian Poetry. *Jascha Kessler,* *tr.* **(1988) Coffee House Press. 190p., pap.**

In contrast to the earlier volume, *Modern Hungarian Poetry,* this work has been translated by only one compiler. There are about half as many writers included, and, of these, only a handful are found in the companion volume. The comparison is inevitable, because Kessler worked with the editor of the earlier collection to arrive at his choices. The translations, though, are his alone. Each of the selections is prefaced with a brief biographical sketch of the author and a black-and-white photograph. István Vas, Sándor Csoóri, and Márton Kalász are most heavily represented, with a dozen or so poems each. All are found with different works in the aforementioned *Modern Hungarian Poetry.* Essentially, then, purchasing one necessitates the purchase of both collections. It is hard to think of interested individuals or libraries who would not require the two.

Modern Hungarian Poetry. *Miklós Vajda, ed.* **(1977) Columbia University Press. 290p.**

"The background of some of the best poems in this collection is nothing less than five hundred years of unjust and debilitating history . . . ," the compiler explains. As editor of *The New Hungarian Quarterly,* Vajda breaks through the past, even across the Iron Curtain, and brings the general reader forty-one poets from Lajos Kassák (1887–1967) to half a dozen who were born slightly before or during the Second World War. William Jay Smith assisted with the translations, as did Ted Hughes, Edwin Morgan, Daniel Hoffman, and a dozen other prominent poets. As commendable as it may be for poets to translate other poets, the question remains of just how faithful they are to the original. Reviews indicate they dutifully respect the Hungarian voices, and some critics believe this volume to be the best of its type. Unfortunately, several of the best poets are overlooked. "This anthology was designed to survey postwar . . . contemporary Hungarian poetry . . . selected from the pages of *The New*

Hungarian Quarterly. Those poets who did not live to see the end of World War II are not included." For example, Miklos Radnoti, who died at age 33, was a Hungarian Jew whose last poems were found on his body after the war, in a mass grave. There is no sign of Miklos Radnoti. A pity. See, too, the companion volume, *Face of Creation.*

INDIAN POETRY

The Golden Tradition; an Anthology of Urdu Poetry. *Ahmed Ali, ed. and tr.* **(1973) Columbia University Press. 286p.**

Urdu originated in the twelfth and thirteenth centuries in India's Western Sectors, but it was not until the seventeenth century that Urdu poetry assumed its present form. Sufficient background is given about the language and the poets by the compiler and translator in the scholarly, well-written introduction that comprises the first hundred pages of the collection. The poems open with eight poets of the eighteenth century and close with seven of the nineteenth. For each of the poets there is a two-to-four-page introduction that not only gives biographical data, but sets the poetry in its place within the history of the form. A brief glossary and index conclude the anthology. As for the translations, they are exact and remain as faithful to the original as possible. "I have left the translations, like the originals, unexplained, so that each reader can interpret the poet in accordance with his own sensibility." A wise decision. The collection is a delight for both expert and layperson.

Poems of Love and War from the Eight Anthologies and the Ten Long Poems of Classical Tamil. *A. K. Ramanujan, comp. and tr.* **(1985) Columbia University Press. 335p.**

Spoken by over fifty million people, Tamil is one of the two classical Indian languages of Tamilnadu State (formerly Madras), in southeastern India. It is spoken, too, in Sri Lanka, Malaysia, and the Fiji Islands. The Ten Long Poems and the Eight Anthologies reflect early classical Tamil literature (c.100 B.C.–A.D. 250). Selections are given from each, along with a detailed commentary on Tamil poetry and poetics. The poems, which came to be known as Cankam poems, vary in length from three to over eight hundred lines. Many are anonymous, while nearly half were by sixteen poets, of whom Kapilar and Ammuvanar are among the most famous. The work is in four sections, with a seventy-five page explanatory "Afterword." The book opens with Akam Poems, i.e., love poems. Next comes Puram Poems, i.e., poems of war, kings, and death. "The third and fourth sections consist of a small sample of late classical poems (c. fifth to sixth century) . . . [that] offers some comic, earthy, even bawdy poems. . . . It also includes an unusual poem on the bull fight contests of the time." The last section is a long hymn to Visnu. The translation captures the tone of the poems, and even someone who is totally unfamiliar with their background will be charmed and thrilled by much of the verse.

The Penguin Book of Modern Urdu Poetry. *Mahmood Jamal, ed. and tr.* (1986) Penguin Books. 170p., pap.

A poet and critic brings together seventeen poets who write in Urdu, the language that developed in northwestern India and traces its roots back to the twelfth century. "One of the peculiarities of Urdu is that, in spite of its being one of the most widely spoken languages of the subcontinent, it has no home in any province." In Pakistan it is a national language, but only a small percentage consider it a work-a-day tongue. At the same time the India cinema, which is widely attended, has come to make Urdu its "official" tongue. This, and much more about the history and modern use of Urdu, is discussed in the fascinating introduction. The editor then goes on to explain briefly his translation techniques and opens with a poet who lived from 1911 to 1984. A short biographical sketch introduces him, and there is one for each poet in the book. Many of them were jailed for civil disobedience, and much of the subject matter concerns human rights. "All of this attention from rulers is an indication of the importance of Urdu poets." Unfortunately, there are neither author nor poetry indexes.

Songs of the Saints of India. *John Stratton Hawley, ed.* (1988) Oxford University Press. 244p.

"The verses of the great poets of medieval north India stand at the fount of the Hindi language, and many would say that they also represent its greatest flowering. Unlike the poems of Chaucer or Donne, which occupy a somewhat similar place in the history of the English language, these Hindi verses are as lively and familiar to Indians today as they were four hundred years ago." This astonishing information derives from the introduction to this volume of verse. The songs of the saints are short, they deal with the various Hindu Gods and a vast variety of human emotions and experiences. They are both exotic and beautiful and are clearly understandable to Western readers. Each of the six saints (Ravidas, Kabir, Nanak, Surdas, Mirabai, and Tulsidas) is given a separate chapter, and each is accorded a careful, substantial introduction that serves as biography and poetic analysis. The lovely poems help to bridge some of the cultural gap that exists between Western experience and Eastern realities. Futhermore, they reveal a part of poetic history that is unknown to most modern readers outside India.

IRISH POETRY

An Anthology of Irish Literature. *David H. Greene, ed.* **(1954) Modern Library. 602p., o.p.**

Random House's familiar Modern Library series preceded the famous portables by Viking (e.g., *The Portable Medieval Reader, Greek Reader, Cervantes*). This is a perfect example of the form. The six hundred pages are literally pocket sized and strike a sound balance between prose and poetry. "The Viking Terror" (seventh or eighth century) is translated from the Gaelic and opens the compact volume. The verse of Louis MacNeice and W. R. Rodgers winds it down, before the bibliographical notes and the index. Myth, sagas, and romance fill the first two hundred pages, while late-nineteenth- and early-twentieth-century prose and poetry take up the remainder. The translations are as lively as the choices of poems and poets: Shaw, W. B. Yeats, "Æ," Synge, O'Casey, for example, are all here with representative pieces. The publishing date has obviously eliminated any of the brilliant voices since 1954, but with that caveat, one would be hard pressed to find a better collection of Irish writing.

The Book of Irish Verse; an Anthology of Irish Poetry from the Sixth Century to the Present. *John Montague, ed.* **(1974) Macmillan; also published as The Faber Book of Irish Verse. 400p.**

The poet and compiler John Montague (b. 1929) gives himself four entries in this collection, and the number is about the same for everyone else. The exceptions are Swift, Merriman, W. B. Yeats, Synge, and Kavanagh, where the number of poems ranges from eight to a dozen. Also, under the broad classifications of "Old Mythologies," "A Way of Life," "A Monastic Church," "Women in Love," "Courtly Love," "The Bards Mourn," and "Songs from the Irish" there are more Irish poems than are usually found in one place. The first sixth- to seventeenth-century poets, often anonymous, account for about a quarter of the volume. Add some dozen poets from the seventeenth and eighteenth centuries and about the same number from the nineteenth, and one is half way through the collection. Properly, and historically, the memorable modern poets from W. B. Yeats to Seamus Heaney make up about half of the volume. The limited number of selections illustrates the problem with any work that tries to cover so much time and so many poets.

Contemporary Irish Poetry; an Anthology. *Anthony Bradley, ed.* **(New and rev. ed., 1988) University of California Press. 526p.**

As the compiler points out, "the range of accomplishment in contemporary Irish poetry is great . . . and my choice of individual poems cannot please everyone." Yes, but it surely comes close. He has included all of the major modern Irish poets, among them Louis MacNeice and Samuel Beckett, as well as Seamus Heaney and Derek Mahon. The fifty or so poets leave almost no one out, and if the compiler errs, it is in including too many; their relative importance, at least in his view, is indicated by the number of poems selected from each writer. He finds John Montague a leader, for example, with more poems than either Heaney or Mahon. Choices like that are open to argument, but the point is that the compiler is here trying to show what he thinks is best, what is more representative. In his witty introduction he points out that when it gets right down to it, the selection must be personal. Each poet has a photograph and a brief biographical sketch. Eavan Boland ("It's a woman's world") is among the women poets, but they are so few they can be counted almost on one hand. There are useful notes and good indexes.

The Faber Book of Contemporary Irish Poetry. *Paul Muldoon, ed.* **(1986) Faber and Faber. 415p.**

This thick volume contains the works of only a handful of famous modern Irish poets, ten to be exact. As a result, many of their verses are printed, and the reader can have a clear sense of their artistic style and attainment. All but two of the poets are alive today. Aside from the deceased Patrick Kavanagh and Louis MacNeice, there are Thomas Kinsella, John Montague, Michael Longley, Seamus Heaney, Derek Mahon, Paul Durcan, Tom Paulin, and one woman, Medbh McGuckian. The decision to print the work of only a few poets means that the quality can be kept extremely high. Ireland, to paraphrase one critic quoted in the Prologue, is the place that pure poetry comes from. Certainly, the poems in this collection are among the finest of contemporary verse. They can be read for the pleasure they provide on their own, or they can be seen as the current flourishing of a perennial literary talent in the Irish.

Irish Poetry after Yeats; Seven Poets. *Maurice Harmon, ed.* (1979) Little, Brown. 231p., pap.

The seven poets are Austin Clarke, Patrick Kavanagh, Denis Devlin, Richard Murphy, Thomas Kinsella, John Montague, and Seamus Heaney. Arrangement is chronological according to the birth of the poet. A fair sampling of work is offered, although, rightly, there are more generous selections for the more important poets such as Kinsella and Heaney. Ten years on, one might have composed a different list, but essentially the choices here represent one man's view of the progress of Irish verse. There is a twenty-one page introduction in which each of the poets is considered and his gifts weighed. The judgments are discerning and generally accurate, although one might argue here and there not only with the poet selected but the reasons given for his place in the ranks. (There are no women included, an oversight not attributable to a lack of talented Irish women.) Each of the selections is prefaced with an indifferent black and white photograph of the poet. There is a lackluster bibliography, but no index. The collection has little new to offer except the odd poem not found in other anthologies.

New Irish Poets. *Devin A. Garrity, ed.* (1948) Devin-Adair. 210p.

The built-in danger of using such terms as "modern" and "new," particularly in a collection of poetry, is evident here. Almost 50 years later, the "new" Irish poets are not so bold, not so young, and, unfortunately, not so well remembered. Of the thirty-seven voices, only a half dozen or so will be immediately recognized, and only half again of these might find their way into a 1990's book of "new" or "modern" Irish verse. So this collection is primarily of historical interest, and a good place to find otherwise difficult-to-locate early Irish poets. By "early," one means those born near the turn of the century or just before the outbreak of the First World War. Delightful features are the down-home photographs of the authors and the brief, yet cleverly written, biographical notes. After this time, how good are the poems? The romantic verse is fairly weak, although the detailed, concrete poems about the history of Ireland are still good. This is a fine reference source in a library, although of limited value to the average reader.

The New Oxford Book of Irish Verse. *Thomas Kinsella, ed. and tr.*
(1986) Oxford University Press. 422p.

This anthology's poems stretch back in time to before the sixth cen-
tury, so astonishingly long is the history of Ireland's poetry. The very
early works are frequently by unknown authors or by those connected
with the Christian Church. Although, as Thomas Kinsella suggests in his
introduction, some of these early works also look back, in their "incan-
tatory character," to a close association with pre-Christian art. Christian
themes took root in the following centuries, to give way only later to
bardic poetry and love poetry. Famous Irish authors of the eighteenth
century are afforded considerable space, authors such as Swift, Gold-
smith, and Sheridan. Folk poems and songs are included as well, along
with ballads. Among the modern poets well represented are W. B. Yeats,
Samuel Beckett, and Seamus Heaney. This selection of Irish poetry is of
the highest order. The range of the poems is vast and serves to give the
reader a clear feeling for the depth of creativity that welled up in Irish
poets over the centuries. A lucid introduction by Kinsella helps place the
poems in their historical context, and notes on each of the poets explicate
the significance of their poetry.

Treasury of Irish Religious Verse. *Patrick Murray, ed.*

See under RELIGIOUS POETRY

ITALIAN POETRY

The Defiant Muse; Italian Feminist Poems from the Middle Ages to the Present. *Beverly Allen, Muriel Kittel, and Keala Jane Jewell, eds.*

See under WOMEN'S POETRY AND FEMINIST POETRY

The New Italian Poetry, 1945 to the Present; a Bilingual Anthology. *Lawrence R. Smith, ed. and tr.* **(1981) University of California Press. 486p.**

The "present" referred to in the title, is 1980. The "new" is divided into: (1) realism, with seven poets, the earliest being Franco Fortini (b. 1917), (2) hermeticism, with only Andrea Zanzotto and Luciano Erba (both born in the early 1920's), (3) experimentation, with four diverse poets, and, finally, (4) avant-grade, with eight voices. Each poet is represented by a half dozen or so choices, although three or four wrote such long poems that there are excerpts from these. The translations are uniformly excellent, but the translator seems to be more comfortable with the poems in the last section. Each poet is introduced with a short biographical/literary sketch. The bilingual arrangement is excellent as are the layout and the typography. Unfortunately, the publisher chose not to include standard indexes, and a search of the table of contents is required to find a given poem or poet.

Poems from Italy. *William Jay Smith and Dana Gioia, eds.* **(1985) New Rivers. 456p., pap.**

The Italian poem on the left, the translation into English on the right — everyone is familiar with a bilingual format. This is a model of its kind. The poet William Jay Smith and his collaborator chose only work that could be translated into English and still retain its beauty. And for translators, they went to the best. Smith and Gioia translated a dozen between them, but in addition one finds the work of Byron, Shelley, Robert Lowell, William Arrowsmith, Gavin Ewart, Richard Wilbur, and just about every major poet/translator from the nineteenth and twentieth centuries. The result is a true, lyrical collection that begins with Saint Francis of Assisi and moves chronologically to the twentieth century and Pier Paolo Pasolini and Rocco Scotellaro. Almost two thirds of the poems were written before 1700, because of the nearly "eight centuries of poetry represented here, the greatest work is clearly from the earlier period, especially the Renaissance." And "in presenting the twentieth century we have concentrated on established writers." There is no better bilingual anthology of Italian poetry available.

JAPANESE POETRY

From the Country of Eight Islands; an Anthology of Japanese Poetry. *Hiroaki Sato and Burton Watson, eds. and trs.* **(1981) Columbia University Press. 652p., pap.**

The earliest poems in this brilliant collection are from the Kojiki (Record of Ancient Matters), compiled early in the eighth century. Another oral-based collection is the Manyoshu, which began about the same time but was compiled over a period of centuries. This, in the words of the editors, "marks the real beginning of the tradition of Japanese poetry and contains poems so powerful in artistic and emotional appeal that they have seldom if ever been surpassed in later periods." Matsuo Basho (1644–1694) is a challenge to that statement in that his poems have great significance for us today, as do the poems of Ryokan (1758–1831), or, for that matter, Takahashi Mutsuo (b. 1937), the last poet in the collection. The development of the sophisticated tradition is traced through the major poets from the eighth to the middle of the twentieth century. In addition to a generous group of poems from each writer or school, the compilers provide a historical introduction that is essential to anyone who wishes to appreciate the background of the poetry. There are brief biographical sketches of the poets and a useful, select bibliography. The translations are outstanding, and they were understandably the winner of the P.E.N. Translation Prize for the year.

Japanese Literature in Chinese. Vol. I: Poetry and Prose in Chinese by Japanese Writers of the Early Period; Vol. II: Poetry and Prose in Chinese by Japanese Writers of the Later Period. *Burton Watson, tr.* **(1975, 1976) Columbia University Press**

It is all a trifle esoteric, but one must quickly appreciate that beyond the imposing titles of these two volumes is exceptionally lyrical and historically fascinating poetry. The compiler explains that these are poems composed by Japanese writers, but in a foreign language, i.e., Chinese. Some connoisseurs are critical of what they see as essentially imitative work. Still, the consensus is that this poetry successfully "transcends the insularity of Japan," particularly before the opening of the country in the nineteenth century. The earliest poet is Prince Otomo, who reigned only a brief seven months in the seventh century. Some 300 pages away, in the second volume, the enthusiasm for Chinese comes to a natural conclusion with the novelist Natsume Soseki (1867–1916). Each section of poems is prefaced by helpful background notes on the time and the poets. There are numerous other guide posts to help the reader who may be as bewildered by the genre as by the period and the poets. The collection is a journey well worth taking.

The Manyoshu. Foreword by Donald Keene. (1965) Columbia University Press. 502p., o.p.

This is the best translation available of one thousand poems from the major Japanese poets who wrote from the pre-Omni and Omni Periods (A.D. 400–673) to the Nara Period (A.D. 710–840). The book is divided into three primary parts. First, there is a lengthy introduction explaining the period, the poets, and the poetry to Westerners who are probably unaware of what the verse represents or its background. Second, there is the body of the work in translation, followed by the text in *romaji,* i.e., mainly modern Japanese. (The complicated translation procedures are explained in the introduction.) Finally there are biographical notes, chronologies, and an index. All of this, helped in no small way by frequent explanatory footnotes, is extremely useful in explaining the full meaning of the poems. The poems are verse, as one poet put it, "on which I never tire to look!"

The Penguin Book of Japanese Verse. *Geoffrey Bownes and Anthony Thwaite, trs.* Introduction by Geoffrey Bownes. (1964) Penguin Books. 245p., pap.

Emperor Onin reigned from about A.D. 270 to 312. The last poet, born in 1931, Tanikawa Shuntaro treats of "Growing Up." Between the two are seventeen centuries, some one hundred and seventy-five poets, and diverse shifts in the sensibility and imagery that capture the elusive Japanese culture. Even today, the Emperor's poetry prize "attracts tens of thousands of entries." The Japanese "delight in their poetry, write for a public, and are not hesitant to stand up and recite it." This enthusiasm translates into subject matter and a style that is easy to appreciate and normally appeals where Western poetry may fail. It is a paradox that while the content seems almost transparent, the layers of meaning often are beyond the American or European comprehension. Tanka and haiku are, for example, simplicity itself. But what does it all really signify? One returns time and time again to the puzzle. Here the brief notes and the scholarly introduction may help, if only in a general way: the reader must choose the appropriate meaning. The translations are uniformally excellent, and the selections are equally good. This is the standard collection for anyone in the West involved with Japanese poetry.

Waiting for the Wind; Thirty-six Poets of Japan's Late Medieval Age. *Steven D. Carter, tr. and ed.* (1989) Columbia University Press. 354p.

The title is as esoteric as the verse, which was composed between 1250 and 1500. The form is the classical *uta,* a "thirty-one syllable lyric that was the major genre of court poetry throughout its history." According to the editor, all of the poets of this period "enriched the poetic heritage in ways that influenced later poets writing in newer genres now fairly familiar to Western readers — including Sogi (1421–1502) and other poets of linked verse, and the haiku poets Basho (1644–1694) and Buson (1716–1783)." The collection includes just over four hundred poems, all in the *uta* form. There are thirty-six poets, of which only four are women. This, again according to the compiler, "is a reflection of the social realities of the medieval period." No one who is interested in the poetic form or the history of its development should miss the extremely well-written introduction. The translations seem equally good. The content puzzles from time to time, but on the whole it consists of topics familiar to everyone. There are biographical sketches of each of the poets and frequent notes to help the reader along the way.

KOREAN POETRY

Anthology of Contemporary Korean Poetry. *Koh Chang-soo, comp.* **(1987) Seoul International. 130p.**

If the reader wishes to become acquainted with Korean poets who are writing today, this is surely the place to do it. There are six poets represented in this anthology, including the editor. They would appear to be in the mainstream of contemporary Korean literature. The poems all tend to be in the lyric mode, and some have an enchanting delicacy about them. Nature imagery plays a large part in their composition. There is something old-fashioned about their tone, perhaps attributable to the translation. The images are frequently sharp and poignant, symbolic of a more rarefied age than ours. For readers who are curious about contemporary Asian poetry, this anthology makes a welcome addition to their library.

LARGE-TYPE ANTHOLOGIES

Best Loved Poems in Large Print. *Virginia S. Reiser, ed.* **(1983) G. K. Hall. 585p.**

There are two primary aspects of this collection. The first, obvious from the title, is that this is a large-print book, and all of the poems are in sixteen-point Times Roman, or about twice the size of the type found in most books. Second, the authors, generally from the nineteenth and early twentieth centuries, are famous, but utterly traditional. This is hardly the place to look for the unusual. The exceptions include Marianne Moore, Wallace Stevens, William Carlos Williams, and W. B. Yeats, but for each poet of this caliber there is an Edwin Markham, Joyce Kilmer, and William Cullen Bryant. So while the compiler is to be congratulated for a major service, one takes some exception with her conventional choices. This volume is fine, of course, if the reader is not too familiar with poetry. The arrangement is by broad subjects, and within each of these the poets are presented chronologically. For example, the part devoted to "Love and Friendship" opens with an anonymous work, moves on to Edmund Spenser and Sir Philip Sidney and concludes with Conrad Aiken, Edna St. Vincent Millay, and Hart Crane. This is a collection that should be in every library and in not a few homes.

Favorite Poems in Large Print. *Virginia S. Reiser, ed.* **(1981) G. K. Hall. 462p.**

This is similar to the compiler's later (1983) collection, *Best Loved Poems in Large Print.* It is arranged by such sections as "Stories and Ballads" and "Nature and the Seasons." Under each of the ten headings are about two dozen poems. The selection is traditional, and, if anything, the collection suffers from the assumption that people who need large print (in this case sixteen point) may not be overly sophisticated. While traditional poetry is fine, a few more modern, avant-garde poets would have been appreciated. The volume is limited, also, to English and American writers, from Edward Lear and Lewis Carroll to Eugene Field and Gelett Burgess (all in the "Humor" section). Where things are a bit more serious, as in the grab-bag section of "Various Themes," the compiler comes up with the estimable Donne, Keats, Emily Dickinson, Amy Lowell, W. B. Yeats, Edna St. Vincent Millay, and Robert Frost.

LATIN AMERICAN POETRY

An Anthology of Twentieth-Century Brazilian Poetry. *Elizabeth Bishop and Emanuel Brasil, eds.* (1972) Wesleyan University Press. 181p., pap.

An exceptionally beautiful and fascinating volume of poetry, this is edited and introduced by Emanuel Brasil and the outstanding American poet Elizabeth Bishop. They open the anthology by discussing the remarkably high position poetry has among the Brazilian elite: the term "poet" is an honor to bestow on a person and has nothing to do with literature. Consequently, poetry is taken very seriously by educated Brazilians. The selection of poetry presented here is by fourteen prominent authors who wrote from the 1920's to the 1970's. The translators of their work are also of the first rank, poets like Richard Wilbur, Elizabeth Bishop herself, Barbara Howes, June Jordan, and W. S. Merwin, to name only some. The poetry is printed both in Portuguese and English in a most handsome format. This is verse that allows the reader to expand his or her vision of the world by entering into the creative experience of poets whose culture is foreign and strange but whose artistry is marvelously developed.

Mexican Poetry; an Anthology. *Octavio Paz, comp.; Samuel Beckett, tr.* (1985) Grove Press. 215p.

There may be more famous poets in literature today than Paz and Beckett, but none so imaginative and so important in shaping twentieth-century thought. While one usually thinks of Beckett as a French-Irish playwright and novelist, not a translator of Spanish, the surprise is pleasant and rewarding. He is a master of translation and responsible for the success of this important volume in introducing the spirit and content of Mexican verse to non-Spanish-speaking readers. Applause, too, to the compiler who had the good sense to arrange the collection in chronological order so that one can fully appreciate the development of Mexican poetry. The book opens with Francisco de Terrazas (1525–1600), who was praised by Cervantes. It concludes with Alfonso Reyes, "regarded as one of the great contemporary writers in Spanish." The forty

151

or so poets are represented by two to ten poems each. Not to be missed are the scholarly introduction by C. M. Bowra and Paz's fascinating history of Mexican poetry. The anthology was first published by agreement between Unesco and the government of Mexico.

The Penguin Book of Caribbean Verse in English. *Paula Burnett, ed.* **(1986) Penguin Books. 446p., pap.**

The scene is set in a forty five-page introduction that details the development of verse in the Caribbean from the oral tradition to the current literary scene. About one quarter of the volume is given to songs, Rastafarian chants, and related material, often by such individual musicians as Bob Marley. This volume is remarkably comprehensive. In the section on the literary tradition, there are close to a hundred poets with four to five poems each. Their content moves from the religious and the agrarian interests of the population to satire and topical poetry. A striking aspect of the poetic form is explained by the editor: "There is almost no major poet of the English-speaking Caribbean who does not have the vernacular as one of the languages of his poetry. . . . The word is still intimately bound up with the music." At the same time, the early poets reflect the prevalent European tastes, following well-established literary models. This can be traced in the chronological arrangement, beginning with Nathaniel Weekes and James Grainger, eighteenth-century poets. The collection is particularly valuable because of the editor's insights and the fact that there has been no substantial anthology of Caribbean poetry for more than a decade. There are a good biographical section, explanatory notes, and a glossary.

Peru; the New Poetry. *David Tipton, ed.* **(1977) Red Dust. 173p.**

Here is the best of Peruvian poetry from about 1959 to 1970. All of the translations are by the compiler and Maureen Ahern. The selection covers all styles and schools of poetry. It is quite amazing to realize how much truly good writing can come out of a single Latin American country in a relatively short period of time. Much of it is shaped by the social-realists and the purists. The former use poems as "a direct weapon in the service of Marxism." The latter seek "verbal and stylistic perfection . . . their poetry claiming to be a song to beauty." There are some fifteen poets represented, with an average of a dozen or so poems each. The volume concludes with a section of statements, "On the Situation of the Writer in Peru," including one by Antonio Cisneros. Biographical notes indicate that most of the poets were born in the 1930's and 1940's.

Volcán; Poems from Central America. *Alejandro Murguía and Barbara Paschke, eds.* **(1983) City Lights Books. 160p., pap.**

When these poems were written, many were banned by their governments. The exception was Nicaragua, but even here there was some check on total freedom of expression. How, then, did the poems from Mexico, Honduras, El Salvador, Guatemala, and Nicaragua reach us in this slim collection? According to the editors, "the poems were often copied by hand and smuggled" into the various countries. Of the thirty-nine poets represented, each grouped under their country of origin, not all had such dramatic lives. The list of credits indicates that at least a few had published their work in literary periodicals, but this is not to deny the danger involved in their work. The effort to bridge the political, cultural gap between the United States and Central America is helped in no small way by the fact that this is a bilingual edition, Spanish on one page and the English translation facing it. While there are numerous poems about love, home, and family, the primary focus is on war, exile, and death. It is neither pretty nor always monumental, but it is real.

LOVE POETRY

A Book of Love Poetry. *Jon Stallworthy, ed.* **(1974) Oxford University Press; also published in Great Britain as The Penguin Book of Love Poetry. 393p.**

All varieties of love are reflected in the poems in this anthology: respectful declarations, vulgar intentions, glorious proposals, adamant denials. The poets come from many different cultures: seventh-century India, ancient Greece, eighteenth-century England, nineteenth-century France. The subject of love has been divided thematically into: "Intimations," "Declarations," "Persuasions," "Celebrations," "Aberrations," "Separations," "Desolations," and "Reverberations," or more or less everything anyone could think of saying about the topic of love. It is interesting to look at these verses in the company of others on their general subject, especially as those observations span the centuries. The authors are all of high quality, with many well-known names set alongside exotic ones from other times and places. John Donne has several entries, as do Robert Burns, Robert Browning, and Christina Rossetti. There is a great deal of food for thought in this volume, and since love is of continual interest, readers should be delighted by the fresh treatment it receives from the scores of writers included.

Dancing the Tightrope; New Love Poems by Women. *Barbara Burford, Lindsay MacRae, and Sylvia Paskin, eds.* **(1988) Peter Bedrick Books. 112p.**

This collection, with its fresh perspective on love, was put together by an eclectic group of women: Barbara Burford is a black woman in her forties who has published short stories and poems; Lindsay MacRae is a poet in her twenties and has worked as a journalist and scriptwriter; and Sylvia Paskin is a writer and lecturer on film, literature, and feminism. The poets in this collection are largely unknown to the general reading public. Besides Burford and MacRae, there are Janet Dube, Fran Landesman, Sue May, and thirty other poets. The only familiar name is that of Medbh McGuckian, an acclaimed Irish poet. Some of the writers

154

are performance poets, and most of them now have their homes in London although several were born abroad. As for the poems themselves, they are a mixed bag: they emphasize sexual love between women and women and between women and men. The best are by Medbh McGuckian, and they are very fine indeed. The others, in rather artless verse, tend to be revealing glimpses into personal moments of their lives. This will be of interest mainly to those who wish to keep up with the periphery of women's writing.

English Love Poems. *John Betjeman and Geoffrey Taylor, comps.* **(1957; paperback ed., 1964) Faber and Faber. 220p., pap.**

Compiled by the estimable poets John Betjeman and Geoffrey Taylor, this volume owes its originality to their rereading the poetical work of a poet — without consulting other anthologies — to find the poems that best express the "different moods of love." As a result, this collection includes a good deal of fresh, rarely encountered poetry: the lyrics, for example, of Philip Ayres and Barnabe Barnes, as well as the more expected selections from Donne and John Gay. This is a tasteful compilation, the verse of high quality and great sophistication. It is arranged chronologically, with each poet represented by up to four poems. At the end of the volume, there are short notes on some of the poets and the poems. They are extremely interesting and sometimes illuminating, noting, for example, that the poet "Michael Field" was actually two women, a writer and her niece who collaborated intimately on all their work. There is excellent poetry in this collection, even for those who think that love is a sentimental subject.

Erotic Poetry; the Lyrics, Ballads, Idyls, and Epics of Love — Classical to Contemporary. *William Cole, ed.* **(1963) Random House. 501p., o.p.**

This is a book of high-quality verse. In his Foreword, well-known poet Stephen Spender suggests that the topics of erotic poetry such as "nakedness, love-making, and sex" are "simply part of the common human condition available to literature." That surely is a sensible stance, but the editor, William Cole, unfortunately subdivides his volume into aggressively playful categories like "Of Women: Virgins & Harlots, Teasers & Losers: the Controversial Sex Is Considered in Its Fascinating and Maddening Variety." Another section concerns "Incitement and Desire: Spurrings of Honest Lust and the Varieties of Sublimation." There is a sense of humor at work here, but the attitude of the editor is openly sexist, an attribute not necessarily true of the poems themselves. These range over an extraordinarily long period of time, from Juvenal's excerpt from "The Sixth Satire" to Ted Hughes's "Secretary." The selection of poems is discerning and astute. Female poets are occasionally heard on the subject of eroticism, but only rarely. The perspective is decidedly male. Poets from other countries are heard: Baudelaire and Mallarmé, as well as Petronius Arbiter. It is interesting to see what serious poets have written on the subject of sex, and here we find the voices of Edmund Spenser, Kingsley Amis, Robert Burns, and Delmore Schwartz — very different voices, some openly sexual, some quite raunchy, others merely sensual.

The Gambit Book of Love Poems. *Geoffrey Grigson, ed.* (1973) Gambit; also published in Great Britain as The Faber Book of Love Poems. 407p.

In an attempt to infuse freshness into a familiar theme, the editor has cleverly arranged his poems into sections that correspond to the various stages of love: "Love Expected," "Love Begun," "The Plagues of Loving," "Love Continued," "Absences, Doubts, Divisions," and, finally, "Love Renounced and Love in Death." That pretty much covers all possible attitudes. The editor remarks that there are two essential kinds of love poems: in-love poems and poems about love. They are both in evidence here, but the former are given more prominence, since they are the more dramatic. Dozens of these poems have been written by anonymous authors over the centuries, and they are joined by the creations of William Barnes, Baudelaire, Blake, Donne, Robert Graves, Robert Herrick, Walter Savage Landor, Thomas Hardy, George Meredith, and many others, including Christina Rossetti and Shakespeare. There are not too many women in this collection, possibly because the emphasis is on poets from other centuries. The quality of the verses is generally very high; the emotion of love seems to have worked its own magic on the writers.

Love Is like the Lion's Tooth; an Anthology of Love Poems. *Frances McCullough, ed.* (1984) Harper & Row. 80p.

Unlike other love poetry anthologies, this one is short and makes no effort to be inclusive. Its actual subject is passion, and its poems are aimed specifically at younger readers, so there tends to be a simplicity about them. Some of the most interesting of these verses are foreign ones, translated from the Azande (of the Congo), from Hungarian, Russian, Japanese. There are famous love poems by Petronius Arbiter, E. E.

Cummings, and W. H. Auden. But many of these poems are rarely collected and will be new to most readers, especially adolescents. Their quality tends to be high, so this is a reliable collection to give to young readers to expose them to fine literature. It is a subject that surely will interest them, and its treatment is refined.

Love Poems from Spain & Spanish America. *Perry Higman, ed. and tr.* (1986) City Lights Books. 243p.

A bilingual anthology with splendid translations, this is a survey of love lyrics in Spanish. The collection opens with anonymous ballads of the sixteenth century and moves alphabetically to Xavier Villaurrutia. Each of the poets is given a brief biographical sketch and placed within the history of Spanish verse. The majority of poems, generally two or three for each poet, are from Spain, although Spanish America is represented by both known and lesser-known figures. Among the poets well known to non-Spanish-speaking readers are Juan Ramon Jimenez, Lope de Vega, Federico Garcia Lorca, Pablo Neruda, Cesar Vallejo, and Jorge Luis Borges. While one might suspect the single theme would soon run its course and there would be a great deal of repetition, this is hardly the case. Each poet and each poem offers a distinct, imaginative response to love. The variations on the theme are quite astonishing, perhaps because of the music of the Romance language or perhaps because of the particular feelings of the poet. The result is a marvelous collection that can be enjoyed by anyone, including young people.

Under All Silences; Shades of Love. *Ruth Gordon, comp.* (1987) Harper & Row. 78p.

According to the compiler, "these poems illuminate the many shadings of love, from its first inception to meetings, discovery, passion, knowledge, and beyond — its place in the timelessness of the cosmic world." The purpose is not an easy one to realize, at least for junior high and high school students who may be more familiar with MTV's version of love than that of Osip Mandelstam, Rainer Maria Rilke, or Paul Verlaine. A wise person, the compiler also includes such popular writers as Joan Baez, Ewan MacColl, and May Sarton. They rub shoulders with both signed and anonymous verse from Egypt, Japan, India, and Greece. All periods, all countries, all situations seem to be dutifully considered. In the jacket copy, Gordon explains: "I am a librarian, but I don't try to teach poetry anymore — it's all too personal." Personal or not, the choice of poems is beyond reproof. Any adult will enjoy them as much, if not more, than the young people who are the target audience.

NATIVE AMERICAN POETRY

Carriers of the Dream Wheel: Contemporary Native American Poetry. *Duane Niatum, ed.* (1975) Harper & Row. 300p., o.p.

The oral tradition dominates these pages. Some twenty Native American (i.e., American Indian) poets draw upon that tradition to explore their past and their present. Unfortunately, all of the poetry is by modern Indians, all written in English. This is within the scope set by the compiler, yet one longs for the roots of that oral tradition, for the voices out of the earlier years. The talents here are uneven, although in the deepest sense they all are reflective of a history that for too many years was forgotten or badly skewed by white American opinion and romance. The editor himself is among the best of the group, followed by Liz Sohappy Bahe, Wendy Rose, and Ray A. Young Bear. Note that few of these names find their way into standard anthologies. Most of the poems were originally published in little magazines or by university presses, neither having the wide audience of commercial publishers. Fortunately, this collection rights a wrong.

A Gathering of Spirit; Writing and Art by North American Indian Women. *Beth Brant, ed.* (1984) Sinister Wisdom Books. 240p.

A special issue of the little magazine, *Sinister Wisdom*, this was issued as a separate book in 1984. The work of accepted, well-known poets from Alaska and America are included, as well as Indian verse from less-familiar writers. The balance is excellent, and what some of the less-accomplished poets may lack in style and authority they make up for in content. Often these humbler voices have much to say about the life and times of a typical Indian woman and her family. But there is more to the collection than poetry. The editor includes telling photographs, drawings, letters, excerpts from novels, and diary entries — just about anything which will complete the picture of Indian life. There is little about the famous white/Indian battles and more on the daily experiences of the poets and writers. Topics move from the adjustments to urban life to the feelings of a child and a prisoner. There are few better collections on this subject.

Harper's Anthology of 20th Century Native American Poetry. *Duane Niatum, ed.* (1988) Harper & Row. 396p.

While there are several collections of American Indian poetry, this is the most comprehensive and the most current. In many ways it complements the same publisher's *Carriers of the Dream Wheel,* 1975, which was also compiled by Duane Niatum. He has brought together the work of "thirty-six poets who attest to the health of both the Native American spirit and American literature. . . . These poets constitute a powerful force . . . one far older, given the oral tradition, than the present republic." One should read the preface and the eighteen-page history, by Brian Swann, to appreciate the work that has gone into this anthology. The result is splendid. Beginning with Frank Prewett (1893–1962) and ending with A. Sadongei (b. 1959), the poets are arranged in chronological order. There are some famous voices, including that of the compiler and Ray A. Young Bear and, of course, Louise Erdrich. Brief biographies of each poet are found at the end of the book, as are notes and indexes to titles and first lines.

New and Old Voices of Wah'Kon-Tah; Contemporary Native American Poetry. *Robert K. Dodge and Joseph B. McCullough, eds.* (1985) International. 144p.

These verses are impressive in their simplicity and directness. They come out of a long tradition of storytelling and poetry developed by Native Americans over many centuries. Since their poetry has been largely ignored by the greater reading public, these works seem especially fresh. The nature imagery in them is extraordinary: the people and the land are strongly interactive. These are poems by Indians and about Indians. Most of the names will be new to general readers; the only really famous poet is Ted Berrigan, who hasn't been particularly associated with Native American culture. The subject matter here is decidedly varied, ranging from going to a dance that ends in a murderous, drunken brawl to a contemplation of Machu Picchu, in Peru. There is a strong sense of being drawn into the visions and experiences of an alien culture, one that is too infrequently taken seriously by the greater American public.

Shaking the Pumpkin; Traditional Poetry of the Indian North Americans. *Jerome Rothenberg, ed.* **(Rev. ed., 1986) Alfred van der Marck Editions. 424p., o.p.**

The title is derived from twelve songs from the Seneca Indians. The poems, which resemble modern concrete poetry in form, are "to welcome the society of the mystic animals." There are extensive "commentaries" at the conclusion to guide the reader. The translation of the visual pattern is typical throughout of a strong effort to match in English not only the words but also the spirit of the poetry. The poet/compiler translates many of the verses himself, but he is helped by a battery of experts, many of whom are themselves poets. Arrangement is by arbitrary sections, with particular attention to religious categories: "I try to establish contexts for the poems where possible or useful, and to carry forward discussions of Indian and tribal poetry, philosophy, or history as lightly touched on in this introduction." Coverage, as the subtitle suggests, is broad. There is verse from the Maya as well as from the Aztec, Navajo, and Eskimo. In truth, the whole of North America is represented. The result is, by and large, the best of the numerous books of Indian poetry, at least in scope and in subject. If only one book in this subject area is possible, this is the choice.

Songs from This Earth on Turtle's Back; Contemporary American Indian Poetry. *Joseph Bruchac, ed.* **(1983) Greenfield Review Press. 295p., pap.**

Entering the era of the powerful, green political parties, this is an ideal guide. Representing slightly over one and a half million American Indians, the poets have a great deal to offer all human beings "who believe in the Earth, in the survival of living things, in the survival of the spirit. Let us listen carefully to their words." Similar in scope to Duane Niatum's *Carriers of the Dream Wheel*, this collection offers different poems of many of the same writers in that 1975 anthology. It has the advantage, too, of offering twice again as many poets, many from a later period. Each of the photographs of the sixty or so poets is followed by a brief autobiographical sketch and usually three to five poems. Many of these have appeared earlier in little magazines or in small press books that tend not to be found either in home or library. The arrangement is in alphabetical order, by author. While much of this is, as Laura Tohe puts it, "living among cedar and sagebrush," it has a message that will involve anyone who bothers to step outside: Treat the earth well and it will care for you.

Voices of the Rainbow; Contemporary Poetry by American Indians. *Kenneth Rosen, ed.* (1975) Viking Press. 232p., pap.

Similar in purpose and scope to two other anthologies, *Songs from This Earth* and *Carriers of the Dream Wheel,* this one features many of the same poets. There are twenty-one Indian voices in the collection. Aside from the "contemporary" aspect of its scope, the editor explains: "My criteria for selection has been simple. If the reader listens carefully, can he or she hear, clearly and directly, the voice of the poet. . . . While I prefer to think of American Indian literature as an integral part of American literature in general, I recognize in these poems a pervasive feeling for the spiritual which resides in the palpable, a common feeling for the land, the climate, the specific place, which infuses this poetry . . ." Little more can or need to be said about the essence of these creative writers.

NATURE POETRY

A Book of Nature Poems. *William Cole, comp.* **(1969) Viking Press. 256p., o.p.**

From Dickens and Coleridge to Frost and Updike, these are personal views of nature that are notable for evoking every season over a number of centuries. The poets celebrate the delights of flowers and trees, night and day, rain and wind, and other aspects of nature seen by the imaginative eye. All of the well-known poets and poems are included, with a particular focus on the modern period. At the same time, Cole includes such lesser-known voices as William Barnes and other early English poets. The black and white illustrations by Robert Parker add little to the collection, but they may help set a mood. Here is a discriminating, fascinating anthology that considers virtually all facets of the natural world. For example, in the index of titles, the first poem is "Afternoon: Amagansett Beach," by John Hall Wheelock; near the end are Robert Frost's "Young Birch" and a Gaelic verse "Welcome to the Moon." It is difficult to think of an aspect of nature not covered.

Moods of the Sea; Masterworks of Sea Poetry. *George C. Solley and Eric Steinbaugh, comps.* **(1981) Naval Institute Press. 300p.**

Originally the quest was to find a book of sea poems for use in the classroom at the Naval Academy. Nothing suitable could be found, and the compilers decided to edit one. It follows several guidelines. First, it includes standard sea poems of England and America, ranging widely from different periods and in different styles. Few long poems are offered complete; many are excerpted. The editors were careful not to include too many poems from such well-known poets of the sea as Herman Melville and John Masefield. The only translations are those from classical sources, such as Chapman's version of Homer's *Odyssey*. Arrangement is thematic, suggested by the poems themselves. The sections are: "Sounds of the Sea"; "Man and the Sea"; "Tales of the Sea"; "The Laughter of the Waves"; "Legends of the Sea"; and "The Sea as Metaphor." There are helpful notes and an index to authors, poems, and first lines. "Each section contains poetry arranged roughly in chronological sequence." It is difficult to imagine a sea poem not here included. A superior collection for the individual and for libraries.

POETRY
Study and Teaching

American Poetry and Prose. *Norman Foerster, Norman S. Grabo, Russel B. Nye, E. Fred Carlisle, and Robert Falk, eds.* (5th ed., 1970) Houghton Mifflin. 3 vols., pap.

This three-volume textbook offers a comprehensive view of American poets and prose writers from the Colonial period through the 1960's. Each volume is divided into several parts. For example, the second volume concludes the "Romantic Movement" begun in the first volume and goes on to "Realism" and "Naturalism." Each chronological period is subdivided by genre. Approximately two thirds of each volume is given over to prose. The periods are introduced by detailed historical, social, and literary essays, with the revised edition strongly emphasizing the literary aspect. In addition, there are suitable introductory statements about the authors and their work. The selection is well balanced, and the compilers note that authority and readability are important criteria in their choices. The design is pleasing, and the three-volume format replaces the unwieldy, cumbersome earlier single volume. This is not the work many people will turn to for entertainment, but it is a useful collection for libraries looking for the best work of hard-to-locate poets and prose writers.

Fine Frenzy; Enduring Themes in Poetry. *Robert Baylor and Brenda Stokes, eds.* (2d ed., 1978) McGraw-Hill. 417p.

The organizing principle behind this volume is one that explores such potent poetic themes as "Exuberance," "Love," "Mutability," "Marriage," "Illusion/Reality," and "Art and Aesthetics." The selection of poems, covering the work of English and American writers from Chaucer to the present, is uniformly high. The reader is able to examine fine poems by more than one writer dealing with the same general topic. While serving as a good introduction for those who are reading poetry seriously for the first time, this volume also contains enough little-known material for the more seasoned poetry lover. The thematic positioning of the poems also increases its potential value: if someone is curious about the way poetry addresses various themes, he or she could turn to this volume and be enlightened. A concluding essay on prosody is helpful for the general reader, and a glossary provides succinct definitions of poetic and figurative terms.

The Heath Introduction to Poetry. *Joseph deRoche, ed.* **(3d ed., 1988) D. C. Heath. 564p., pap.**

Drawing upon the comments and suggestions of teachers of poetry in colleges throughout the United States and Canada, the compiler has added fifty-one selections to the third edition, including the work of such poets as Stephen Spender and Seamus Heaney. In the standard format for college textbooks, arrangement is chronological with particular emphasis given to the twentieth century. The twenty-eight-page introduction to the rudiments of poetry is well done and easy enough to understand. The Northeastern University professor offers what amounts to an effective lecture on the joys and, yes, the difficulties of poetry. An index of terms helps the student locate necessary units in the introduction. There are brief remarks before each of the six sections but little or no effort to employ footnotes. One applauds a decision that helps one think more about the verse than about the explanation. Choices are excellent and, on the whole, this is one of the better textbooks of its type.

How Does a Poem Mean?. *John Ciardi and Miller Williams, eds.* **(2d ed., 1975) Houghton Mifflin. 408p.**

In eight chapters that range from "The Image and the Poem" to "The Words of Poetry," the distinguished poet and critic John Ciardi explains the art form to the layperson. (A translator, Williams serves to balance Ciardi's opinions, but it is primarily the poet whose voice is heard throughout the guide.) The technique they employ is simplicity itself. A poem is given in full, then followed by one, two, or three pages of comment about its meaning and how it illustrates a certain poetic principle. In chapter seven, "The Poem in Motion," "Buick," by Karl Shapiro, precedes an analysis that, among other things, includes a basic explanation of iambic pentameter and the trochee — always with Shapiro's poem as witness and example. The illustrative selections cover all periods, all styles, all countries. The result is an exemplary teaching device and a constant source of pleasure. The rare combination reminds one of Wallace Stevens's "Anecdote of the Jar," which is considered here under the topic "Rippling Pools." This guide, like the jar, takes "dominion everywhere." Highly recommended for home and library.

An Introduction to Poetry. *X. J. Kennedy, ed.* (6th ed., 1986) Little, Brown. 480p., pap.

X. J. Kennedy is one of America's most lively and imaginative poets. He happens to be, too, an excellent teacher. The combination is reflected in this basic guide to poetry. It is one of the best available and should be found in all libraries and in many personal collections. In the Preface, opening with the question: "What is poetry," Kennedy explores the answer and addresses such other common questions as "Who needs it?" Speaking to the average college student, the compiler then moves on to examples of the best poems in the English language. The guide is in three sections. The first explores the quality of verse from "Listening to a Voice" and "Reading a Poem" to "Symbol," "Evaluating a Poem," and "Poems for the Eye." Here, as throughout, each part opens with an explanatory section, gives some examples, and after each poem poses four or five questions. Where there are no questions, there often are brief notes. The second part is called simply "Anthology: Poetry" and is an alphabetical arrangement of over one hundred poets, from John Ashbery and W. H. Auden to W. B. Yeats. A subsection, "Anthology: Criticism," has brief prose remarks by a dozen or so poets and critics, including Samuel Johnson and Barbara Herrnstein Smith. The "Supplement" is primarily an aid to writing a paper about poetry and, finally, provides information on the mechanics of writing a poem. Selection, comments, and focus are first rate. The anthology cannot be praised too highly.

An Introduction to Poetry. *Louis Simpson, ed.* (3d ed., 1986) St. Martin's Press. 640p.

One of the strong points of this anthology is its extremely complete glossary of poetic terms. In addition, it provides a guide to understanding poetry in a series of introductory essays. These cover the significant aspects of poetic composition: metaphor, rhythm, sound, and meter. The introductory remarks are fairly brief and are followed by a long, very well-selected anthology of poems dating from Chaucer in the fourteenth century to the contemporary poets. The editor confines himself to poetry written in English, but he chooses from poetry of all centuries. There are long selections from Edmund Spenser, Shakespeare, Donne, Pope, Byron, Keats, and Emily Dickinson, among scores of others. The editor's judgment in selecting poems is outstanding. People who love poetry will find many of their favorite poems here. And for those who are not especially familiar with the genre, this is an excellent volume to dip into and sample some of the great poetic achievements in English in the past seven centuries. After the brief introduction the readers are, however, on their own: the poets are not individually introduced nor are their poems individually discussed.

Invitation to Poetry; a Round of Poems from John Skelton to Dylan Thomas. *Lloyd Frankenberg, ed.* **(1956) Doubleday. 414p.**

The approach taken by this anthologist is a congenial one, particularly for those who are just beginning to experience the joy of reading poetry. He prints a variety of poems and then writes a series of comments upon those works. For example, after "Kubla Khan," by Samuel Taylor Coleridge, he provides approximately four pages of observations about the history of the poem, his aesthetic response to the verse, the sounds of the poem, and, finally, the possible meaning of the poem. He is quite sensitive to issues of tone and quite unauthoritarian about his judgments. In fact, many of his comments are questions to stimulate the reader to think about what has just been read. Not all of his comments are long, but they are always intelligent and probing. They help to shed light on poems as diverse as a sonnet by Shakespeare and a lyric by E. E. Cummings. His choice of poems is astute, his selections evenly divided among the sixteenth, seventeenth, eighteenth, nineteenth, and twentieth centuries.

Messages; a Thematic Anthology of Poetry. *X. J. Kennedy, ed.* **(1973) Little, Brown. 386p., o.p.**

This thematic anthology is divided into twelve sections: The Nature of Poetry; Cities; Environments; Life Styles; Identity of a Woman; Peoples; Nightmare and Apocalypse; Journeys; Magic; Solitude; Loving; and Enduring. Weirdly, the poems are printed without giving the names of the authors; those are provided at the very back of the book. The Preface explains that this is done so the reader can make up his or her own mind about the worth of a poem without being influenced by the reputation of the writer. This seems a precious arrangement, but the selection of poems is, none the less, very good. At the end of the volume, there are also a section on the lives of the poets and a glossary of poetic terms that is short but helpful. Many modern writers are included in this anthology, and the thematic arrangement makes for an interesting context in which to read their poems. There are also selections from writers of Shakespeare's time to the present, but the emphasis seems to be on twentieth-century verse.

Modern Poems; an Introduction to Poetry. *Richard Ellmann and Robert O'Clair, eds.* **(1976) W. W. Norton. 526p., pap.**

An acclaimed biographer of Joyce and Wilde, Richard Ellmann joins forces with a professor of English to introduce college students to a wide range of modern poetry. The poems move "from the easily accessible to the more difficult." The guide opens with a remarkably well-written and clear introduction on "Reading Poems." Some fifty pages in length, it considers everything from imagery to figurative language, usually with examples. Walt Whitman is the first poet. He is introduced by a biographical and literary sketch, a practice common for all of the poets included. There then follows a half dozen poems. Where necessary, there is a footnote to explain a particular situation, word, or phrase. A brief essay, "Modern Poetry in English," a bibliography, and an index close the anthology. There are some one hundred poets included. As the book draws close to the 1970's the number of poems for each writer decreases to about two or three. Still, these are representative. There is a fair balance between American and English poets, although the Americans rightly take up more space, and there are more of them included. While this is not as ambitious or as useful as such related works as X. J. Kennedy's *Introduction to Poetry* or Brooks and Warren, *Understanding Poetry,* it is extremely good for the modern authors. See also *The Norton Anthology of Modern Poetry.*

The Norton Anthology of American Literature. Vols. I–II. *Nina Baym and others, eds.* **(2d ed., 1985) W. W. Norton.**

These two massive volumes (each is over 2,500 pages) are a "collaboration between editors and teachers" involved in educating college students about American literature. The format, size aside, is familiar. There are six divisions in the two volumes. Each is introduced by a preface of five to ten pages, followed by examples from the work of the leading American authors. Each author is given a page or so of introduction, and there are short, useful footnotes to explain situations, persons, or places in the selections. Most of the focus is on prose, not poetry. For example, in the second volume one is given an overview of American Literature, 1865–1914, followed by the writings of Samuel Clemens and about twenty more writers, not one of whom is a poet. While there are several poets in the next chronological part, it is only at the end that more than three hundred and fifty pages are devoted to "American Poetry 1945–." Indeed, the major poets are given a good deal of space throughout, but essentially the two volumes concentrate on prose. The collection cannot be recommended either to the library or to the individual as a selection of poetry. Still, it is a marvelous overview of American writing.

The Norton Anthology of English Literature. Vols. I–II. *M. H. Abrams, general ed.* (5th ed., 1986) W. W. Norton.

An extremely comprehensive survey, this anthology comprises two enormous volumes. Volume I covers "The Middle Ages," "The Sixteenth Century," "The Seventeenth Century," and "The Restoration and the Eighteenth Century." In the second volume we find "The Romantic Period," "The Victorian Age," and "The Twentieth Century." Each of the individual periods is treated in great depth. From the Middle Ages, for example, there is a long selection of Old English poetry, including "Beowulf" and Caedmon's "Hymn." That is followed by long selections from Chaucer's *The Canterbury Tales,* several of which are included in full. From the seventeenth century, there is a multitude of poems by John Donne, Ben Jonson, Milton, Andrew Marvell, and Robert Herrick. Each century is treated with the same meticulous attention to the great figures and many minor figures who comprise the genius of the age. This is an excellent survey. Those who read it seriously can participate, in essence, in a university course in English literature.

The Norton Anthology of Modern Poetry. *Richard Ellmann and Robert O'Clair, eds.* (2d ed., 1988) W. W. Norton. 1863p., pap.

Among the numerous Norton anthologies, this is one of the best. The reason is twofold. First, the editor, Richard Ellmann (ably assisted by Robert O'Clair) insisted on rigorous selection practices, and he provided copious notes to help the student. (Ellmann died only a few months before the second edition was published.) Second, there is more here than in other collections of this type — more poems, more explanation, more biographical material, and close to two thousand pages representing every major poet writing in English in the twentieth century. If only one anthology of modern poetry were to be purchased, this would be the first choice. The selection begins with the late nineteenth century and Walt Whitman, Emily Dickinson, Gerard Manley Hopkins, and Thomas Hardy. Cathy Song (b. 1955) is the last writer included. Her name reminds the reader that the compilers "have provided a generous selection of poets less celebrated but still of commanding interest."

The Norton Anthology of Poetry. *Alexander W. Allison and others, eds.* **(3d ed., 1983) W. W. Norton. 1452p., pap.**

Among numerous Norton anthologies, this is one of the most famous and most comprehensive. In close to fifteen hundred closely packed pages, the compilers "provide readers with a wide and deep sampling of the best poetry written in the English language, from early medieval times to the present day." The first four poems are anonymous lyrics from the thirteenth and fourteenth centuries. Some two hundred poets and more than a thousand poems later the anthology ends with three poems by Leslie Silko (b. 1948). There is a clear, twenty-page explanation of versification at the end of the volume, as well as an index of authors, titles, and first lines. What makes this edition outstanding for all readers, and a useful guide for college students, are the numerous notes. These may range from two or three for a poem, to long, in-depth comments. The beginning reader will, therefore, have no difficulty understanding esoteric persons, places, and metaphors. Most commendable is the discriminating choice of new poets, women poets, and Afro-American poets. In addition, "there is a significant increase in poems written in English in other countries." All and all, this is an ideal collection for individual and libraries alike.

The Norton Anthology of World Masterpieces. Vols. I–II. *Maynard Mack, general ed.* **(5th ed., 1985) W. W. Norton.**

These whopping volumes could probably help readers develop muscles in their arms as well as improve their minds. There is a massive amount of poetry here: the work of Homer, in long excerpts from *The Iliad* and *The Odyssey;* and entire verse plays, such as *Agamemnon,* by Aeschylus, *Oedipus the King,* by Sophocles, *Medea,* by Euripides, and Aristophanes' *Lysistrata.* Then there are the poems of the Latin poet Catullus, Virgil's *Aeneid,* and selections from Ovid's *Metamorphoses.* All of these were from the section "Masterpieces of the Ancient World." There follows "Masterpieces of the Middle Ages," with some of Dante's *The Divine Comedy.* In "Masterpieces of the Renaissance," there is Petrarch's verse and essays by Montaigne and Cervantes, and so on and so on, until we come to the contemporary writings of Samuel Beckett. Throughout the ages, prose is featured along with poetry, and there is a great effort to recognize extraordinary writing on all the continents. This anthology could serve as a textbook for many college courses. The poetry it provides is of the highest quality.

The Norton Introduction to Poetry. *J. Paul Hunter, ed.* **(3d ed., 1986)**
W. W. Norton. 576p., pap. $15.95

As with a majority of the familiar Norton anthologies, this is directed
to the college student or the adult who wishes to learn more about the
basics of poetry. It also is a useful anthology of primarily nineteenth- and
twentieth-century English and American poetry; but the arrangement,
theme, explanations, and notes are for the classroom. The third edition
includes nearly five hundred poems, most of which are familiar. There
are, however, a few of "the forgotten and the seldom anthologized, for
one of the pleasures of reading — for teachers as well as students — is the
joy of discovery." The fifteen primary sections are arranged to introduce
the reader to the fundamentals of poetry. "Experiencing Poetry" is the
first part, followed by major sections devoted to text and context. Ap-
proximately half way through the anthology, the structure is broken a bit
with "Poems for Further Reading," followed by some fifty pages discuss-
ing poetry and its many forms. This helps the reader not only to un-
derstand the poem, but enables her or him to write critically about a
specific work. Throughout, there are numerous notes and added expla-
nations about particular poems or about the topic of the given section.
The selection of poets, as in all Norton anthologies, is excellent.

Poetry in English; an Anthology. *M. L. Rosenthal, general ed.* **(1987)**
Oxford University Press. 1196p., pap.

In another massive volume for the college student, there are six sec-
tions with seven editors, including the general editor. Only one is from
England, Beryl Rowland, of York University, who was editor of "The
Middle Ages." Canadian and United States scholars are about evenly
spread over the five other parts: the Sixteenth Century; the Seventeenth
Century; the Restoration and Eighteenth Century; the Nineteenth Cen-
tury; and the Twentieth Century, divided between the Early Moderns
and the Late Moderns. The final section is devoted to explaining versi-
fication. Editorial annotations, which are frequent in the earlier sections
and less so later on, appear at the bottom of each page. Preceding each
poet is a short biographical and literary/historical sketch by the editor of
the section. In terms of balance, one hundred and twenty-five pages are
devoted to the Middle Ages, while the twentieth century opens with
Thomas Hardy and closes nearly four hundred pages later with Seamus
Heaney. The explanation of poetic form, i.e., versification, is extremely
clear and should be of great assistance to layperson and student alike. It

is a working volume that will be of great value to librarians and to others seeking representative verse of well-known poets. Of particular value are Rosenthal's remarks about the Early Moderns.

Poetry: Past and Present. *Frank Brady and Martin Price, eds.* **(1974) Harcourt Brace Jovanovich. 527p., pap.**

Professor of English, a literary critic, and editor, Brady brings a thorough understanding of the needs of college students to a basic introduction to poetry. The detailed introduction explores the critical aspects of English and American poetry. The text is written in an extremely clear, easy-to-understand fashion. It serves as a good explanation of the subject not only for students, but for involved laypersons. The techniques and theories of poetry are considered, as are the various elements that set off an acceptable piece of work from mere sentimental verse. There is the usual detailed glossary. Of particular interest is the thematic and generic table of contents that should help the beginner find a way through more than four hundred poems. Arrangement is chronological, from Chaucer to Sylvia Plath. The hundred and fifteen poets are primarily English, but there are enough of the American masters to make this a suitable introduction to American-English poetry.

The Practical Imagination; an Introduction to Poetry. *Northrop Frye, Sheridan Baker, and George Perkins.* **(1983) Harper & Row. 500p., pap.**

While essentially a college textbook, the collection, with its numerous notes, comments, and data on the various poets, will be of considerable interest to the involved layperson. It covers the forms and varieties of poetry "moving from the simple elements to the more subtle and complex, with principles explained and questions provided to guide the students' progress." After a brief background introduction on the aesthetic pleasure and the sound and meaning of poetry, the compilers open with a discussion of the lyric and narrative forms. The short but informative text preceding each section and many of the poems themselves help make the point over and over again that such concepts as symbols, allegory, and metaphor can be understood and appreciated with a little study. The compilers avoid the simplistic, but they are able to convey some difficult lessons in relatively easy to understand terms. Coverage is generous of American and English poets from early anonymous works through to Wordsworth, W. B. Yeats, Philip Larkin, and E. E. Cummings.

Sleeping on the Wing; an Anthology of Modern Poetry with Essays on Reading and Writing. *Kenneth Koch and Kate Farrell.* **(1981) Random House. 313p.**

While serving as an anthology of modern poetry, this book performs the further function of introducing readers to the genre of poetry. After an introduction in which such ideas as how to read and talk about poems are considered, the work of twenty-three poets is printed, each being allotted from four to ten pages. These poets range from Walt Whitman, Emily Dickinson, and Gerard Manley Hopkins to Ezra Pound, John Ashbery, and Amiri Baraka. After each of their sections of poems, there is an essay on their work written by the editors. These essays tend to be fairly brief, sometimes only a page in length; they also include a poetry-writing exercise for the reader to undertake. One of the delightful aspects of the essays is their precise, sincere appreciation of the particular genius of each poet. This sense of devoted admiration is contagious. Still, the very simple nature of the essays probably makes them more appropriate for younger audiences in high school and college.

Sound and Sense; an Introduction to Poetry. *Laurence Perrine, ed., with the assistance of Thomas R. Arp.* **(6th ed., 1982) Harcourt Brace Jovanovich. 342p.**

For several decades a popular introduction to poetry for college and advanced high school students, this is an exploration of poetic concepts as well as an anthology of poetry. Throughout, there is a clear sense of what constitutes fine writing, and the choice of poetry reflects that high degree of critical judgment. Poets whose work is featured in the great detail include Emily Dickinson, A. E. Housman, and Robert Frost. Following each of the poems in the general text, there are questions to provoke the reader to consider particular aspects of the poem. They tend to be sharp, probing inquiries about the essential nature of the work. The elements of poetry that are explored through brief discussions of the concepts, with close examinations of individual poems, are: denotation and connotation, imagery, figurative language (including metaphor, personification, metonymy, symbol, allegory, paradox, overstatement, understatement, and irony), allusions, meaning and idea, tone, musical devices, rhythm and meter, and so forth. The thoroughness of the approach and the excellence of the poems that are explicated make this a fine introductory textbook for those starting out on a quest to understand poetry. A glossary of poetic terms is included.

Twentieth-Century Poetry; American and British (1900–1970). *John Malcolm Brinnin and Bill Read, eds.* **(Rev. ed., 1970) McGraw Hill (Text edition entitled The Modern Poets). 515p., o.p.**

Not another textbook for college students? Yes, and while the selection is much the same as that found in other anthologies, it is blessed with some distinguishing features. First, the compilers have attempted to include pleasurable poetry, eliminating that which is "dense, tough, and technically adventurous." Second, and this does set it apart, there are "informal commentaries" at the end of each section whenever they are needed to explain the poem and the poet. There are also the customary, brief biographical sketches for each writer. Third, and the most charming aspect of the whole collection, there are full-page, black-and-white photographs of the poets by Rollie McKenna that are highly individualistic and worth the price of the volume. There are no better portraits of Wallace Stevens, Vernon Watkins, James Merrill, Marge Piercy, and scores of others in the collection. More than a hundred poets are represented by from three to ten poems each. There are a good bibliography and an index.

Understanding Poetry. *Cleanth Brooks and Robert Penn Warren, eds.* **(4th ed., 1976) Holt, Rinehart and Winston. 602p., o.p.**

Many authorities correctly believe this to be the best single, modern guide to poetry for student and layperson alike. Prepared as a textbook, with a justifiably famous "letter to the teacher" in the first (1938) edition, it is the skilled work of two famous critics, poets and, yes, teachers. "This book has been conceived on the assumption that if poetry is worth teaching at all it is worth teaching as poetry." The guide is divided into such broad sections as "Dramatic Situation" and "Theme, Meaning, and Dramatic Structure." Each section has a foreword that explains the particular aspect of poetry. The editors then cite examples from Shakespeare, Robert Lowell, and almost every famous American and English poet to emphasize their point. Approximately a quarter to a third of the poems are analyzed within the sections. Questions to stimulate further study sometimes are included. The analyses presented in the early part of the book are relatively simple, as are the poems. They grow progressively more difficult and sophisticated as the book progresses. The arrangement is based on "aspects of poetic communication, and on pedagogical expediency." In the course of numerous editions, the compilers have added comments that dutifully explain their slight changes in direction, as well as their additions and deletions. These are based as much upon changes in critical judgment as upon the expressed needs of students and teachers. There may be other places for the close study of poetry, at least for beginners and laypersons, but none is as celebrated, or as free of the burden of jargon. An absolute must in libraries and for many individuals. For a similar approach, see *How Does a Poem Mean?*

Western Wind; an Introduction to Poetry. *John Frederick Nims, ed.* **(2d ed., 1983) Random House. 639p.**

The last two hundred pages of this introduction to poetry are an anthology that begins with some of the earliest English ballads and ends with contemporary writing. The choice includes many of the masterpieces of poetic discourse, with great poems by Donne, Milton, and Blake. The contemporary authors range from Derek Walcott to Katha Pollitt. This collection of poems is preceded by a stimulating introduction organized around the senses, the emotions, words, sounds, rhythms, and the mind. As the editor suggests: "The book begins, as our lives do, with sense impressions and the emotions they arouse. It then proceeds to the words with which the poet, like the rest of us, has to express such images and emotions. It goes on to consider the qualities of these words as poets use them: their sounds as well as their meanings, the rhythms they assume, the forms . . . in which they find expression." This methodical approach reaps real benefits when it comes to analyzing difficult or puzzling poems, such as Wallace Stevens's "The Emperor of Ice Cream." Nims's leading questions (under his heading "Exercises and Diversions") and his canny definitions and illustrations of poetic terms help to explicate his own and many other compositions. As an introductory text, this is highly recommended.

POLISH POETRY

Postwar Polish Poetry; an Anthology. *Czeslaw Milosz, ed.* (3d ed., enl., 1983) University of California Press. 192p.

Three points distinguish this unusual collection. First, it is selected and edited by one of the century's greatest poets, Nobel Prize-winning Czeslaw Milosz. Six of his poems are reprinted here. (Zbigniew Herbert, on the other hand, whom he greatly admires, is represented by at least twice as many works.) Second, the translations, primarily by the compiler, are as sensitive as they are reflective of Polish thinking since the Second World War. Third, Milosz includes only poems that he believes are adaptable to English translations. And, finally, the third revised edition has several poems that he "translated especially for the occasion." Aside from the poets mentioned, among the twenty-five others are Aleksander Wat, Witold Gombrowicz, and Anna Swirszczynska. Each poet is presented with a brief biographical sketch and the compiler's evaluation of his or her place in the history of modern Polish literature. The work's "mixture of macabre and humorous elements, its preoccupation less with the ego than with dramas of history . . ." give it wide appeal for any Western reader. A highly recommended collection for individuals and libraries.

POLITICAL POETRY

Anthology of Poems on Affairs of State; Augustan Satirical Verse, 1660–1714. *George de F. Lord, ed.* **(1975) Yale University Press. 800p.**

How many people read the political poems of the Augustan period? Today, not many. The verses are limited to the purview of scholars and specialists. More the pity. The lines originally were written as lampoons and satires for popular consumption. The subjects ranged from kings and queens to actresses and "orange wenches and leaders of the court, as well as more momentous matters of state." Thanks to these verses, we now know more about the loves of Charles II than about the secretive foreign policy of the day. Even Charles's friends had to admit the king had more than a few personal weaknesses! In order to give the proper background to the individual poets and their works, each is introduced by a short essay and often an engraved portrait. Each and every line that might give the reader pause is explained in easy to follow footnotes. Given these numerous crutches, one has the pleasure not only of splendid poetry but also of an actual history lesson. In fact, the primary arrangement is by historical topic, from church affairs to Defoe's and Swift's comments on the Act of Union.

The Faber Book of Political Verse. *Tom Paulin, ed.* **(1986) Faber and Faber. 482p.**

Dante is the first on the poetical platform, with his biting appraisal of Count Ugolino. He is followed by Thomas Wyatt, Milton, Swift, Wordsworth, Walt Whitman, and Robert Lowell. In between are close to a hundred other poets, the majority English or American. But one does find selections from Osip Mandelstam, Hans Enzensberger, and other outstanding Russian, German, and Italian poets. The book makes two points. First, a considerable amount of verse can be classified as political. Second, as Tom Paulin points out in his introduction, there are at least seven distinct types of such verse: popular, monarchist, Puritan-Republican, Irish, Scottish, American, and the anti-political. It is to be expected that Milton is given more space than almost any other poet.

(Paulin has a strong preference for the Puritan-Republican tradition). Others who are judged almost as important, at least in terms of space, include Blake, Wordsworth, and W. H. Auden. A surprise is Arthur Hugh Clough, who the compiler believes is a much neglected voice, and quite up to the best work of the others. The collection spans six centuries, and its scope cannot be faulted. It is the best single place to turn to for representative political verse.

RELIGIOUS POETRY

American Hymns Old and New. Vols. I–II. *Albert Christ-Janer, Charles W. Hughes, and Carleton Sprague Smith, eds.* **(1980) Columbia University Press.**

A magnificent reference work, this is in two volumes. The first, as the preface points out, is "a generous selection of hymns with suitable tunes." The music covers four centuries of American religious song. The second volume is in two major sections. The first two hundred and eighty pages offer advanced scholarly commentaries on the individual hymns. The equally fascinating second part prints "biographies of authors and composers." A bibliography winds it all up. The first volume begins in the seventeenth century where there is a brief, general introduction to the century, and shorter prefaces for each subdivision: psalters; English devotional verse; devotional verse of the Dutch, Germans, and Italians. The same general pattern is followed throughout, concluding with the twentieth century and a brief section on "commissioned hymns." There are five indexes, including tunes, meters, and bible verses. In the second volume the notes on the hymns are arranged alphabetically by their first lines and are abundantly documented. This definitive work is an absolute must for libraries and for many individuals.

An Anthology of Catholic Poets. *Shane Leslie, ed.* **(Rev. ed., 1952) Macmillan; later published by Newman Press. 378p.**

A highly personal selection, here are Catholic poets and Catholic verse from almost the beginning of the Church to the early part of the twentieth century. Arranged in an orderly fashion by subject and time, the collection represents poets who are spiritually, and sometimes aggressively, devoted to the Roman faith. In the main, though, the work is more a collection of Catholic poets than Catholic themes. As a consequence, most of the verse may be read and appreciated by anyone who enjoys imaginative, intellectual poetry. The introduction should be read for its marvelous survey of Catholic poets and for the personal insights of the compiler. Most of the poetry is limited to Great Britain and Ireland, with few modern writers included. The scope, then, is restricted as much by time as by place and subject. Note that in the revised edition the compiler has added Hilaire Belloc and G. K. Chesterton. Lack of title and author indexes is a bother.

The Best Loved Religious Poems. *James Gilchrist Lawson, comp.* **(1933) Fleming H. Revell. 253p.**

With confidence the compiler observes that "this is probably the most complete anthology of favorite Christian poems yet offered to the public." Some 50 years later the claim is no longer true. Still, the collection has been in print for many years and has a regular following. There are close to 500 poems, for the most part brief. Selection is based "not on literary merit, but because of popularity and heart appeal." The arrangement is by religious, even sentimental, subject headings. We find atonement, brotherhood, giving, humility, heart purity, satisfaction, security, and the like. Hymns, oddly enough, are limited to a single page. The index of authors indicates the compiler was true to his own conviction: Most of the work "offered to the public" is from religious newspapers and "several hundred monthly church magazines," and, in consequence, the authors are less than household names. "Anonymous" and the Bible, as might be expected, have by far the most entries, followed by Annie Johnson Flint, Frances Ridley Havergal, and John Oxenham. Elizabeth Barrett Browning, Bunyan, Kipling, and Tennyson are limited to one or two poems each. This may or may not "help in deepening the spiritual life and character of its readers."

Contemporary Religious Poetry. *Paul Ramsey, ed.* **(1987) Paulist Press. 227p., pap.**

It is hard to predict which contemporary American poets would show up in a book of religious poetry. As it happens, several of the authors here are well known. There are Amiri Baraka, John Berryman, T. S. Eliot (a more obvious choice), X. J. Kennedy, Frank O'Hara, Theodore Roethke, Richard Wilbur, and William Carlos Williams, to name only the most famous. The editor has divided his anthology into such subjects as "Against the Wind of Time," "By Light and Sorrow," "Epigrams and Light Verse and Kin." This proves a very fruitful arrangement. It allows small poems to be read with others that are concerned with the same subject matter. In this volume are poems written from the 1950's to the 1980's. Although all the verses have religious themes, the religion is not always Christian: Jewish poets, Muslim poets, and others are included. It is interesting to see how contemporary authors handle a topic virtually as old as poetry itself, although somewhat eclipsed in recent years.

The Earth Is the Lord's; Poems of the Spirit. *Helen Plotz, comp.* **(1965) Thomas Y. Crowell. 224p., o.p.**

Despite the somewhat simplistic introduction, the well-known compiler succeeds again in offering an intelligent, imaginative, and wide-ranging collection of poetry for young people. The theme is evident, but the scope goes beyond Judaeo-Christian themes. Even a cursory examination of the five sections, all of which are oddly named, indicates the scope of the collection. For example, under "Praise Doubt" or "The Vision Splendid," or "Our Daily Bread" one discovers short entries from Joseph Addison, Martin Luther, and Henry Vaughan. There are adequate translations of Pindar, The Book of the Dead, a Dahomean song, and Zen parables. Plotz rightly conceives of an eternal God with a world vision. True, the vast majority of poems do concern the Christian religion, but they are so well chosen as to seem, as one poet puts it, to be "rising into sunlight/out of soil and darkness." The result is a close to perfect summary of religious verse for readers of all ages and backgrounds.

The New Oxford Book of Christian Verse. *Donald Davie, ed.* **(1981) Oxford University Press. 320p.**

This anthology in no way skimps on artistic quality. In fact, in his introduction, Donald Davie remarks that he chose to exclude any kind of devotional poetry that could only be called mere verse and not poetry. The writers whose work is particularly featured include the great hymn writers, Isaac Watts, Charles Wesley, and William Cowper. The other authors, too, adhere to the Christian dogma in their poetry, the anonymous poets who wrote from the seventh through the sixteenth centuries, as well as Donne, George Herbert, Milton, Anne Bradstreet, and Henry Vaughan. Emily Dickinson is also on hand with several poems of a Christian nature. Modern poets include Sir John Betjeman, W. H. Auden and Elizabeth Jennings. This anthology should prove extremely satisfying to those readers concerned with Christian faith; it provides some of the finest literary expressions of religious experience.

News of the Universe; Poems of Twofold Consciousness. *Robert Bly, comp.* **(1980) Sierra Club Books. 305p.**

One of America's leading poets here gathers together poetry that reaches out beyond the self and human ecology to the very heart of nature and the universe. The hundred and fifty poems are arranged in six parts, but it is the last section in which Bly addresses himself to the modern individual in quest of "an interior unity." Each of the sections includes a splendid introduction, followed by the poems. The "Old Position" leads off — the time when people had little or no appreciation of nature and its way. There were exceptions, of course, and these are the quoted poets — Gotthold Lessing, Pope, Milton, and Swift. "The Attack on the Old Position," one finds, is a much longer section, with such writers as Blake and Walt Whitman. Throughout the volume numerous poems are translated by Bly, as expert a translator as he is a poet; the work is thus given an added dimension. This is evident particularly in the final section where he translates poems from numerous cultures: "I've included Eskimo, Ojibway, Zuni poems here, early Anglo-Saxon poetry, and some medieval ballads." There is an index of authors and poems.

Tongues of Fire; an Anthology of Religious and Poetic Experience. *Karen Armstrong, ed.* **(1987) Penguin Books. 352p., pap.**

The title comes from an English television series that explored the relationship between poetry and religion. While most of the focus is on Christianity, the divisions of the book (and, indeed, the series) try to emphasize ideas and emotions rather than particular religious groups. The collection is divided into ten sections. In each, one finds standard, and not so standard, poets and poems which celebrate and explain the topic. "Sex and Religion" has eighteen poets and about as many poems. The balance is much the same in the other sections. One finds the work primarily of English poets — Donne, Blake, Milton, Thomas Hardy, and Robert Browning are typical. On the other hand, there are the words of Czeslaw Milosz (one of the poets who helped with the series), Ibnu 'l-Arabi, and Teresa of Avila. So, while it would be wrong to say an exact balance has been struck between faiths, at least they are represented. Each section opens with a brief introduction that attempts to show the relation between the poetry and the subject, a device that is sometimes a bit simplistic. On the whole the collection is for the generalist.

The Treasury of Christian Poetry. *Lorraine Eitel, comp., with others.* **(1982) Fleming H. Revell. 182p.**

A number of distinguished poets set apart this collection of popular religious verse. Among those present, and not that often found in competing collections, are W. H. Auden, Ezra Pound, and W. B. Yeats. One also finds, of course, such earlier poets as Ben Jonson and John Donne. The better-known writers are represented by some of their lesser-known poetry. Be that as it may, the poems are first rate and show a side of the poet that may be unfamiliar. The standard Christian verses are counterbalanced by the not-so-standard, and usually much better, poems. The compilers arrange the works under broad subject headings that are sometimes less than descriptive. There is a combined author-title index, and the compiler says all of the works may be delivered orally — a matter of opinion — but in no way does it detract from a superior religious anthology.

Treasury of Irish Religious Verse. *Patrick Murray, ed.* **(1986) Crossroad. 295p.**

According to tradition, some hundreds of years before Christ the Irish poet Amergin composed the first Irish poem, "Leabhar Gabhala," or "Book of Invasions." This collection opens with an excerpt from that work called "The Mystery." (Actually, this might well be the title for the entire anthology that, after a chronological presentation, concludes a good two thousand years later with Seamus Heaney's "St. Francis and the Birds.") After one or two anonymous poems, the work takes a leap forward with a poem attributed to St. Patrick in the fifth century. After that, there is no holding back the Irish bards who sing more of nature and the ordeal of loss in relation to Christianity than of religious experiences as such. Little of these early verses remain, so it is no accident that most of the book is involved with the eighteenth, nineteenth, and particularly the twentieth centuries. Many of "the later poems recall the dark days of persecution and suppression." This sometimes results in inartistic verses, as the compiler observes, but they do show the anguish of the times as no other writers do and for that reason are valued. There are brief notes on the authors, and a most useful index of themes.

A Treasury of Poems for Worship and Devotion. *Charles L. Wallis, ed.* **(1959) Harper. 378p., o.p.**

Here are over four hundred poems written by several hundred poets, most of them unknown to the general reader or scholar. Their work is organized by such Christian religious themes as "To God the Father," "The Varied Ministries of Nature," and "Petitions of Doubt and Protest." This book is clearly aimed at a religious audience, one that wishes to increase spiritual experience through the power of poetry. This volume ignores the interest of more secular readers by printing only excerpts from longer poems by such accomplished poets as Robert Browning and William Cowper. For the full flavor of their handling of religious experience, one must consult their collected works. If a reader desires to sink into a pool of potentially popular, overly simple, and aesthetically unchallenging religious verse, then this treasury will fill the need. A more sophisticated approach to religious utterance can be found elsewhere, such as in *The New Oxford Book of Christian Verse.*

The World's Great Religious Poetry. *Caroline Miles Hill, ed.* **(1954) Macmillan. 836p., o.p.**

First published in 1923, here is a standard work that groups the poems of primarily Christian poets under broad subject headings. One finds suitable verse arranged by period, from Pre-Christian to Medieval and modern, as well as by such topics as "Trees" and "Animals." The editor admits in earlier editions that "this collection . . . is not all great [literature] and it makes strange combinations and sequences." Hymns, for example, may be side by side with the poetry of Lord Byron. And Gustavus Adolphus's "Battle Hymn" and "O Mother Dear, Jerusalem," are here alongside Sara Teasdale. Work from the nineteenth and twentieth centuries dominates, although one finds the basic Christian poetry from earlier periods. Very little space is given to other faiths. This is the last place to turn for a true picture of the "world's great religions." Still, as far as it goes it is an adequate aid for individuals and librarians attempting to locate hard to find songs, poems, and poets. There is an index of titles, authors, and first lines.

RUSSIAN POETRY

An Age Ago; a Selection of Nineteenth-Century Russian Poetry. *Alan Myers, comp. and tr.* **Foreword and biographical notes by Joseph Brodsky. (1988) Farrar, Straus and Giroux. 171p.**

Aside from the eleven poets represented here, no one should miss the foreword and the impressive biographical notes by Joseph Brodsky. The Nobel Prize-winning poet writes a revealing essay on the nineteenth-century poets. "Most belonged to the class of impoverished gentry — the class which is almost solely responsible for the emergence of literature everywhere.... Looking through the little window of this anthology onto the nineteenth century, we should try to see it for what it was, for what it felt about itself." And that is made much easier by the careful selection and the sensitive translations. Certainly, most readers will instantly recognize Pushkin and Lermontov, but few will have read such excellent renditions of their poems into English. Brodsky sets the stage for such lesser-known writers as A. A. Fet, "a lyrical poet of the highest acumen." In no other collection will the reader better see what has come to be known as the steam engine that carried Russian writers into the twentieth century.

The Oxford Book of Verse in English Translation. *Charles Tomlinson, ed.*

See under WORLD POETRY

186

SCOTTISH POETRY

The Golden Treasury of Scottish Poetry. *Hugh MacDiarmid, ed.* (1941) Macmillan. 410p

The great poet Robert Burns, the ballad form, and the talented anonymous writers are the best-known features in the wide field of Scottish poetry. All three sometimes need explanation, and to that end this anthology supplies a useful glossary and a lengthy introduction. The collection draws upon the whole history of the land. Translated from the Gaelic, for example, "The Path of Old Spells" is an early entry in the book. Here the choice is a prose translation that makes more sense of the verse but fails to convey the elementary power of the poetry. Be that as it may, no one can fault the collection for lack of proper choices. Everything is here, even "Auld Lang Syne," which opens rather than ends the anthology. Among the ballads, "The Bonny Earl o' Moray" may be the most familiar, but a real treat is "Rare Willie Drowned in Yarrow." And so it goes. The familiar rub shoulders with the lesser known, and often the latter is the more exciting, the more vibrant. This is true as well of poets who may have only one or two poetic claims to fame. If they are not of the caliber of Burns, they still are distinctive voices. Along the way one acquires a marvelous profile of Scottish history.

The Oxford Book of Scottish Verse. *John MacQueen and Tom Scott, comps.* (1966) Oxford University Press. 633p.

According to the compilers, the purpose of this collection "is to lay the greater emphasis on verse written in Scots as opposed to English." This is done in an anthology that begins in the thirteenth and moves to the mid-twentieth century. The poems are arranged chronologically by author, and the focus in on poetry of literary, rather than social or historical, importance. The editors often give readers some help by defining and explaining Scottish words. When published, it was the best one-volume anthology of its type, and over the years there have been no serious competitors. If there is any criticism to be made, it is in the decision to devote almost a quarter of the book to poets born since 1880.

There seems to be an overemphasis on the Scottish Renaissance; there are, on the other hand, solid offerings of all the great figures, no matter what century they were born in.

Poems of the Scottish Hills; an Anthology. *Hamish Brown, comp.* **(1982) Aberdeen University Press. 202p., o.p.**

A famous fisherman, Norman MacCaig, writes in the foreword of the feeling of freedom found in "the natural, physical world." It is that part of Scotland the compiler, who climbs mountains and writes poems, celebrates in this collection. "This is a collection for the hill goer's pack rather than a literary or historical study. . . . Come to it as we do to the hill, with rambling opportunism." Divided into sections, the two hundred or so poems tend to be short and deeply involved with the out-of-doors. In "Questions and Answers," which leads off the book, one finds Archie Mitchell's "Hills of the Middle Distance," Leen Volwerk's "Bog," and Kathleen Raine's "The Wilderness." So while the setting is Scotland, most of the poems can apply in spirit to other parts of the globe. Few of the poets are that well established, but if the names lack familiarity, there is no lack of skill and enthusiasm. Most of the writers are modern and Scottish, but a few are from other sections of the United Kingdom.

SPORTS POEMS

American Sports Poems. *R. R. Knudson and May Swenson, comps.* (1988) **Orchard Books. 226p.**

Drawing upon the sports which are best known to young people, the compilers have collected poems that demonstrate the thrills of both the players and the spectators. Baseball, running, football, swimming, basketball, and gymnastics are a few of the popular sports considered. There are short notes at the end of the volume that give information on the particular sport and the poet. There is an occasional interpretation, but on the whole the poems are left to speak directly to young people through high school. Among the contributions are numerous favorites by Ogden Nash and Shel Silverstein, for example. May Swenson's image of a rodeo is one of the best, as is Howard Nemerov's "Watching football on TV." Among the other poems are John Updike's "Ex-basketball Player," Lucille Clifton's "Jackie Robinson," and Arnold Adoff's "Wrestling the Beast." A totally satisfying collection that can be enjoyed by adults as well.

Sprints and Distances; Sports in Poetry and the Poetry in Sport. *Lillian Morrison, comp.* (1965) **Thomas Y. Crowell. 212p., o.p.**

What a good idea! Collecting sports verse, particularly with an eye towards involving younger people, seems clearly justified. Still, the compiler does briefly make a case for the relationship between sport and poetry. The unique approach covers any and all periods, poets, and areas, so long as they deal with sports. Furthermore, the editor warns, "Nor are all the poems in praise of sport. Some are critical, some satiric." The real measure for inclusion is quality and the appeal to young sportspersons. (At the same time, as with most poetry collections for the younger reader, there is little verse that will not be enjoyed by an adult.) The primary concern of most sport poets is the race, and much of the book is given over to runners and field sports. Still, there is plenty of space for fishing, swimming, skating, and baseball, among others. There is a most useful index by sport. Yeats considers the fisherman, Euripides the poor athletes, and Kipling the delights of skating. Anonymous is here in force, as are numerous other poets whose only real claim to fame is a single poem. No matter, the overall selection is close to perfect for the subject.

This Sporting Life. *Emilie Buchwald and Ruth Roston, eds.* **(1987) Milkweed Editions. 176p., pap.**

The arrangement is almost ideal for the reader who enjoys participating in or watching sports. Each section's half dozen to a dozen poems are devoted to specific sports. They are: Life Is Water: Swimming, Diving, Canoeing, Sailing; Climbing the Air: Rock Climbing . . . to Parachuting; Tennis and Squash; Play Ball — Baseball, Basketball, Football; Running, Jogging, Skating, Skiing; Blood Sports: Hunting, Fishing, Boxing, Wrestling. After that are three broad sections that are catchalls: Coaches; Playing the Game; and This Sporting Life. All of the poets are contemporary Americans. Among the more famous are Maxine Kumin, Thomas Lux, Richard Hugo, James Wright, Donald Hall, and Robert Bly. The eighty or so other names may be familiar only to those who are avid poetry readers, particularly in little magazines. Most, as the compilers claim, "give vivid language to wordless experience." The collection is as suitable for young people as it is for adults.

TRAVEL POETRY

The Faber Book of Poems and Places. *Geoffrey Grigson, ed.* (1980) Faber and Faber. 387p., pap.

The distinguished poet and critic Geoffrey Grigson looks back on "poems and places" and offers the reader a delightful view of his sense of reality and of imagination, often inseparably linked. The introduction is only three pages long, but it pinpoints the scope of the anthology: "I have chosen verse about places in England, Wales, Scotland and Ireland, and the Channel Islands, into all of which our emotion flows outward, to be returned to us gladly or reflectively as well." In addition, Italy and France are considered, as are French poems about the English and their country. "I know little of comparable Italian poetry." The content is arranged by locality, and begins with a prologue and then moves to "The South." There are sections on London, Oxford, Cambridge, the Lake Country, Scotland, and Ireland, and about forty pages of translated French and Italian verse. The poets are predominantly English, from the eighteenth and nineteenth centuries. There are few modern voices — air flight seems to have done away with much of the mystery of places, particularly in Europe. Some useful notes and references are included, as well as an index of first lines.

The Oxford Book of Travel Verse. *Kevin Crossley-Holland, ed.* (1986) Oxford University Press. 423p.

Under the heading "En Route," one begins to travel with Sir Richard Grenville (1541–1591). Midway through his poem, he explains the joys and profits of travel, this time by sea, with the line "I must abroad to try my lot." The other one hundred or so poet/travelers are of a similar mind. Arranged geographically, the poets take to the high roads of Europe (by far the favorite route) and of Africa, Asia, Oceania, and North and South America. All of the voices are British, including Scottish and Welsh poets "and those Irish writers not averse to union with their English peers in an anthology of this kind." The poets write from direct experience. Every travel poem paints a sometimes glorious, sometimes quite terrible picture of the places where the poet has wandered. Within each of the primary sections and subsections, the dozen or so poems are arranged chronologically. One of the earliest (c. 1425) is an anonymous poem about Iberia. A comparative youngster, Frank Ormsby (b. 1947), is of the contemporary school. Threading their way through the descriptions are every emotion, from humor and joy to grief and longing. The selection is representative of the best travel poetry, as least as practiced by English writers, and can be recommended as a companion volume to Geoffrey Grigson's *Faber Book of Poems and Places*.

VAMPIRE POETRY

The Vampire in Verse; an Anthology. *Steven Moore, ed.* **(1985) Dracula Press. 196p., pap. $7.95**

If the subject matter here needs an explanation, it should be noted that the press that published this slim volume is an important part of the "Count Dracula Fan Club." The publisher has issued numerous related works, from *Dracula Made Easy* to the current volume. The intentions and aims of the society are much the same as the one evidenced in this collection — "good fun." The compilation celebrates the fact that many poets, and not a few of them excellent, have fallen under the vampire spell. Goethe, for example, is represented here by "The Bride of Corinth," and Byron, Keats, Théophile Gautier, Baudelaire, and even James Joyce and Rudyard Kipling are included. There are about fifty poets with approximately the same number of poems. They are arranged in chronological order and with a few exceptions are primarily American and English. One should note, too, that while much of the verse is fun, "I have avoided all light verse." In fact, especially during the Romantic period, many of the poems are deadly serious; only by the time of the twentieth century is the vampire more amusing. There is also a strong component of sublimated sex and violence, nicely explained in the copious notes.

WAR POETRY

Chaos of the Night; Women's Poetry and Verse of the Second World War. *Catherine W. Reilly, ed.* **(1984) Virago Press. 150p., pap.**

When one thinks of "war poets," women writers may not spring immediately to mind. In fact, when the editor of this volume explored prestigious anthologies of war poetry, she found that women were strikingly underrepresented. In this volume, she seeks to redress a wrong. This collection focuses on women's responses to the Second World War in Great Britain, where they were intimately involved in battles that sent shells crashing through their houses or into their Armed Forces. Some of the authors of these poems are familiar: Ruth Pitter, Edith Sitwell, Stevie Smith, and Sylvia Townsend Warner are some of the most famous, but most of the eighty-seven poets whose verses appear here are unknown. Their work was discovered by the editor in the course of her researches at the Bodleian Library at Oxford, where the holdings provided her with material neglected by other anthologies. These poems are fascinating, eye-opening accounts of women's reactions to the utter turmoil and intense suffering of a war brought to their doorsteps.

Men Who March Away; Poems of the First World War. *I. M. Parsons, ed.* **(1965) Viking Press. 192p., o.p.**

Can the horrors of battle ever be caught in poetry? Besides Homer and the later epic poets, the answer is a resounding NO. There are numerous gallant efforts, and some of the near successes in this volume captured the terrors and emotions of the trenches in the First World War. Yet, for anyone who has been under fire, the poem is only a shadow of the reality. Obviously the compiler of this volume would not agree, although numerous front-line poets are the first to admit that only a proximity to the dreadful truth of war is all that is possible. The poems dealing with casualties actually do attain higher proportions of poetic truth than do other sections. The editor points out that "Ivor Gurney's 'To his love' [and] F. W. Harvey's 'Prisoners' . . . are cases in point. But the established names inevitably predominate. Here are Rosenberg's terrifying 'Dead Man's Dump,' Robert Graves's 'Last Post,' Sorley's sonnets, Sassoon's 'The Death Bed,' and the great poems of Owen's maturity." The compiler's divisions, from "Visions of Glory" to "The Dead" and "Aftermath," trace the evolution of thought about the First World War. As such, the volume is a tribute to the power of poets to capture the emotions of common people in the hurricane of war.

The Oxford Book of War Poetry. *Jon Stallworthy, ed.* (1984) Oxford University Press. 358p.

In his introduction, Jon Stallworthy writes that "there can be no area of human experience that has generated a wider range of powerful feeling than war." His selection of poems effectively bears out that contention. Stallworthy traces the significance of war over the centuries in the different societies that nurtured the authors, and he comments on their lives and accomplishments. He has chosen works from many different countries and times (including a few from ancient Greece and Rome, as well as later ones from France, Germany, and Russia), but modern poems are primarily English and American. Stallworthy arranges the verses in chronological order according to the wars that inspired their creation. His taste and judgment are splendid: the range of poems is broad, their quality fine, and he has included a few works by women. But the emphasis on the theme of war is so relentless — and not really so varied — that the reader must be truly fascinated by the subject for these verses not to pall.

War and the Poet; an Anthology of Poetry Expressing Man's Attitudes to War from Ancient Times to the Present. *Richard Eberhart and Selden Rodman, eds.* (1945) Devin-Adair. 240p.

Published in the time of war, this selection of poems is exceptional in its scope. Most anthologies are limited to a single period, a single war, or certainly to English-speaking poets. Here, United States Navy officer (Eberhart) and Army of the United States sergeant (Rodman) begin with the Asiatic campaigns of Thutmose III (about 1450 B.C.). The first fifty or so pages, in fact, deal with military matters before the Dark Ages. Part II carries the poetry up to the First World War, and the final section highlights verse from the Second World War, as well as anti-war poetry. Both of the compilers are, of course, well-known poets as well as war veterans. Their choices reflect "man's varying reactions to war through the centuries." There are a few odd choices. Basho, for example, normally associated with seventeenth-century Japanese poetry of peace, has a three-line poem. Among the scores of poets, there are only one or two women, including Emily Dickinson. There are subjective notes about each of the poets and an index to first lines.

The War Poets; an Anthology of the War Poetry of the 20th Century. *Oscar Williams, ed.* **(1945) John Day. 485p., o.p.**

With regard to the title, one can now say that its extent is not quite the twentieth century. When this was edited, the century was only half over; the Korean and Vietnam wars and other concentrated intense ideological battles were yet to rage. The editor can hardly be faulted for an accident of time; and, even nearer the end of the same century it is still hard to locate poetry that does justice to the years after the Second World War. Given, then, the limitation of time, the editor has done all readers a great service. He has included Sgt. Randall Jarrell's familiar "The Death of the Ball Turret Gunner" and poems by Wilfred Owen, Rupert Brooke, and Vernon Watkins. Divisions are by the two World Wars and, more imaginatively, by "Poems by the Men in the Armed Forces of England and America" and "War Poems by the Civilian Poets," one of which Williams counts himself. The unique approach is reason enough to consider the volume, but what is better is the selection of poems rarely reprinted, little known, and deserving of wider attention. One may argue with his conclusion that "our war poetry as a whole is perhaps the document of our time that will outlive all the rest," but one must applaud this different and, for the most part, compelling anthology.

WELSH POETRY

The Oxford Book of Welsh Verse in English. *Gwyn Jones, comp.* (1977) **Oxford University Press. 313p.**

Welsh is an ancient Celtic language, and the Welsh poetic tradition is the oldest in the British Isles. This anthology of Welsh verse begins at the beginning, in the Heroic Age of Britain. In his scholarly introduction, Gwyn Jones sketches the history of the enduring poetic tradition in Wales during the ever-changing political realities of the land. The most ancient poet in this collection dates from the sixth century and is named Taliesin. He is represented by a tale of battle and a death song. Most of the older poets will be entirely new to readers, but they are steeped in a creative, rich literary tradition. Poets from the seventeenth century begin to sound more familiar; George Herbert, Henry Vaughan, and Christopher Smart frequently appear in anthologies of English verse, and are deservedly well known. Of the more modern poets, there are John Cowper Powys, Edward Thomas, Wilfred Owen, David Jones, and, most famous of all, Dylan Thomas. This collection affords an extremely long, but deep, view of the wealth of poetry produced in the Welsh language and by Welsh poets writing in English. The contribution of these men and women to the general tradition of English verse is indisputable, and it is remarkable to see it collected in one place.

WOMEN'S POETRY AND FEMINIST POETRY

Ain't I a Woman! a Book of Women's Poetry from around the World. *Illona Linthwaite, ed.* **(1988) Peter Bedrick Books, 195p.**

There are contrasting literary styles in this volume of poetry, written by women about their lives. The material is organized thematically according to the essential events that make up most women's lives: childhood, love, marriage, and, finally, old age. The authors come from different cultures, and several of them are historical figures. Well-known poets are among the contributors: Elizabeth Jennings, Audre Lorde, Rosemary Tonks, and Elaine Feinstein. But the emphasis is on mixing the voices of white poets with those of black poets from around the world. Many of the works are in simple, everyday language, or in the vernacular of the street; others are in more elevated speech. So this anthology, which grew out of a stage play dramatizing the experience of women through their poetry, catches the variety of voices and experiences that the poets sought to express. This is an interesting way of gaining entry into the imaginative experiences of creative women.

A Book of Women Poets from Antiquity to Now. *Aliki Barnstone and Willis Barnstone, eds.* **(1980) Schocken Books. 613p.**

According to the editors of this anthology, the earliest known writer on earth was female, a Sumerian priestess from the third millennium B.C. Some of her poems are in this book, as are long selections from the great Greek poet Sappho, ancient Sanskrit works from India, early Persian poetry, and Chinese verses. The sampling of women's writing here is remarkable both for the length of the time period covered, and for the numbers of countries surveyed. Beginning with the Sumerian poet Enheduanna, this volume also presents anonymous Egyptian hieroglyphic texts, ancient and modern Hebrew poems, ancient Greek, Byzantine Greek, and modern Greek poets. There are also verses in several different languages of the Indian subcontinent, various traditional African poems, and extremely long selections from Chinese and Japanese writers, stretching once again from ancient to modern times. The section on Spanish poets includes old and new verses from Spain, Mexico, Puerto Rico, El Salvador, Peru, Argentina, and Chile. Finally, there is a long section of English writers from Great Britain, the United States, Canada, and Australia. For breadth, length, and excellence in translation, this volume of women's poetry is hard to surpass.

Bread and Roses; an Anthology of Nineteenth- and Twentieth-Century Poetry by Women Writers. *Diana Scott, comp.* **(1982) Virago Press. 282p., pap.**

After a general introduction, each period of women's poetry in the nineteenth and twentieth centuries is given a separate introduction, as are each of the poets. The editor states early on that she has compiled the book both for the accustomed reader of poetry and for the novice. Both should be able to enjoy the approach to these poems. The anthology is divided into four main sections. "We Who Bleed" and "A Vaster Knowledge" are devoted to British poetry of the nineteenth and the early part of the twentieth centuries. Such poets as Emily Brontë, Elizabeth Barrett Browning, Christina Rossetti, Charlotte Mew, and Alice Meynell are featured. The final two sections are: "The Meeting: On Reading Contemporary Poetry 1920–80," with such writers as Frances Cornford, Stevie Smith, Elaine Feinstein, and Ruth Fainlight; and "The Renaming: Poetry Coming from the Women's Liberation Movement 1970–80," with such poets as Mary Coghill, Diana Scott, and Astra. This arrangement is effective, in that it explores the work of acknowledged, superbly talented poets alongside the efforts of a newer literary, and finally, a newer political, generation.

Chaos of the Night; Women's Poetry and Verse of the Second World War. *Catherine W. Reilly, ed.*

See under WAR POETRY

Dancing the Tightrope; New Love Poems by Women. *Barbara Burford, Lindsay MacRae, and Sylvia Paskin, eds.*

See under LOVE POETRY

The Defiant Muse; French Feminist Poems from the Middle Ages to the Present. *Donna C. Stanton, ed.* **(1986) Feminist Press. 207p.**

There are now several collections of women's poetry from different countries and different eras, but there is nothing quite like this series: feminist poems in various languages over the ages. This volume of French feminist poems reflects the editor's "determination to exclude poems that privilege *kinder, kirche, küchen,* extol conjugal bliss, passively bemoan seduction and abandonment, and seek escape into transcendent saintliness or the beauty of flora and fauna. Conversely, the decision was made to include poems that showed an awareness of the scenes and acts of 'the femininity plot' and opposed or tried to subvert them with a different script." As a result, although many of these verses were written long before any women's movement was conceived, they rebel against any marriage and the political institutions that keep women in a subservient position in society. They are bold statements against the status quo, made by courageous and imaginative poets who realized that society had dealt them cards from a marked deck. The first poets in this collection date from the twelfth and thirteenth centuries and the last are contemporary authors. All the texts are printed in both French and English. It is a brave, astonishingly relevant volume of poetry.

The Defiant Muse; German Feminist Poems from the Middle Ages to the Present. *Susan L. Cocalis, ed.* **(1986) Feminist Press. 163p.**

Another astonishing bilingual collection of virtually unknown and neglected female poets, this one features German authors from the early part of the thirteenth century to the present day. The thing that these women have in common is their purported feminist perspective on life. The editor warns that "when approaching a collection of feminist poetry . . . the reader must suspend all previously learned and instinctively applied aesthetic criteria, as well as any preconceptions about the meaning of the term 'feminist literature' in order to reach a deeper understanding of the emancipatory nature and poetic accomplishment of the texts presented." In fact, the editor has stretched the term "feminism" to apply to any "nuances, or thematic or formal aberrations from traditional norms, or lapses that suggest a new consciousness of the poet's situation as a woman, and specifically, as a woman writer." This is a slippery definition at best, but it allows the editor to choose very interesting poetry, indeed, even if it is not always convincingly "feminist." The poets here deserve a wider audience regardless of their categorization, and they are given a fine forum here. They are a fascinating lot, and libraries should own all of these collections.

The Defiant Muse; Hispanic Feminist Poems from the Middle Ages to the Present. *Angel Flores and Kate Flores, eds.* **(1986) Feminist Press. 145p.**

This is, once again, a bilingual volume of poems written by women through the ages that can be generally categorized as feminist. These editors suggest that "to be a feminist means to be not only sensitive to the reality of women's lives, but courageous enough to do something about it, to speak out, to criticize." The poets in this collection date from thirteenth century Spain, and the poems start with anonymous ballads. The recorded poets from the next several centuries also lived in Spain, but beginning in the nineteenth century, there are poets from Ecuador, Bolivia, Uruguay, Chile, and Argentina. Twentieth-century poems come from Nicaragua, Mexico, Panama, Cuba, and Puerto Rico. This is another excellent collection in the Feminist Press series of women's poetry, featuring overlooked but highly developed artistic voices. They are sensuous, astute, and deeply conscious of their place in these Spanish-speaking countries. As usual, short biographies of the poets are placed at the end of the volume. Once again, a superior anthology.

The Defiant Muse; Italian Feminist Poems from the Middle Ages to the Present. *Beverly Allen, Muriel Kittel, and Keala Jane Jewell, eds.* **(1986) Feminist Press. 150p.**

The editors here examine the nature of feminist poetry as it occurs in a body of literature. They conclude that "whatever the historical context, the fact that these poems are written at all may itself be viewed as a feminist act." How that actually differs from the category of plain and simple "women's poetry" remains puzzling, but the collection once again is outstanding. The first poet, La Compiuta Donzella, dates from the thirteenth century with a series of sonnets. There is a rich collection from the sixteenth century, a couple from the seventeenth and eighteenth centuries, and then many diverse voices from the nineteenth and twentieth centuries. Once again, all these writers will be new to the general American reading public, and they ought to be much better known. The poems have universal appeal, and all larger libraries should own the entire collection of *The Defiant Muse*.

Early Ripening; American Women's Poetry Now. *Marge Piercy, ed.*
(1987) Pandora Press. 280p.

This anthology offers an exciting view of the state of women's poetry
writing in America today. The work of many women from various mi-
nority communities has been featured: there are Chicana writers (Bar-
bara Brinson Curiel and Lorna Dee Cervantes), black writers (Lucille
Clifton, Jayne Cortez, and Thulani Davis, among many others), and Na-
tive American poets (Linda Hogan). Many of the authors are lesbian.
Each writer is represented by several poems, so it is possible to sense the
flavor of her work. There is great diversity here: some of the poets are
accomplished, older, and well known; others are still developing their
craft; and others are simply lacking in talent. Among the well-known
writers whose work is included are Denise Levertov, Mona Van Duyn,
May Sarton, Adrienne Rich, Maxine Kumin, June Jordan, and Amy
Clampitt. It is fascinating to see what they, and the scores of other au-
thors, have been writing in the 1980's.

The Faber Book of 20th Century Women's Poetry. *Fleur Adcock, ed.*
(1987) Faber and Faber. 330p.

Fleur Adcock, herself an eminent poet, has compiled this selection of
women's verse that explores their output from the time of Charlotte
Mew (1869–1928) to that of Selma Hill, who was born in 1945. The poets
all write in English but hail from America, Canada, England, Australia,
New Zealand, and Ireland. Most are represented by two to four poems,
but several particularly prominent poets, such as Marianne Moore, Eliz-
abeth Bishop, Stevie Smith, and Sylvia Plath, are accorded much more
space. Those are the only exceptions, and this judiciousness in the se-
lection of the best representative poems allows the editor to include the
work of over sixty women. Her choices are very discerning, the poetry of
the highest quality. She thus manages to introduce a select number of
the best poets writing in English in the twentieth century. In a thought-
ful, perceptive introduction, Adcock intelligently addresses the central
questions about women's creative writing and cogently speaks about the
accomplishments of the poets she has featured in this volume.

**A Gathering of Spirit; Writing and Art by North American Indian
Women.** *Beth Brant, ed.*

See under NATIVE AMERICAN POETRY

I Hear My Sisters Saying; Poems by Twentieth-Century Women. *Carol Konek and Dorothy Walters, eds.* **(1976) Thomas Y. Crowell. 295p., o.p.**

After a fairly saccharine introduction, this anthology is divided into sections that correspond to the stages of a woman's life: "It took my childhood before I could see"; "This man, this stranger in my arms"; "I am trying to think how a woman can be a rock"; "What have I made"; and so forth. The poems that follow these evocative lines are fresh and exciting. They are written by a variety of women, well known and little known: Barbara Howes, Susan Fromberg Shaeffer, Denise Levertov, Adrienne Rich, Gwendolyn Brooks, Joyce Carol Oates, and Sarah Youngblood. Many of the poems are strong, sure, and evocative, but they are mixed in with dozens of weak verses that seem to be included because they fill out the thematic scheme of the volume. None the less, there are fine poems about the experiences of American women. Many of the works are by women of color, and one section is devoted to lesbian poetry. But if one is looking for a generally higher quality of women's poetry, they might better consider *The Faber Book of 20th Century Women's Poetry, Early Ripening: American Women's Poetry Now,* or *No More Masks! an Anthology of Poems by Women.*

No More Masks! an Anthology of Poems by Women. *Florence Howe and Ellen Bass, eds.* **(1973) Doubleday Anchor Books. 396p., o.p.**

In her foreword, Florence Howe voices a sentiment that still holds true today, although to a lesser extent: "Few volumes [of poetry anthologies] have included more than a token woman — Emily Dickinson or Christina Rossetti — and fewer still, if any, their poems about women." This book set out to right the record by presenting dozens of poems by American women about both men and women. The compilers begin with Amy Lowell, who wrote in the late nineteenth and early twentieth centuries, followed by Gertrude Stein, Elinor Wylie, "H.D." (Hilda Doolittle), Marianne Moore, and Edna St. Vincent Millay. That first section of earlier poets also contains the work of Gwendolyn Brooks and May Swenson, as well as lesser known poets. The second section begins with Mona Van Duyn, threads through the work of Denise Levertov, Maxine Kumin,Anne Sexton, Adrienne Rich, Sylvia Plath, as well as many other modern day poets. This anthology is extremely rich. The authors are represented by approximately one to five poems, so one is often able to gain an accurate sense of their work. And the cumulative effect is startling: one wonders how anthologists could have overlooked such creativity?

The Other Voice; Twentieth-Century Women's Poetry in Translation.
Joanna Bankier and others, eds. **(1976) 218p., pap.**

This fascinating selection of women's poetry in translation begins with
an introduction by the highly regarded American poet Adrienne Rich,
who says of this collection, that while it "offers only a hint of the world-
wide efflorescence of poetry by women in this century," still, "its
strengths and richness are astonishing. It reinforces my sense that
women of whatever class, nation or race share a common sensibility — a
sensibility that is complex, subversive, and heterodox." The volume is
organized thematically: "Being a Woman"; "Women and Men"; "Medi-
tations"; "Speaking for Others"; and "Visions." Most of the poets will be
entirely new to contemporary readers, but some familiar names surface:
Anna Akhmatova and Marina Tsvetayeva, the great Russian poets, Nelly
Sachs from Germany, and Dahlia Ravikovitch of Israel. Short biograph-
ical sketches and bibliographical notes can be found at the end of the
book. In general, the quality of the poetry is exceptionally high, and it
is fascinating to see how women from different cultures and different
times have handled similar subject matter. Readers are bound to agree
with Adrienne Rich that the discoveries to be made in this collection are
profound.

The Penguin Book of Women Poets. *Carol Cosman, Joan Keefe, and
Kathleen Weaver, eds.* **(1978) Penguin Books. 399p., pap.**

This comprehensive anthology of women poets begins with anony-
mous love poems composed in Ancient Egypt in the fifteenth century
B.C., travels around the world and through the ages in Greece, Ireland,
Wales, India, Japan, and many other countries, to arrive finally in the
twentieth century in such countries as Russia, Finland, Denmark, Spain,
Korea, the Ivory Coast, and Zaïre, as well as the United States. The scope
of this volume is, therefore, vast. Each author, nonetheless, is given an
ample introduction that is helpful in understanding her work. The ed-
itors have chosen a great deal of little-known poetry, much of it in trans-
lation, and have compiled an excellent and fascinating anthology that
sets those obscure poets alongside the more familiar ones. Approxi-
mately half the book is allocated to pre-twentieth century poets, and half
to modern ones. Many authors are accorded space for more than one
poem so that something of their range can be discerned. That there have
been so many fine women poets through the ages and across the world
is a revelation. It serves to balance, in a modest way, the many anthol-

ogies that lean so heavily (and sometimes even exclusively) on male creativity.

Tangled Vines; a Collection of Mother and Daughter Poems. *Lyn Lifshin, ed.* (1978) Beacon Press. 95p., pap.

This slim volume focuses on a particular aspect of women's poetry: the transformation into art of feelings about daughters and mothers. The poets who contributed to this anthology are all contemporary Americans who come from various segments of the community. There are several black authors represented, as well as lesbians. Some of the poets, including Maxine Kumin, Sylvia Plath, and Sharon Olds, have more than one work reprinted. Many of the writers are well known. Aside from the ones just mentioned, there are Anne Sexton, Audre Lorde, Erica Jong, Lucille Clifton, and Anne Waldman. Others are little known. The theme of relationships between mothers and their daughters will capture the interest of many readers. These are intimate poems that register the intensity of this primal relationship. They tend to be simple, easy to comprehend, and to relate to one's own experiences.

Watchers and Seekers: Creative Writing by Black Women in Britain. *Rhonda Cobham and Merle Collins, eds.* (1988) Peter Bedrick Books. 157p.

Written by contemporary Black women in Britain, this collection presents poems written generally in open forms. Often, they represent the experiences of the writers, and deal with questions such as prejudice, male/female incompatibility, relations with children, and romantic feelings. The subject matter is very down to earth, but the treatment is not very fresh or original. Some of the strongest poems are those that one can imagine being performed, sounding a bit like strong expressions of rap music lyrics in their protest of the status quo. Many new poets are on view here, several of them very young and just beginning their careers. It is possible that as they mature their art will, too.

The Women Poets in English; an Anthology. *Ann Stanford, ed.* (1972) McGraw-Hill. 374p., o.p.

One might think, given the title of this volume, that it is concerned with women in the past two centuries. Not so. In fact, the first poem included dates from around A.D. 800 and is written in Anglo-Saxon by an anonymous poet who writes in a woman's voice, from a female perspective. Other very early writers in English include Marie de France, who dates from the twelfth century, with "The Lay of the Honeysuckle," and a poet known only as The Lady of the Arbour, who wrote in the middle of the fifteenth century. We are shown an excerpt from her long poem entitled "The Flower and the Leaf." This older period also features such royal authors as Queen Elizabeth of York and Queen Anne Boleyn, as well as Queen Elizabeth I. Later writers who achieved some fame are included: Anne Bradstreet, Aphra Behn, and Anne Finch, Countess of Winchilsea. They are followed by the still more famous Elizabeth Barrett Browning, Emily Brontë, Christina Rossetti, and Emily Dickinson. Each is represented by several poems, and they are interspersed with dozens of less-well-known writers. In the modern section, we have the work of Charlotte Mew, "H.D.,"Marianne Moore, Edna St. Vincent Millay, and scores of others, finally arriving at contemporary writers such as Adrienne Rich, Sylvia Plath, and Margaret Atwood. This is a balanced and exciting anthology, filling in, as it does, so many gaps in traditional literary history.

Women Poets of the World. *Joanna Bankier and Deirdre Lashgari, eds.* **(1983) Macmillan. 442p., o.p.**

This anthology seeks to place over two hundred female poets, from 2300 B.C. to the present day, within their particular culture. The volume is organized according to the country of origin of the poet — China, Japan, India, Iran, Sumero-Babylonia, the Arab World, Ancient Greece, Israel, Medieval Europe, Europe in the sixteenth and seventeenth centuries, Europe in the eighteenth and nineteenth centuries, Europe after 1914, Africa, Latin America, North America (which is subdivided into: Euro-American, Afro-American, Asian/Pacific American, and Chicana), and Native American poetry. Each of these sections is accompanied by an introduction to the writing by women in that culture. This is an ambitious project, and it is marked by meticulous attention to the historical aspects of women's lives and to the artistic nature of the poets' accomplishments. The editors understand that it is hopeless to comprehend fully an artist's work unless you can also understand the culture in which that artist works, and so this volume seeks to impart a sense of the culture before exposing the reader to the poems themselves. All in all, this book provides a fascinating overview of women poets of the world and through the ages.

The Women Troubadours. *Meg Bogin, ed.* **(1980) W. W. Norton. 192p., pap.**

Women troubadours sounds like an oxymoron: being a troubadour *means* being a man. So one might have thought before picking up this anthology. In fact, very few of these female troubadours have been translated or studied before this anthology that rides on the current wave of women's studies. Women troubadours, like their male counterparts, were serious court poets, and their poetry had a seminal relationship to subsequent European poetry: it established the convention of romantic love, it used the vernacular speech for literary purposes, and it spawned imitators wherever the songs were heard. In her introduction, Meg Bogin explores the meaning of the troubadours' work and its relation to the state of women at the time it was being composed. After lengthy essays on the historical background of these poets, about the nature of courtly love, and about the women troubadours themselves, the poems of eighteen women troubadours are printed both in ancient Provencal and in English. The context the editor provides is helpful in deciphering these verses that grew out of such an alien culture. It is fascinating to hear what women had to say about life in a culture that seems to have been defined by men.

WORLD POETRY

An Anthology of World Poetry. *Mark Van Doren, ed.* **(Rev. and Enl. ed., 1936) Reynal & Hitchcock. 1468p.**

Bulky, and chock full of familiar verse — that is a capsule summary of one of the most frequently used anthologies. It is not particularly appropriate, however, for the average reader. Not only is it too heavy, but some translations are dated, and the selection is somewhat conventional. With that said, the advantages can still be named. First, the scope is impressive, from Chinese literature to Roman and American. Second, the translations may be dated, but they remain some of the best, for example, Waddell, Waley, Pound, Dryden, and Rossetti. Third, the selection is of the first-rate, most-accepted verses, and while there are few surprises, there are even fewer omissions. There are, too, standard indexes. Everything is easy enough to find in this indispensable reference work. Van Doren was a man who knew what he was about: he devotes only four or so pages to a descriptive introduction, in this case, that is more than enough.

Collected Translations. *William Jay Smith, comp.* **(1985) New Rivers Press. 152p., pap.**

One of the best-known and most highly skilled translators, William Jay Smith declares that he has gathered together "translations that I have done over the past several decades of poems in the Romance languages — Italian, French, Spanish, and Portuguese." The selection includes both major and minor poems, but they are "all poems that have delighted me in one way or another." An anonymous thirteenth-century Italian work begins the collection. There are then nine more Italian poets, ranging into the twentieth century. The chronological organization is followed in the French section, which comprises at least half the book, and in the Spanish and Portuguese sections. Among the poets one finds Eugenio Montale, Théophile Gautier, Arthur Rimbaud, Jules Laforgue (of whom Smith seems particularly fond, as he is given more space than any of the others), Paul Valery and Federico Garcia Lorca. In his brief introduction, Smith explains his approach to translation. "Translating poetry . . . is like converging on a flame with a series of mirrors, mirrors of technique and understanding, until the flame is reflected in upon itself in a wholly new and foreign element." The compiler's handling of mirrors is as deft as the poems themselves.

Confucius to Cummings; an Anthology of Poetry. *Ezra Pound and Marcella Spann, eds.* **(1964) New Directions. 353p., pap.**

Famous for his *Guide to Kulchur,* in which he attempted to teach poetry, Pound followed through many years later with this volume. Here, then, are the poets, from Confucius to T. S. Eliot, Basil Bunting, and E. E. Cummings. This time there is no text, no guidance. As Pound explains briefly, "The active student may enjoy figuring out when and how they [i.e., earlier poets] got into the minds of later poets, if at all; and with what degree of light or muddle. . . . We assume the reader who has been able to get into a junior college will be able to put our mosaic together to her, or to his satisfaction." The chronological arrangement is as satisfactory as the choices, many of which are truly eccentric. The imaginative selection makes this unique. Particularly interesting are the translators whom Pound chooses: Chapman for Homer, Hardy for Sappho, and himself for Sophocles, to name only a few of the early entries. The nineteenth century is fairly well represented, but there is little, indeed, from the twentieth. Pound seemed particularly fond of Browning and enjoyed Whittier's "Barbara Frietchie." Anyone who is curious about Pound should read this collection for a better understanding and appreciation of the poet.

The Faber Book of Useful Verse. *Simon Brett, ed.* **(1981) Faber and Faber. 254p., pap.**

The introduction to this volume clarifies the meaning of its title. "Groucho Marx once condemned as useless all poetry, except for the six line verse which begins 'Thirty days hath September' . . . whose usefulness was obvious." Brett soon found he would have to go a bit beyond this definition. "I have extended the field of usefulness to include verse which is instructive or functional." Given this scope, several fascinating points surfaced. First, most of the useful verse appeared in the eighteenth century. It was a time dominated by poets in quest of a meaningful topic. Second, the Romantic Movement killed, or badly wounded, useful poetry. Finally, the loss of a classical education meant the loss of verse used as a mnemonic device to learn Latin and Greek. There are twenty-five subject headings, opening with "Useful for Dates," then "Weather Forecasts," then "Lovers," etc. The chronological list of writers begins with Hesiod's eighth-century masterpiece "Book of Work and Days" and closes with the new math as explained by the satirist Tom Lehrer. "The process of selection has been an enormously enjoyable one." The same sentiment should be experienced by any reader who ventures into these pages. An exceptionally enjoyable anthology.

The Oxford Book of Verse in English Translation. *Charles Tomlinson, ed.* **(1980) Oxford University Press. 608p., pap.**

This is a book for erudite poetry enthusiasts. The editor has organized his material according to the chrolonology of the translators. One may, therefore, read many different versions of Ancient Greek literature as it has been translated over the ages. This is, indeed, a sophisticated pleasure for poetry lovers. The volume opens with a translation by fifteenth-century Gavin Douglas, selections from his version of Virgil's *The Aeneid.* Several Biblical translations follow, and eventually, in the sixteenth century, such familiar names as Edmund Spenser (with translations from French and Italian) and Christopher Marlowe (with his version of Ovid) follow. Famous writers abound in this volume; modern ones include Ezra Pound, Marianne Moore, Czeslaw Milosz, Robert Lowell, and Ted Hughes. There are English versions of Navajo and Chippewa poems, as well as Chinese, German, French, Polish, Italian, and Icelandic works, but the emphasis seems to fall on Ancient Greek and Latin poetry. The reader is provided with many selections from Chapman's celebrated sixteenth-century version of Homer's *The Iliad,* and *The Odyssey;* Dryden's translations of *The Iliad,* Virgil's *The Aeneid,* Ovid's *Metamorphoses,* and Juvenal's *Satires;* and Pope's translations of *The Iliad* and *The Odyssey.* The Bible is presented in several versions from the early sixteenth century, translated by William Tyndale, Miles Coverdale, Sir Thomas Wyatt, and Mary Herbert, Countess of Pembroke, as well as from the Authorized Version of 1611. These are expert translations of great literary works.

P.E.N. New Poetry I. *Robert Nye, ed.* **(1986) Quartet Books. 196p.**

The compiler explains: "My brief from P.E.N. was straightforward, to assemble in three months of early 1985 an anthology of mostly unpublished verse of which one third would be by known poets and the rest by the little known or unknown." The result is an anthology with just over a hundred and fifty poems by fifty-four poets. A glance at the "biographical details" at the end of the book confirms the success of the mission. While Dannie Abse, John Ashbery, George Barker, and numerous others will be recognized immediately, the remainder are "little known or unknown." This hardly detracts from the quality of the verse, and some of the best entries are from this group. The majority are English, although there is a scattering of poets from other parts of the globe. Nye, himself, is one of the best poets around, and his choices reflect an interest in the new. Tony Harrison and Sacha Rabinovitch are among the outstanding contributors to a fascinating overview of modern poetry. The selections, two to four per poet, are arranged in an orderly fashion, and one poem seems to complement the next.

Under Another Sky; an Anthology of Commonwealth Poetry Prize Winners. *Alastair Niven, ed.* **(1987) Carcanet. 106p., pap.**

Beginning in 1972, the London-based Commonwealth Institute began to offer prizes for the best, newly published poetry in a Commonwealth language. This is a collection of the poems that extends from the 1972 joint winners (Chinua Achebe and George McWhirter) and commended winners (Richard Ntiru and David Mitchell) to the joint winners and regional winners for 1986. Some thirty-five poets are found here, with two or three representative poems for each. All parts of the Commonwealth are represented, and while most of the poets are not well known, there are a few who have international status. Each of the poets is introduced by a short biographical/bibliographical paragraph. There are numerous issues raised in the poems, but one of the more surprising, for those not involved with Commonwealth affairs, is the role of English as a common language. It is a great controversy, possibly not helped by the fact that "all the poets who have won or been commended . . . write in English, either because they have no alternative or because it is the tongue best suited to their intentions. . . . A poet can use English and be true to a local culture." No matter, the poetry is well worth reading and is particularly interesting for the dominance of so-called third-world poets.

The World Comes to Iowa; Iowa International Anthology. *Paul Engle, Rowena Torrevillas, and Hualing Nieh Engle, eds.* **(1987) Iowa State University Press. 295p.**

The title is explained by the editors: "This anthology celebrates the twentieth anniversary of the International Writing Program . . . [which] brings to Iowa writers not only of many languages and countries, but also of the newest forms of the literary imagination, those about to appear in next week's book or magazine." The Engles give detailed accounts of the program in their twenty-page introduction and describe their part in insuring the success of the unique gathering of international poets, many of whom are young and not that well known. The collection of nearly a hundred poets follows a distinct format. There are individual or group photographs of most of the writers before their work. This is followed by letters, usually addressed to the compilers, in which the authors explain themselves. And while the collection is focused on poetry, a good two thirds of it is prose — criticism and memoirs. Biographical notes conclude the volume. It is difficult to find a country, East, West, South, or North that is not represented, and the anthology is truly a world collection.

A World Treasury of Oral Poetry. *Ruth Finnegan, ed.* **(1978) Indiana University Press. 548p., o.p.**

Oral poetry from thirteen cultures is gathered here to demonstrate that "unwritten poetry can offer much that, at its best, can parallel the written poetic forms." Apart from *The Odyssey,* "Beowulf," and some individual works by English and Irish poets, the song and verse are primarily anonymous, so much a part of the culture that the original author is lost to time. Each of the thirteen sections is prefaced by a brief introductory comment, giving an outline of the background and explaining the local poetic forms and symbols. These include the epigrammatic and lyric, as well as the epic and narrative. Sometimes brief notes are given with the poem, and the translator is dutifully noted. Among the traditions represented are the Gond, Mongol, Malay, Somali (often with a credit to a specific poet), Zulu, Yoruba, Irish, Pueblo, Eskimo, Hawaiian, Maori, Australian Aborigine, and English. The epic and narrative poetry of Homer ends the volume, along with an index of titles and first lines. Anyone interested in oral poetry and its tradition should not miss the fine introduction.

YOUNG ADULT POETRY

The Cherry Tree. *Geoffrey Grigson, comp.* **(1959) Phoenix House. 518p.**

Although edited for young people, this volume is for anyone who is imaginative enough to appreciate the delights of different poetic forms and modes. What has the title to do with the twenty-nine sections of English-language poems that start with "Idle Fyno," move on to "The Cherry Fair," and end with "I Think You Stink"? Well, anyone who recognizes the name of the compiler, an English poet of no mean talent, will understand. Grigson takes a broad-minded, universal view of his art and thinks reading aloud, to yourself or to others, is just fine as long as it is poetry. Subject matter, is not important. "I have always liked — and now offer — a large book of poems of all kinds, arranged according to mood and subject; a book of so many poems that there is room inside it for endless exploration and new discovery." This journey offers many delights, and while numerous poets and poems are well known, others are new to the world of anthologies. "Idle Fyno", for example, is full of nonsense verse with a bitter, yet amusing, edge. The selection makes for fascinating bed partners: Edwin Arlington Robinson precedes Shakespeare and D. G. Rossetti — or vice versa depending on where one looks. The grab bag or cherry tree is joy for the browser and offers numerous opportunities to draw new readers to poetry.

Eye's Delight; Poems of Art and Architecture. *Helen Plotz, comp.* **(1983) Greenwillow Books. 150p.**

In his poem "Thanksgiving for a Habitat," W. H. Auden writes; "To you, to me,/Stonehenge and Chartres Cathedral,/the Acropolis, Blenheim, the Albert Memorial/are works by the same Old Man/under different names." Under different names, the compiler brings together over one hundred poems by almost as many famous poets, writing about much the same thing — art. The poems are neatly divided into four sections, poems about pictures, poems about sculpture, and two last parts on architecture. Much of the focus is on such modern writers as Muriel Rukeyser, W. H. Auden, Richard Wilbur, Elizabeth Bishop, and others of the post Second World War period. There are the obvious, exceptional voices from the past, such as Keats ("On Seeing the Elgin Marbles") and Melville ("Art"), but they are in the minority. The compiler is an expert at bringing together poems. She has a half dozen or more anthologies to her credit, and her skill is obvious here. The volume is a work that can be enjoyed by young people and by adults.

Favorite Poems Old and New. *Helen Ferris, ed.* **(1957) Doubleday. 589p., pap.**

A book of favorite poems aimed at young adults needs an organizing principle that would allow readers to locate favorite poems for themselves. Here this principle is a thematic one. The sections are labelled "Myself and I," "My Family and I," "My Almanac," "It's Fun to Play," "Little Things that Creep and Crawl and Swim and Sometimes Fly," "Animal Pets and Otherwise," "On the Way to Anywhere," to name a few. In each of the sections, there are dozens of poems by well-known and unknown authors: Shakespeare rubs shoulders with Hilda Conkling, Amy Lowell with Humbert Wolfe. The poems in this volume are readily accessible to the general reader and the high school student; it might provide them with some delightful moments as they locate poems about subjects that interest them. The humorous poems in the section "Almost Any Time Is Laughing Time" are particularly appealing. This could prove an effective book for introducing newcomers to poetry.

Going Over to Your Place; Poems for Each Other. *Paul B. Janeczko, comp.* **(1987) Bradbury Press. 157p.**

A teacher of high school English, and a consistent winner of American Library Association prizes for "best books for young adults," the compiler here offers over one hundred poems. They all reflect the familiar, everyday preoccupations of young adults in such poems as Stanley Kunitz's "First Love" or David Evans's "The Sound of Rain." There are almost as many poets as poems, beginning with Elizabeth Bishop and Richard Eberhart and concluding with May Swenson and John Updike. Most of the authors are not that famous or well known. Poets are chosen for what they have to say about matters relating to youth. There are no introduction, no preface, no prefatory remarks for the four sections; the compiler lets the poems speak for themselves. As the jacket copy puts it, "Listen — and be won."

The Golden Journey; Poems for Young People. *Louise Bogan and William Jay Smith, comps.* **(1965) Reilly & Lee. 275p., o.p.**

Compiled for high school students by two distinguished poets, both of whom are represented here, this is an ideal collection for high school students. The compilers have excellent taste, a grasp of the development of poetry, and an appreciation for what young people enjoy. "The poems we have selected cover a wide range — all the way from simple rhymes on the slightest of subjects to supreme flights of the imagination. Some were written by the greatest poets of the past, British and American; others are the work of recent, and, in some cases, unknown poets." There are over twenty sections that cover everything from "The Sea" to "Ballads" to "Birds, Beasts and Flowers." Among the greatest poets included are Blake, Emily Dickinson, T. S. Eliot, Robert Frost, Robert Herrick, Wallace Stevens, Tennyson, Wordsworth and W. B. Yeats. Excellent, if less famous, poets also find a place in this marvelous anthology. There are author and title indexes. A good acquisition for any library serving teenagers and suitable for many adults, as well.

Golden Numbers. *Kate Douglas Wiggin and Nora Archibald Smith, eds.* **(1902) Doubleday, Doran. 687p.**

Almost a century old, this "book of verse for youth" tells more about early American educational activities than later collections for the same group. First, it is assumed all readers are Christians. There is a final section devoted almost entirely to Christmas and "the glad evangel." Here, as elsewhere, the selection of poets is uneven. There are the well known, the "classic" voices from Herrick to Southwell and, yes, Shakespeare, but at the same time one is forced to wade through the sometimes less than felicitous verse of William Drummond of Hawthornden and Felicia Hemans. The message, then, counts considerably more than the style. Still, when style and content can be wed, the two compilers are not bashful about asking the young reader to master ballads, Emerson, Ben Jonson, Keats, Kipling, Scott, and all. In terms of coverage, Shakespeare leads, followed closely by Sir Walter Scott, James Russell Lowell, Milton, and Tennyson. And the choices are delightful reminders that several generations back, young people were expected to master the work of the classic poets, American and English. There are no "foreigners" to speak of and no translations. It is English, American, Christian, or out! The numerous headings remind one of an optimistic age, which was equally innocent: "A Garden of Girls", comes just before "New World and Old Glory" and "In Merry Mood."

Imagination's Other Place; Poems of Science and Mathematics. *Helen Plotz, comp.* **(1955) Thomas Y. Crowell. 200p.**

While this is compiled for junior high through high school readers, most of the poetry can be enjoyed by younger people and by adults. It is the subject matter that is important. Blake's "Auguries of Innocence" opens the first section, titled simply "In the Beginning." He is followed by a brief selection from T. S. Eliot's "Four Quarters." Other poets in this section, one of four, include Emily Dickinson, Shelley, Emerson, and A. E. Housman, not to mention Shakespeare and portions of the Book of Job. No one can fault the compiler here, or in numerous other works of hers, for underestimating either the taste or the skill of the average reader. Weaving the themes around mathematics, astronomy, anthropology, and aspects of general science, the collection may be used for browsing or for selecting just the appropriate poem or stanza to illustrate a scientific point. There is an index of first lines, but no subject index.

Love Is like the Lion's Tooth; an Anthology of Love Poems. *Frances McCullough, ed.*

See under LOVE POETRY

The Music of What Happens; Poems That Tell Stories. *Paul B. Janeczko, comp.* **(1988) Orchard Books. 188p.**

Story poems often appeal to teenagers, and this volume works on that safe assumption. Here one finds about fifty poets and about as many poems. As is the custom in the other compilations by this high school teacher, few of the poets are famous, and the primary emphasis is on the poem not on the name of the poet. There are no introduction and no notes. Again, this is Mr. Janeczko's custom. As the jacket copy says, one may turn here for "ghosts, lovers, dreamers, zanies; young Civil War soldiers, classroom cutups, grandchildren, step children, and the childless." The opening poem, by Jared Carter, sets the stage for "The Purpose of Poetry." After that, mostly young, modern Americans tell the teenager what life is all about in poetic form. There is an index of poets, but, unfortunately, no subject index.

100 More Story Poems. *Elinor Parker, comp.* **(1960) Thomas Y. Crowell. 374p., o.p.**

The story poem is a popular kind of verse, and there are numerous collections available, all reflecting the distinctive outlook of their compilers. In this anthology, Elinor Parker is not so much concerned with content and style as with her audience. The hundred poems included here are directed to young people, and primarily those in junior high and high school. One suspects that the poems may have been selected for teachers who must try to point out the joys of poetry through the story they tell in easy to understand verse. Why else, for example, would one bother with Frederick Whittaker's "Custer's Last Charge." On the other hand there is the traditional Scottish ballad about "The Battle of Otterburn," and if Homer is not in evidence, Kipling is here in force. On balance the selection is fair, although one can see signs of a desperate effort to involve youngsters. At the same time, because it does include some downright peculiar poems, this volume is a marvelous source of hard-to-find works.

Poems That Live Forever. *Hazel Felleman, ed.* **(1965) Doubleday. 454p., pap.**

This general anthology is the self-confessed "potpourri of favorite poems (with a few prose selections)" by one of the former editors of *The New York Times Book Review.* She divides her material into stories and ballads, love, friendship, home and family, patriotism and war, humor, nonsense and whimsy, the ages of man, death, reflection and contemplation, faith and inspiration, nature's people, and so forth. Many of the poets are little known today, while others are quite familiar. This is disparate, unfocused collection of verse, and the quality of the poems varies widely. But many popular poems can be found here, and this volume might serve as a useful introduction for young readers, or others, who are unsure about exactly what attracts them in a poem. Here the variety is so great, and the quality so diverse, that any reader is bound to find something to appeal to his or her sensibility.

Poetspeak; in Their Work, about Their Work. *Paul B. Janeczko, comp.*
(1983) Bradbury Press. 238p.

Chosen as one of the "best books for young adults" by the American
Library Association, this anthology is compiled by a high school teacher
who has by now almost a half dozen such anthologies to his credit. Here,
as with the others, the primary audience is the high school student. The
theme is in the title — poets explain their work to young people. Maxine
Kumin's "Fräulein Reads Instructive Rhymes," for example, is followed
by a three-paragraph explanation of its meaning and background. "It
came up directly from my childhood memory," she writes. Not all of the
sixty or so poets care to comment on each poem, but there are editorial
remarks after every third or fourth entry. As is his custom, the compiler
offers no introduction or any help. He lets the poems and the poets
speak for themselves. This works quite well. Few of the poets are that
well known, but all are modern, and all are writing about matters of
concern to young people. The result is an extremely pleasing book that
will involve the reader.

Postcard Poems; a Collection of Poetry for Sharing. *Paul B. Janeczko,*
ed. **(1979) Bradbury Press. 106p., o.p.**

The title comes from the fact that each of the hundred poems is brief
enough to fit on a postcard, and "each lively enough to inspire mailing
to comrades and lovers." Furthermore, according to the compiler, "the
poems in this collection are gifts from the poets, meant to be shared. . . .
If you like the poems, pass them on!" While this may be among the most
unusual justifications for an anthology, it seems to work. Most of the
authors are modern and American, a few English, and some European.
Rainer Maria Rilke opens his "Closing Piece" with a stark sentence,
"Death is great." While one might pause before sending this on a post-
card, most of the other verses are at least appropriate, particularly X. J.
Kennedy's "Epitaph for a Postal Clerk" and David Ignatow's "The City,"
which has only three lines: "If flowers want to grow/right out of the
concrete sidewalk cracks/I'm going to bend down to smell them." This
may not be the most comprehensive or selective of collections, but it is
one of the more unique.

Rhythm Road; Poems to Move To. *Lillian Morrison, comp.* (1988) **Lothrop, Lee & Shepard. 148p.**

This distinguished Young Adult Services librarian knows her audience, and here she brings together poems that "sway, twist, glide, ride, rock, dive, lurch, loop, fly." The nearly one hundred poems succeed in conveying the essence of motion, and they are "an invitation to what might be called a poetry workout." The novel idea brings to the pages a great number of modern poets, although here and there one finds such earlier writers as W. S. Gilbert, Lewis Carroll, Edgar Allan Poe, and Gerard Manley Hopkins. Hilaire Belloc opens the rhythm road with "Tarantella," followed closely by Edith Sitwell's "Daisy and Lily" and Marianne Moore's "Slim dragon fly/too rapid for the eye/to cage — / contagious gem of virtuosity — make visible, mentality." The sixty-seven other poets and some anonymous verses are equally engaging. While particularly suited for young people, most of the poetry will be equally enjoyed by adults.

Room for Me and a Mountain Lion; Poetry of Open Space. *Nancy Larrick, comp.* (1974) **M. Evans. 191p.**

This differs from other collections of nature poetry in that most of the poets are modern. The entries are suitable for older children and teenagers, although all may be enjoyed by any age. Celebrating the joys of open spaces and the delights of nature are such poets as Robert Frost, Ted Hughes, Maxine Kumin, William Stafford, Theodore Roethke and D. H. Lawrence, to name only a representative few. The compiler, an imaginative teacher, was assisted in the selection by her students who chose poems they thought would be of interest to others who have "a need for freedom to breathe pure air, climb rocky trails and observe the tiniest creatures." While the focus is on poetry of the twentieth century, there are long selections from Whitman, some eighteenth-century Chinese poetry, and Indian and Eskimo verse. There are also some indifferent photographs. For ages eleven to sixteen.

Under All Silences; Shades of Love. *Ruth Gordon, comp.*

See under LOVE POETRY

The Wind and the Rain; an Anthology of Poems for Young People.
John Hollander and Harold Bloom, eds. **(1961) Doubleday. 264p.**

A distinguished poet (Hollander) and a famous critic (Bloom) collaborated to select poetry for children. The two, who are now Yale professors, are relentless in their search for quality, and the result is a varied, intelligent, and always imaginative collection. The arrangement is suitable for the audience. The poems are divided by seasons, and they indicate the human moods these evoke. For children in junior high and high school this will be both a challenge and an awakening. The challenge is to grasp the meaning of some of the more difficult poems without the aid of notes from the compilers. The awakening comes from reading Shakespeare, Jonson, Rossetti, Tennyson, Blake, and others of the English school who bring pleasure and insight to verse. Unfortunately, the twentieth century is not represented, and the editors fail to say in the introduction why they drew the line at the close of the nineteenth century. No matter, what is selected is about as distinguished as anyone is likely to find in a collection for children and teenagers. The editors have a high regard for their audience and refuse to print anything which is not first rate. As a result, the collection may be enjoyed by adults as well. There is an index of first lines, authors, and titles.

HIGHLY RECOMMENDED ANTHOLOGIES

The following anthologies are recommended as the best of the best by the group that selected the basic volumes for the ninth edition of THE COLUMBIA GRANGER'S® INDEX TO POETRY.

Anthologies in the first group are recommended for all libraries and recommended as first choices for individual readers.

Anthologies in the second group are recommended for all medium to large libraries, although, of course, small libraries will wish to consider them.

All Libraries

An Anthology of World Poetry
The Harvard Book of Contemporary American Poetry
An Introduction to Poetry (X. J. Kennedy, ed.)
The New Oxford Book of English Verse
The Norton Anthology of Poetry
The Norton Book of Light Verse
The Penguin Book of Women Poets
The Poetry of Black America
The Random House Book of Poetry for Children
Talking to the Sun; an Illustrated Anthology of Poems for Young People

Medium to Large Libraries

American Folk Poetry
American Hymns
The American Poetry Anthology
Best-Loved Poems in Large Print
The Best Loved Poems of the American People
Black Sister
The Book of Irish Verse
A Book of Love Poetry
Breaking Silence
The Cherry-Tree

Collected Translations
The Columbia Book of Chinese Poetry
Contemporary Chicana Poetry
Ecstatic Occasions, Expedient Forms
The Faber Book of Ballads
The Faber Book of Nonsense Verse
The Faber Book of 20th Century Women's Poetry
Fine Frenzy
From the Country of Eight Islands
Golden Treasury of the Best Songs & Lyrical Poems
Harper's Anthology of 20th Century Native American Poetry
How Does a Poem Mean?
The Longman Anthology of Contemporary American Poetry
The Morrow Anthology of Younger American Poets
The New Oxford Book of American Verse
The Norton Anthology of Modern Poetry
The Norton Introduction to Poetry.
The Oxford Book of American Light Verse
The Oxford Book of Children's Verse in America
The Oxford Book of Twentieth Century English Verse
The Oxford Book of War Poetry
The Oxford Nursery Rhyme Book
The Treasury of American Poetry
The Treasury of English Poetry

INDEX